CONTENTS

INTRODUCTION

The average American spends about 55 per cent of his or her time in a household environment. That includes fifty-six hours of sleeping and resting each week, twenty-five hours working, relaxing, and studying, five hours in visits to friends, and seven hours washing, cleaning, and dressing. But many people are not average and all of us go through periods of our lives when even more time is spent indoors. The sick, the elderly, and infants are often only rarely outside the confines of their residence. Also, about one fifth of the population are housewives who spend much of their working day in the home. In short, the household indoor environment is where we spend a major portion of our lives.

Ecology consciousness and Earth Day stressed the outdoor environment—that is, the air we breathe, the water of our rivers and streams, and the landscape. In fact, our federal government and industries have spent about $29 billion cleaning up this outdoor environment. In the early days of the environmental movement we equated pollution and environmental problems with dirty exterior air, contaminated water, and dumped garbage. We realized that dirty rivers meant unclean tap water, and smog-filled urban areas meant soiled curtains. Nevertheless, we still thought that the sacred confines of the home could be protected from those "other" outdoor polluters.

In the beginning of the 1970s we became a little more sophisticated about environmental problems. We began to speak about occupational health, which quite often meant the workplaces of chemical and textile workers, foundry workers, and blast-furnace operators. This often was an indoor phenomenon. Workers in coal mines were exposed to the dangers of black lung disease, those in cotton mills to brown lung, and chemical workers who cleaned vats of plastic factories could get liver cancer from the vinyl chloride. Asbestosis afflicted asbestos plant workers, those living near the plants, and finally the inhabitants of homes into which workers carried asbestos dust on their clothing.

The growing awareness of occupational hazards in our modern industry and business soon led to governmental intervention which was partly catalyzed by aroused labor unions, public-interest groups, and concerned citizens. The Occupational Safety and Health Act was passed, and the federal government set up the Department of Health, Education, and Welfare's National Institute for Occupational Safety and Health (NIOSH), the Department of Labor's Occupational Safety and Health Agency (OSHA), and the Department of Interior's Mining Enforcement and Safety Administration (MESA). The health of workers, their families, and persons living near workplaces was seen as part of the total ecological picture.

Today, however, the home still remains beyond the consideration of many environmentalists. The regulatory agencies have done little or nothing, even though isolated researchers within those agencies have deplored the lack of attention to this vast area of human contact. Our research team at the Center for Science in the Public Interest (CSPI) asked five of the regulatory agencies what they were doing about household pollutants. The Food and Drug Administration (FDA) replied that the Governmental Interagency Taskforce of which FDA is a member was beginning to tackle such problems, but the examples cited were not indoor household pollu-

THE
HOUSEHOLD
POLLUTANTS
GUIDE

by the Center for Science
in the Public Interest

General Editor: Albert J. Fritsch

Contributors:

Elaine Burns   Thomas Conry   David Fry
Andy Gottesmund   Peter Haas
Edward Haggerty   Fred Smith

ANCHOR BOOKS

ANCHOR PRESS / DOUBLEDAY

GARDEN CITY, NEW YORK

Anchor Books Edition: 1978

ISBN: 0-385-12494-5
Library of Congress Catalog Card Number 77–76269

ACKNOWLEDGMENTS

CSPI researchers on this project were hindered by the scattered and incomplete nature of research materials. Thus the help of other persons was paramount to completing this book. The research team is indebted to the technical staff of CSPI and the Technical Information Project for invaluable assistance.

Special credit is due to:

— the Maryland Lung Association for an initial grant to investigate the household pollutants area;

— Dennis Darcey and Barbara Hogan for work on general pollutants and especially aerosol sprays;

— Alan Okagaki, Andy Keeler, Angela Iadavaia-Cox, and Elizabeth Dodson Gray for editorial suggestions;

— Cheryl Tennille for reviewing household survey questions;

— Father Fred Middendorf and the biology class of St. Xavier High School in Cincinnati for household surveying;

— Fred Panzer for alerting the team to certain valuable references;

— Drs. Art Purcell and Bill Millerd for assistance in the garbage and radiation sectors;

— and Catherine Mills and Julie Shearer, interns from Bethany College, West Virginia, for collecting brand-name labels.

tion areas. The Federal Trade Commission (FTC) mentioned mandatory disclosure of possible fire hazards from synthetic insulation in mobile homes and trailers, but admitted FTC could not ban products from the market place, though it did require full and truthful disclosure of cautions, warnings, and accurate performance claims. The Environmental Protection Agency (EPA) acknowledged the possible problems of indoor pollutants; EPA said it was starting to conduct some preliminary research to determine the extent of the problem.

The lack of current awareness and assembled data on household pollutants is the reason for this book. It is the first —not the last—word about indoor pollution of the home. While accompanying governmental action is needed to preserve a clean home environment, individual citizens may learn to recognize danger spots in their home, find out how extensive these are, and take certain remedial steps. All the while, we must exercise our civic responsibility by prodding the government into action.

Most Americans suffer from the illusion that the more modern and expensive the home, the healthier the environment. This may not necessarily be so, for modern conveniences, building practices, and chemicals used as cleaners and polishes all have associated dangers which must be recognized and eliminated. Shaking one's faith in modern housekeeping should not result in undue alarm, but it should lead us to take positive steps to make our homes more wholesome places in which to live.

The first step is to learn about the chemicals present in the home—be they furniture polishes, oven cleaners, or detergents. More chemicals are found in the average home than in chemical laboratories of a century ago. Many homemakers know little about these chemicals and even less about their toxic effects when mixed or misused. Labels contain only partial listings of ingredients which are often unpronounceable and mysterious. It is commonly assumed that product-makers know best about what can be safely used in the home, and, as a fallback, a vigilant government supposedly checks on any irresponsibility by these manufacturers.

Just for a start, look around and count the various chemicals found in various parts of the house. Over the course of the year the average home will contain forty-five aerosol sprays, another two dozen nonaerosolized cleaners, and several insect killers and repellents. Add to this paints and paint thinners, solvents, motor vehicle products, inks, deicing agents, caulking compounds, spot removers, and on and on. One look at the household counter in a local supermarket or hardware store reveals how consumers treat themselves in their homes.

Danger lies in not only the variety but the sheer quantity of chemicals used in the home. A few drops of a solvent may do little harm, but an open can evaporating over a period of time may be fatal to inhabitants.

The problems presented by the variety and amounts of household chemicals are compounded as various products are used in enclosed spaces—whether kitchenette, closet, or bathroom—within short periods of time. The toxicity of two household chemicals may not be pronounced when used separately, but when mixed together may produce a "synergistic effect," where the total effect is greater than the sum of the two effects taken independently. Vapors from one cleaning may linger because of poor ventilation, which may then combine with acids and bases used in subsequent cleanings— thereby catalyzing toxic chemical reactions. In fact, in an average American home, at least once a day two aerosols are used within one-half hour of each other. Heated stoves and heaters may likewise catalyze the formation of toxic by-products.

It is often virtually impossible for inexperienced homemakers to handle a chemical properly. One homemaker lugged her small oven outdoors since the aerosol spray oven cleaner always gave her a headache, in hopes that the plentiful air supply would carry away the basic vapors. That it did, but a gust of wind sent the spray right into her eyes, almost blinding her.

No conscientious chemist would handle chemicals such as pesticides and oven cleaners without laboratory hood and rubber gloves, nor dispense aerosolized caustic materials through the laboratory. What professionals won't do through an acquired respect for the danger of most chemicals, the manufacturers of household chemicals instruct the average homemakers to do "with care" using their products. Only an alert and informed citizenry can bring about the proper sharing of responsibility for safe use of chemicals.

Construction practices employed in making and refurnishing modern homes only exacerbate indoor pollution problems. Modern homes are cooler in summer and warmer in winter than those of a few centuries back. But this comfort has its price. In order to save expensive fuel, insulation is installed, many types of which can be dangerous to the insulator, or fire hazards. Yet replacing the airy home of yesteryear by a snug modern one also means the accumulation of household chemicals.

The lack of proper ventilation becomes a more serious problem when homes are refurnished or painted. Solvents and thinners evaporate quickly and fill the enclosed space with toxic vapors. Some people even close the windows and use air-conditioners when doing indoor painting. A CSPI staff person called in to help determine the solvent which killed an artist found the small room filled with open cans of solvents and paints.

Artists are not the only victims of their materials. Hobbyists such as stone polishers and metal sculptors, potters, and photographic buffs are all potential victims of accumulated chemicals in the cozy workplaces they make in the house. And so are the growing crowd of do-it-yourselfers who sand, varnish, paint, and polish their homes. A heater or an air-conditioner may make work more comfortable, but indoor air also becomes laden with toxic fumes and dust. Lead dust from scraped paint, mercury paint fumes, and newly installed polyvinyl chloride tile may be potentially dangerous materials without proper ventilation.

About one third of the public smokes and most of the other

two thirds must endure the aroma of the burning tobacco. Likewise all must inhale to some degree the dust which naturally accumulates in the home. Allergic people seldom realize that the lack of fresh air supply exacerbates their problem, for dust may accumulate more in a tightly enclosed home.

Heating and cooling systems are potential sources of dangerous fumes. Accidents are rare involving carbon monoxide leakage from furnaces or ammonia, sulfur dioxide, or fluorocarbon leakage from refrigerating units. Nevertheless, heating and cooling systems occasionally leak when old or poorly maintained. The microwave oven may contain a faulty door and leak harmful high-energy radiation.

Modern lifestyles introduce new and exotic materials into the home. Because many of the new synthetics used in furniture and clothing are combustible, manufacturers have been required to insert flame retardants, which are often toxic materials themselves. Drinking water flowing through pipes made from asbestos, lead, or PVC (polyvinyl chloride) adds harmful materials to our body burden. Decorative habits may include potentially harmful materials. Many plants brought into our homes may be poisonous. Motor vehicle fuels are often stored around the home. And last of all, garbage, the end product of our affluence, gives off its odors before saying good-by to the household.

This book is an action manual wherein conscientious homemakers may detect, understand, and substitute for harmful household materials. In Chapter 1 a method is detailed for detection of harmful pollutants both in the reader's home and in the neighborhood market so the consumer will understand dangers in household products which affect the entire public.

Chapter 2 takes one through the ABCs of pollutant categories and gives selected available information on toxic effects of many household materials and practices. Merely locating pollutants is not enough. Often they must be properly used and disposed of, and examples of misuse are thus worth knowing.

Each section also discusses substitutes and remedies for the specific problem areas. How do we remove or reduce dangerous household materials and practices and still preserve a high-quality lifestyle? Good housekeeping is the key, and forethought allows for practices which are both more economic and healthy.

The book is divided into an ABCs of household pollution—in detection, in identification, and in remedy. It is not to be read from cover to cover at one sitting, but studied over a reasonable time period so that a consciousness of household problems might develop.

This book was written for the individual consumer, but citizen action is always implied. Knowledgeable persons engaged in home safety practices can initiate legislative and regulatory actions to improve all homes. The extension of environmental consciousness into all homes requires an awareness of dangers both to self and to neighbor, and the recognition of potentially dangerous consumer products in neighborhood stores. This book is a first step in exposing and cleaning up the household environment.

On Terminology

A note of caution must be made for readers concerning the terms *toxic and toxicity*. Often consumers use these terms to refer to *hazardous* substances, which has a far broader meaning (see Appendix 1). Scientific literature refers to toxicity in terms of a response to a given dose of a "poisonous" substance, or one which damages or endangers our bodies or any living tissue. In one sense any chemical substance can be harmful when overused, and thus the challenge is to define overuse. In this book addressed to average consumers the authors attempt to establish a middle course between common usage and scientific terminology. Normal household use is set as a standard. Thus extreme toxicity should mean never to use the material in the home, high toxicity means use only when necessary and with listed precautions, moderate toxicity means use only when substitutes are not readily available, and slight toxicity means never overuse. Toxicity is thus a warning flag to the consumer about immediate (acute) danger and readily confirms the adage "respect all chemicals when using them."

Unfortunately, toxicity may not adequately point out long-term (chronic) dangers from repeated chemical usage. Some substances may be only slightly toxic when handled once, but may be long-term poisons. Chronic toxicities are often not discussed for household products listed in this book, since information exists on relatively few of them. When chronic dangers are not discussed, extra care should be exercised in repeated use of a household product, especially one which has been on the market for a short period of time.

CHAPTER 1

WHAT IS IN OUR HOMES?

Recognizing the extent of actual or potential household pollution takes some systematic searching and general knowledge. The "hot spots" of pollution are there but we often overlook them. This chapter asks hard questions about home environment. While the simpler the home, the less likely there are severe pollutants present, modern convenience items and a variety of household chemicals seem to tempt all levels of society, and to transcend class and economic differences. More than likely there is something for everyone to discover in this survey.

The procedure for home surveying is in three parts: to survey the home in a preliminary manner before reflecting on possible dangers; to survey the home with a set of questions which might reveal many unthought-of pollutants; to survey the market place for subtle pressures and products which lead to further pollution of homes. The preliminary survey really shows how aware we are of certain dangers. It establishes what we know and makes us cognizant of our ignorance. A second survey will alert us to the full range of pollutants in our home. Finally, becoming more familiar with consumer products, even those we don't buy, makes us more aware of what threatens the health and safety of all home dwellers.

A PRELIMINARY HOME SURVEY

Finding the pollution "hot spots" in our home means knowing the place where we live. It means reviewing what we buy and use as household products, what the design and materials are which compose our house, and what specific lifestyle practices might be harmful.

Let's begin with a rough sketch or floor plan of the house. Include all the key living areas where pollutants might be found. Don't overlook any part of the total home. The precise floor measurements are not necessary, nor the exact placement on the plan of doors and windows. Realistic approximations, however, might answer some questions about indoor air quality. The following areas should not be overlooked:

1. Kitchen
2. Closets and storage areas
3. Living and dining room area
4. Bathroom and showers
5. Bedroom and sleeping area
6. Garage (whether attached or detached)
7. Utility area for clothes washing and drying apparatus
8. Furnace room or area
9. Work, study, hobby area
10. Recreation area
11. Attic
12. Back porch and yard (technically out-of-doors but the source of pollutants which may seep into the house).

Overcome any reluctance about a preliminary survey. It is a valuable exercise. Maybe the family can make a game out of the survey. It is a grown-up's hide-and-seek. See who comes up with the greatest number of possible and actual pollutants. An unopened can of toxic material is a potential pollutant, whereas an open one is actual hazard. Give each person as much time as necessary.

With sketch in hand move throughout the house and immediate environs and note where all boxes, chests, cans, and bottles of chemicals are located. Check window sills, tool chests, closets, and dresser drawers. Keep a running list of all aerosol cans and see whether your home exceeds the national average of forty-five units. Note whether any of these were unused in the last three months, whether any have corroded, and whether they are near heated areas. Check for damaged chemical containers and spilled chemicals, for these are truly pollutants.

Read the labels of a variety of boxes and cans in the household for warnings to users. Does the manufacturer tell whether the contents are dangerous? In listing pollutants in each area of the house, underline those materials which the surveyor thinks are either toxic or unsafe in some form of application. Highlight those which are difficult to dispose of or might be spilled easily.

Circle materials which could be mishandled by the children. Even if no children are present, make such a marking since many visitors bring inquisitive children who might wander unattended through the home.

Check the building materials used in the home. Remember to check for heating and cooling practices and to inspect the furnace room and the ventilation system. Note the fireplace and kitchen stove areas. Check insulation in the attic areas.

Go through your storage sections of the home. You might be surprised to find out what you've stored there. If there are detached outside buildings, search them also, together with the back porch, garage, and garbage area. Check for fuel and oil storage, and especially check garden supplies.

After the survey has been taken, mark down letters for the class of pollutant from the following listing (don't study before taking the survey):

AEROSOL SPRAYS (A)

BUILDING MATERIALS (B)

CLOTHES AND FABRIC CARE PRODUCTS (C)

DUST (D)

EMISSIONS FROM HEATING AND COOLING
   DEVICES (E)

FURNITURE AND FLOOR POLISHES (F)

GARBAGE AND SOLID WASTES (G)

HOBBIES, ARTS AND CRAFTS (H)

INSECTICIDES AND OTHER CHEMICAL
   PESTICIDES (I)

GERMICIDES AND DISINFECTANTS (J)

KITCHEN AND LAUNDRY SOAPS AND DETER-
   GENTS (K)

LEAD (L)

MOTOR VEHICLE PRODUCTS (M)

NOISE POLLUTION (N)

OVEN AND OTHER CLEANERS (O)

PLASTICS AND PLASTICIZERS (P)

QUICKSILVER (MERCURY) AND OTHER
   METALS (Q)

RADIATION POLLUTION (R)

SOLVENTS (S)

TOBACCO SMOKE (T)

UTENSIL COATINGS (U)

VEGETATION IN THE HOME (V)

WATER CONTAMINANTS (W)

EXTRA CHEMICALS AROUND THE HOME (X)

YULETIDE AND OTHER DECORATIONS (Y)

ZOOLOGICAL WASTE AND DISEASE (Z)

These are the basic classes of pollutants into which the
book is divided.

How many of these are found on the preliminary survey?
Are some categories omitted and overlooked? Are there some
which are unclear? The second survey may help answer some
questions about the category contents. (See sample floor plan
indicating likely location of pollutants.)

Places Where Pollutants Might Be Found

MAIN FLOOR

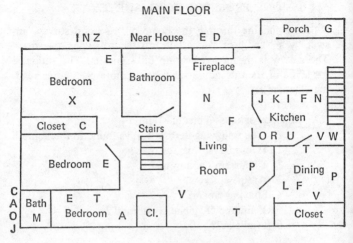

ATTIC

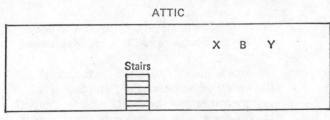

BASEMENT

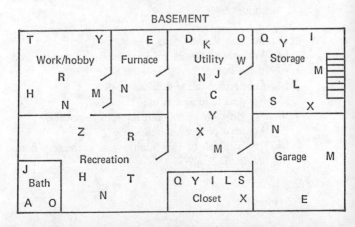

IN-DEPTH HOME SURVEY

Before moving through the home on a second survey, answer "yes," "no," or "uncertain" to the following questions. The survey is meant to clear up uncertainties. The rationale for some of the questions will become more clear after reading Chapter 2.

A AEROSOL SPRAYS (Personal Items)

Are the following aerosol sprays found in the home:

1. Hair sprays, tints, or dyes?
2. Underarm deodorants?
3. Antiperspirants?
4. Shaving cream?
5. Feminine "hygiene deodorant"?
6. Medicines?

B BUILDING MATERIALS

7. Is the home insulated with asbestos products?
8. Are these asbestos caulking materials around the home?
9. Are caulked surfaces sanded in the house?
10. Are air vents or ducts lined with fiber glass?
11. Are home repairs made with asbestos shingles?
12. Are loose asbestos materials stored around the house?

C CLOTHING AND FABRIC CARE PRODUCTS

13. Are spot removers or dry-cleaning materials used in the home?
14. Are aerosol fabric finishes used?
15. Are antistatic agents used?
16. Are gloves worn when using spot removers?
17. Are aerosol spray starches used?
18. Do members of the family wear extremely flammable clothing?

D   DUST

19. Does dust accumulate in various parts of the house? (Be honest.)
20. Is vacuum cleaner in poor running order?
21. Do sweeper bags become overfilled?
22. Are air-conditioner filters left unattended?
23. Are collector screens in clothes driers neglected?
24. Does drier vent fail to reach the outside?
25. Does ragweed grow near the house?
26. Is the ash chute unattended?

E   EMISSIONS FROM HEATING AND COOLING DEVICES

27. Is there a coal, natural gas, or heating oil furnace?
28. Has it been checked this year?
29. Is there a gas stove without an exhaust hood? Was the pilot light for water heater or kitchen stove checked today?
30. Is there an attached garage?
31. Do family or neighbors ever warm up cars (let them idle) for long periods on cold mornings?
32. Is the house near a heavily traveled highway?
33. Does the refrigerator or air-conditioner leak coolant?
34. Is there a kerosene stove, lantern, or camping stove in the house?
35. Is there a fireplace which occasionally emits smoke in the house?
36. Are glowing charcoals ever carried indoors?
37. Is trash burned in the back yard?

F   FURNITURE AND FLOOR POLISHES

38. Is aerosol floor polish, wax, or cleaner used?
39. Are aerosol furniture polish and wax used?
40. Are metal polish and cleaners used (silver, aluminum, brass, and copper) without gloves?
41. Is rust remover kept around the house?

42. Are tarnish-preventing materials used?
43. Is aerosol rug cleaner or tack-down material used?

G GARBAGE AND SOLID WASTES

44. Are there open garbage bags at the kitchen counter?
45. Are garbage cans left open?
46. Are garbage cans left uncleaned especially during hot weather?
47. Is "junk" mail permitted to be sent to the house?
48. Is a garbage service used instead of mulching?
49. Do neighborhood pets get into the garbage?
50. Does garbage stand overnight in the kitchen?
51. Is a garbage disposal unit used?
52. Is an automatic trash compressor used?
53. Is there a failure to defrost and clean out the refrigerator often?
54. Are rotten and stale vegetables and fruits left in the storage room?

H HOBBIES, ARTS AND CRAFTS

55. Is paint (oil-based) used for artistic work at home?
56. Is the hobby area poorly ventilated?
57. Are rocks polished without the use of a facial aspirator?
58. Is film developed in the house?
59. Is pottery baked at home?
60. Are home photographic, painting, and etching supplies stored outside a chemical hood?
61. Are wood lacquers in furniture finishing used?
62. Is metal work such as sculpting, welding, or etching done at home?
63. Are fast-fixing glue and cement kept in the house?

I   INSECTICIDES AND OTHER CHEMICAL PESTICIDES

64. Are insecticides stored in the household?
65. Have any of these ever spilled?
66. Are garden pesticides used?
67. Are rooms used within three days after fumigation?
68. Are pesticides ever used before reading the instructions?
69. Are herbicides used?
70. Is the house unclosed when neighborhood trees are sprayed?
71. Is petroleum-based fly spray used in place of pest sticking paper?
72. Are doors and windows unscreened?
73. Is No-Pest Strip used?
74. Are mothballs stored where small children can get to them?
75. Are aerosol insect repellents used?

J   GERMICIDES AND DISINFECTANTS

76. Are aerosol air fresheners or room deodorizers used?
77. Are aerosol disinfectants used?
78. Are germicides and disinfectants near where children are playing?
79. Is there a failure to aerate rooms after use?
80. Is the family overly germ-conscious?

K   KITCHEN AND LAUNDRY SOAPS AND DETERGENTS

81. Are strong soaps used in kitchen or laundry?
82. Are detergents used?
83. Are brighteners used?
84. Are laundry soap or detergent overused (beyond instruction amounts)?
85. Are soaps and detergents beyond the reach of infants?
86. Are rubber gloves worn when using strong soaps?

87. Are there spilled laundry soaps and detergents in the house?

L LEAD

88. Is indoor lead-based paint present in the house?
89. Is lead paint removed without proper ventilation?
90. Is any of the paint cracking, peeling, and chipping?
91. Is a blowtorch used for removing the paint?
92. Are there old lead-based paint cans around the house?
93. Are unglazed pottery mugs for coffee, tea, fruit juices, or soft drinks used?
94. Do children habitually play within fifty feet of a heavily traveled highway or where dirt is contaminated with leaded gasoline emissions?

M MOTOR VEHICLE PRODUCTS

95. Is gasoline stored in the house or garage?
96. Are aerosol antirust or lubricants in the house?
97. Are there waste oil cans in the house?
98. Is oil changed near the house?
99. Are commercial deicing agents used?
100. Has leaded gasoline been spilled on carport or in garage?
101. Is antifreeze kept away from children?

N NOISE POLLUTION

Are the following used at home:
102. Typewriter?
103. Hair drier?
104. Loud vacuum cleaner?
105. Stereo?
106. Radio?
107. Television?
108. Electric mixer?
109. Power drill?

110. Leaf chopper?
111. Children's toys?
112. Power chain saw?
113. Power lawn mower?
114. Metal garbage cans?
115. Lathe?
116. Vibrator?
117. Motorcycle?
118. Do persons have a habit of making phone calls late at night?

O OVEN AND OTHER CLEANERS
Are the following in the reach of children:
119. Oven cleaners?
120. Glass cleaners?
121. Bleaches?
122. Toilet bowl cleaners?
123. Scouring powders?
124. Are ammonia and bleach or acid cleaners ever mixed in the home?
125. Are rubber gloves worn when working with cleaners?
126. Are a large variety of cleaning agents purchased?
127. Are aerosol drain cleaners used?
128. Are aerosol oven cleaners used?

P PLASTICS AND PLASTICIZERS
129. Are large amounts of plastic furnishings used around the house?
130. Is the family unaware of toxic emissions from burning plastics?
131. Does the car have a film (from plasticizers) on the windows?
132. Are furnishings made from PVC (polyvinyl chloride)?
133. Are PVC containers used for food products?

Q   QUICKSILVER (Mercury) AND OTHER METALS

> 134. Are antifungicide paints used which contain mercury?
> 135. Has spilled mercury ever come from a broken thermometer?
> 136. Are mercury-treated seeds around the garden supplies?
> 137. Is there liquid mercury in the house?

R   RADIATION POLLUTION

> 138. Is an old microwave oven used?
> 139. Does the microwave oven work improperly?
> 140. Do any family members sit quite close to a TV set?
> 141. Are there ultraviolet lamps in the house?
> 142. Is the house near high-tension electric wires?
> 143. Are black lights in the home?
> 144. Do members oversunbathe?
> 145. Is the home near locations containing powerful transmitters or defense electronic equipment?

S   SOLVENTS

Are the following stored in the house?

> 146. Paint solvents?
> 147. Paint thinners?
> 148. Paint removers?
> 149. Lighter fluid (charcoal or tobacco)?
> 150. Butane lighter containers?
> 151. Kerosene?
> 152. Are aerosol paint products used?
> 153. Are oily rags stored around the house?
> 154. Are there open cans of petroleum-based solvents with paint brushes?
> 155. Are cement solvents used?
> 156. Is the house aerated after painting until fumes decrease significantly?

T TOBACCO SMOKE

Is smoking allowed in the following:

157. Bedrooms?
158. Bathroom?
159. Living room?
160. Kitchen?
161. Recreation area?
162. Do smokers fail to honor nonsmoker rights?
163. Is the house aired out after smoking and parties?
164. Is marijuana smoking permitted in the house?

U UTENSIL COATINGS

165. Are aerosol utensil coating materials used?
166. Is the household ignorant of the use of utensil coatings by teen-agers for sniffing?

V VEGETATION IN THE HOME

167. Are there any poisonous plants in the house?
168. Are any in the reach of children?
169. Are fertilizers kept around the house?

W WATER CONTAMINANTS

170. Is the drinking water below standards for purity?
171. Is hot water used for cooking purposes?
172. Do drinking water pipes contain asbestos?
173. Do they contain lead?
174. Do they contain PVC (polyvinyl chloride)?
175. Is the house near a heavy industrial area?
176. Are the gutters dirty or downspouts blocked?
177. Are pool cleaners stored around the house?
178. Are water-conditioners kept around the house?
179. Is there a water-purifying device in the house?
180. Do the toilets ever back up into the bathtub?
181. Does the water have a cloudy look when taken from the tap?

X EXTRA CHEMICALS AROUND THE HOME

Are the following around the house:

182. Lye and other corrosives?
183. Fireworks?
184. Matches?
185. Aerosol medicines such as decongestants and antifungus agents?
186. Are medicine cabinets unlocked or within reach of children?
187. Are medicines stored near food?
188. Are any old unmarked medicine bottles around?
189. Are any members of the household habitual users of drugs?
190. Are fire extinguishers left unchecked from year to year?
191. Is salt used to melt snow on walkways and drive?

Y YULETIDE AND OTHER DECORATIONS

192. Has there been a cutoff Christmas tree in the house this year?
193. Are aerosol decorative materials or cocktail chillers used?

Z ZOOLOGICAL WASTE AND DISEASE

194. Are there rats or other rodents in or near the house?
195. Are dogs, cats, or other large pets allowed indoors?
196. Do children play near dog or cat litter or in pet pens?
197. Is the pet ever infested with fleas or ticks?
198. Is there a protective screen on chimney to prevent bug and rodent entry?
199. Are there bird nests in rafters or bird droppings near the house?
200. Do the children have pet turtles?

Obviously all 200 questions do not pertain to each household situation. Some may not have pets or a yard or children. But if this is an average American home, about 160 do pertain to you and your household. If the answer to half of those which are pertinent is yes the chances are quite high that potential household pollution problems are present. Mere storage of toxic material may not mean that an actual hazard exists, but the chances for accidents are increased. If one says yes to only about one fifth (40) of the questions, then the degree of pollution potential is low. However, the weight of each question varies with the individual potential for dangers. A person with a habit of using aerosol oven cleaners (⌘119) is in far worse shape than a childless household using matches (⌘184).

Honesty is needed for a complete household survey. But we are prone to stretch the truth, especially after realizing that affirmative answers betray a poorer quality of household environment. Remember, no household is perfect. There are simply too many dangerous materials around to expect any household to be absolutely free.

Besides the yeses and noes, it is highly significant just how many "uncertain" answers have been tallied. The areas of uncertainty are where one should seek further information. The meaning of a danger may not be understood. For instance, why is a fast-fixing glue dangerous? Or maybe the surveyor cannot detect asbestos insulation or whether particular clothing is extremely flammable. At least the survey will pinpoint major uncertainties and lack of information. It may be best to go directly to the sections of Chapter 2 which answer these uncertainties.

Through the survey we might find that we fit into one or other of the following categories: impulsive mixers, overusers, hasty cleaners, sloppy maintainers, and compulsive hoarders.

Some people like to use combinations of spices and herbs in cooking and eating. When they extend their culinary propensities to household chemicals, trouble is brewing in the mixing bowl. Chlorine bleach when mixed with toilet bowl cleaners, ammonia, or drain cleaners can cause deadly gases to evolve. Mixing acids and bases with water can cause severe splattering and resultant burns.

Some people are so caught up in our consumer culture that they believe that if a little substance is good, more is better. Such logic helps commercial sales but is hard on consumer health. For instance, too much acid-type drain cleaner can eat away the pipes. Heavy use of a paint thinner can fill the house with toxic fumes. Overuse of detergent will simply add to the water treatment load on the municipal plant and not produce any cleaner clothing.

It is always a problem to get amateur chemists to take time when handling toxic materials to avoid serious spills. Some people simply underschedule cleaning chores and thus the axiom of haste making waste applies. Take time to read the label; plan how to open, pour, and mix household chemicals. Aerate the workplaces and don't do the operation until the weather co-operates. Hasty people also fail to clean up after painting and using solvents, an operation as important for health and safety as painting itself. Take time before beginning to buy the proper protective gear—goggles, gloves, face masks, or aprons.

Some remember the Fibber McGee and Molly radio show and how the closet door opening signaled a plethora of spilled pots and pans. Generally someone in every household has the "sloppiness" problem. Poor maintenance of such sensitive apparatus as furnaces can be fatal because of emitted carbon monoxide fumes. Failure to clean up spilled chemicals adds to the toxic dust levels. Highly flammable liquids may produce heavier-than-air vapor clouds which creep along the floor and can be ignited by a careless smoker or a pilot light. Thus the sloppy storer must be reminded often to store flammable materials outside. Drugs and poisons should be securely locked and high out of the reach of inquisitive children. Since metal cans rust in humid places and leak products, they should be checked frequently. Unlabeled items should be properly and promptly disposed of even though they may be important and expensive household materials. It's better to store only what we are certain of. The dangers of storing toxic materials near food and beverages hardly need repeating, but almost every survey uncovers one or more examples of this problem. Chapter 2 will treat these dangers in greater detail.

MARKET PLACE SURVEY

In order to become knowledgeable about household pollution, one should learn what is commercially transported, stored, and sold. Merely examining our own shopping list does not tell the whole picture. Our neighbors also go to the store, are tempted to purchase items, and succumb to commercial allurements. By studying the whole panorama of household market products we see the field of possibilities. Some people complain that they do not know of available substitutes for their aerosol sprays—which interestingly, were introduced into the home only two decades ago. The ignorance or shortened memory of consumers makes them prey to consumer rip-offs.

Among the things to look for in taking a consumer market survey are the following:

Advertisements: Collect several weeks of sales notices from drugstores and supermarkets. Find out how many are household products and exactly how many are needed. Are all specialized cleaners needed, or will only a few simple chemicals (baking soda, salt, ammonia, etc.) satisfy the many cleaning needs? Are the items on sale really cheaper than alternatives which are often pushed into the background?

Store Promotion: After getting permission from the store manager—it makes you feel more unhurried and accepted—find out where the product is placed in relation to cheaper and higher priced substitutes. Are the shaving soap and creams more remote from the consumer's reach than the aerosol can? How much prominence is given the various brand items?

Variety: Does the store carry all environmental and consumer quality items and brands, or is the selection restricted to poor-grade and wasteful items? Are the higher priced decorative items displayed and more imaginative and cheaper items simply absent?

Spillage and Contamination: Toxic materials may be in containers in supermarkets which allow for intentional or accidental opening. These may contaminate food, especially fresh produce. Spillage may also occur at check-out counters. (In a consumer survey of a local supermarket, one of our researchers observed a youth taking a household pesticide off the shelf, holding it close to his nose, and sniffing the ejected contents. Apparently the smell did not suit him, for he placed the opened container back on its shelf hardly twenty feet from food products. Our researcher found the label filled with warnings about toxic effects to careless users.)

Consumer Education: Does the store make an effort to tell consumers about the dangers of materials purchased? Quite often the salespersons do not know about materials sold. Find out if they read the labels. Is there any effort to provide displays or instructions for consumers about relative merits of various household products? Does the manager know whether a plastic item is PVC?

Product Placement in Store: Often there is an interspersion of food and toxic household materials in a grocery store or supermarket (e.g., pesticides in supermarkets). Many dangerous items are within reach of small children who often accompany parents.

Besides these general practices one should also look at the specific items sold. Make a listing of a particular product line (e.g., oven cleaners). Read and copy down label instructions. Note the warnings given. Note company name, price, and net weight of materials sold.

Complete knowledge about what is sold enables us to apply pressure to change precise sales practices. Organize a boycott of aerosol sprays or asbestos products. Make the store display safer, more wholesome, and longer-life products to encourage wiser purchasing.

A consumer survey must not stop at general and specific

store management practices but should also include consumer attitudes. Why do consumers purchase a particular product? Do they read labels? Do they compare prices? Do they feel enticed by heavier weighted packages with less net product? Are they influenced by location and sales displays? How much do sales and advertisements influence their buying a particular product line? Do they know about substitutes? While consumer attitudes may aid in understanding the dynamics of the market place, determining these attitudes is beyond the expertise of the average surveyor. It is a whole field of social or consumer psychology.

The market place surveyor may note at times that products with long shelf life often do not conform to updated regulations. Discovering this and making it known to the proper persons may be a beneficial side effect of the market place survey. One area of special note is current regulations for child-resistant containers. The following are now so required:

1. Aspirin—containing products intended to be taken by mouth.
2. Furniture polishes containing 10 per cent or more of petroleum distillates.
3. Liquids containing more than 5 per cent of methyl salicylate (oil of wintergreen).
4. Products containing any substance controlled under the comprehensive Drug Abuse Prevention and Control Act of 1970 such as depressants and stimulants.
5. Dry household substances containing 10 per cent or more of sodium and/or potassium hydroxide (lye), and all other household substances containing 2 per cent or more of sodium and/or potassium hydroxide.
6. Liquid household substances containing 10 per cent or more by weight of turpentine.
7. Prepackaged liquid kindling and/or illuminating preparations, such as fuel for cigarette lighters, charcoal, camping equipment, torches, and decorative or functional lanterns, which contain 10 per cent or more by weight of petroleum distillates.

8. Liquid household substances containing 4 per cent or more by weight of sulfuric acid (not including wet-cell storage batteries).

9. Household substances containing 10 per cent or more by weight of sulfuric acid (not including wet-cell storage batteries).

10. Oral prescription drugs unless specifically exempted.

11. Household substances in liquid form containing 10 per cent or more of ethylene glycol.

The survey may reveal certain repetitions in label warning which will signal to the alert surveyor that a federal agency is now requiring a standardized label warning. With this in mind the person may discover older products on the shelf which do not conform to that label requirement. Such a discovery should be made known to the store management and/or regulatory agency.

A single interested consumer can only do so much. Pretty soon the call for help goes out to neighbors. Tapping into voluntary human resources is a powerful move. The first place to look is within the family for home surveying as mentioned earlier. But there are ways of enlisting a wide range of assisting hands by using some ingenuity.

The millions of high-schoolers, especially those in biological and social science classes, are often more than willing to gather data and information as part of the course requirements. Work through the teachers, not the students. Teachers are often eager to discover ways students can collect meaningful information and still learn about the scientific method in the process. Ask teachers to develop a systematic surveying of the student's home as part of regular course work. This should be done early in the course before routine subject matter piles up. Elementary chemistry courses are also opportunities for both home and market place surveying. Map out stores for different students to prevent store managers from becoming angry at large numbers of noncustomers looking over the wares.

Have boy or girl scouts engage in home surveying. Make merit badges for home environment. There is no need that all of the surveys be done at the place where they live—an agreeable neighbor's home may be a ripe place to gain an environmental merit badge for discovery of pollutants. Another exercise for these younger children is to have them review catalogues of merchandise for dangerous or potentially harmful products.

For college and graduate school students, perhaps a more sophisticated level of action is needed. These students may initiate the following regulatory actions regarding poor consumer practices by manufacturer, distributor, and individual stores:

- Petition corrective labeling to the FTC.
- Expose potentially dangerous commercial items to the CPSC.
- Bring an unforeseen indoor environmental hazard to the attention of the EPA.

CHAPTER 2

KNOW AND CURB POLLUTANTS IN THE HOME

Pinpointing potential dangers may be a nice home game, but a more thorough knowledge of home hazards is required. Ecology deals with the relationships of living organisms "in" or "to" their environment. Household ecology is somewhat complex since the risks of certain homemaking practices must be balanced with benefits including a better quality of home living (cleanliness, warmth or coolness, etc.), which is a matter of subjective value judgments. It is also difficult to determine the seriousness of the various potential hazards. Which problem should be tackled first requires environmental knowledge and understanding.

Furthermore, the individuality of homes makes generalizing about indoor ecology more difficult. Some of the factors which accentuate that individuality include:

- Outdoor pollution surrounding a given home environment (how near a heavy-trafficked highway, a heavy-polluting industry, an airport, etc.).
- Indoor cooking, cleaning, and smoking practices which may be partly affected by habit and customs.

- Home maintenance practices both internal and external (garbage collection).
- Home heating, ventilating, and air-conditioning systems.
- Meteorological conditions (humidity, winter and summer temperatures, air currents).
- Geographic factors (proximity to mountains, lakes, sea-shores, etc.).
- Building location (on hillside, in a valley, or near woods).
- Building type (apartment, single dwelling in town or country, etc.).
- Building construction and design.
- Energy conservation practices (degree of insulation).
- Neighborhood practices and ordinances (amount of noise allowed).
- Lifestyle practices and number of inhabitants within a dwelling.
- Permeability of the dwelling.

Since these factors go beyond the scope of this book, it is important that the reader understand the basic dangers of each pollutant and then apply them to his or her specific home environment.

Merely exposing the many dangers and potential dangers which are present in the average modern home is not sufficient. Some things can be done when the household pollutant is discovered and exposed, and some must wait until a substitute is found. The remedy needed in each case varies considerably, and so it is misleading to say that substitutes are easy to buy or make or apply. In the case of aerosol sprays substitutes are easy and a low investment, but in the case of household building materials it requires the replacement at considerable expense of a floor or an insulation system. And even the act of replacing potentially polluting materials may prove dangerous.

Costs are not the only hurdles in choosing substitutes. In some of the groups of pollutants the cure or substitute is a new practice which may go beyond some people's notions of free choice of lifestyle, and requires other judgments than merely purchasing or refurbishing materials. For instance, hobbyists may have to change their pastimes, noisemakers become silent, and homemakers restrict their choices of pets. This is an invitation to examine the substitute as an option which might lead to a healthier and higher quality home environment.

Not every substitute is listed, and in some cases the ideal one has not yet been pinpointed even if it could be determined theoretically. However, selections have been made based on the following:

- Proven safety in handling
- Lack of all health effects to maker or user
- Minor disposal problems
- Low drain on nonrenewable resources
- Availability at low cost to consumer

Some obvious substitutes are omitted for not fulfilling these criteria. Likewise some partially tested substitutes are noted and the tentative nature of these suggestions pointed out.

A. AEROSOL SPRAYS

The first living creature to die from an aerosol spray was a mosquito in 1942. Since then the American aerosol spray industry has cast its eyes far beyond pesticides to include a variety of consumer products (see listing at end of this section). The industry has grown to be an $8-billion monolith, annually producing about 3 billion aerosol spray cans. The injury to human beings and the environment has grown. The death toll has mounted. Aerosol sprays didn't just stop mosquitoes. In 1975 at least seventy-nine aerosol spray fatalities in humans were reported, a number which is perhaps on the conservative side. The greater part of this toll was from intentional sniffing of aerosol fumes by teen-agers.

However, other dangers exist. One government account documents the death of a Willowgrove, Pennsylvania, woman who was killed when an aerosol spray can hidden in a wastepaper fire exploded, severing her jugular vein. More gruesome incidents exist. Aerosol sprays present multifaceted dangers to human beings, and many consumers are becoming aware of these dangers through use. In 1975 alone, 5,626 people were treated in hospital emergency rooms for aerosol spray related injuries. Even more disconcerting is that this was a 26 per cent increase over 1974, with 1976 continuing the increase in reported injuries.

Why the dangers? One problem rests with the basic design of how the aerosol spray works. Aerosol sprays contain an active ingredient (deodorant, window cleaners, etc.) and liquid or gaseous propellant that are packed under pressure (40 psi). The pressure is needed to expel the mixture of the propellant and active ingredient in the form of a fine mist.

Pressurized cans are dangerous, however, because when heated or left lying around in a warm room they have the potential to become like powerful bombs. This explosive quality is a major cause for concern. In addition, so are the more insidious effects on human health and the environment.

Health Effects

Contrary to what many citizens believe, it is not necessary for the manufacturer to demonstrate an aerosol product's safety in order to put it on the market. Even in the case of medical products for which preliminary experiments are required, there is no absolute guarantee of safety (remember thalidomide). Most aerosol products such as personal items and cleansing agents are marketed with few if any restrictions on product safety. In effect, the consumer becomes the test animal in the laboratory of the home to determine the ill effects associated with the use of aerosol sprays.

Aerosol sprays are a major source of air pollution within our homes. Aerosol mists spread out into the surrounding air making it unfit to breathe. This is especially true in closed quarters such as the bathroom where concentrations of propellant reach dangerous levels. A study completed by Du Pont Laboratories measured the amounts of fluorocarbon (Freon) propellant in the air in front of the faces of users of hair spray and deodorant in a room ventilated with an exhaust fan. They found concentrations of propellants as high as 460 parts per million in ventilated rooms—levels of considerable health concern. Unfortunately, the recent fluorocarbon replacements (hydrocarbons) are of even greater health concern.

The use of aerosol sprays intensifies hazards due to inhalation of certain chemicals and creates new problems as well. Health hazards are increased because the small size of aerosolized particles makes it possible for chemicals to be inhaled deeply into the lungs and quickly absorbed into the bloodstream. Thus, a chemical that is harmless to external parts of the body may be extremely dangerous if inhaled as an aerosol mist. The combined effect of the ingredients common in most aerosol spray products is another area of grave concern which has not been thoroughly investigated.

A gradual accumulation of clinical data is beginning to link aerosol use and misuse to a variety of medical problems. The most serious potential dangers include the induction of cardiac arrhythmias, or "sudden death," birth defects, and lung cancer. In addition, research studies done at universities, medical colleges, and hospitals across the country have associated headaches, nausea, dizziness, shortness of breath, eye and throat irritations, skin rashes, burns, lung inflammations, and liver damage with aerosol spray products.

A serious misuse of aerosol spray products that occurs commonly among teen-agers trying to get "high" involves the forced inhalation of aerosol spray fumes in a severely restricted space such as a plastic bag. Inhaling the mist can be very dangerous because it quickly enters the lungs and is transmitted easily into the bloodstream. The primary ingredient that yields these highs is the common aerosol propellant HHP (halogenated hydrocarbon propellant or fluorocarbon). Some solvents and active ingredients also contribute to the toxic effects.

Teams of researchers throughout the country have devised tests using laboratory animals in which the HHP doses of human "sniffers" are simulated. Fifty to 90 per cent of the animals died suddenly. Analysis of the hearts of these animals and of the heart muscles directly subjected to HHP has led to an understanding of how the heart is affected. Adrenaline, which normally speeds the heart rate, is enhanced by HHP. The pacemaker of the heart is overstimulated and its control over the heart muscles is lost. As a result there is a loss of natural rhythm, fibrillation, and, finally, heart arrest and death.[1,2,3,4]

Dr. Nancy Flowers, of the Veterans Administration Hospital in Augusta, Georgia, and Dr. Leo G. Horan, of the Medical College of Georgia, have done research to find out why only some of the HHP sniffers die. The researchers exposed dogs to the fumes of HHP simulating the conditions of human abuse. Thirteen dogs reacted with slower heart rate and irregular beats. Another thirteen went into fibrillation and suffered cardiac death. The blood of the latter group, before and during the experiment, had higher bicarbonate levels than the survivors. Flowers and Horan conclude that "these data suggest that one factor in determining the likelihood of survival or death in young people who sniff aerosols deliberately may relate to the acid-base response of the host to the inhalant."[5] Thus since these responses differ in individual people, the dangers vary also from person to person.

Laboratories associated with aerosol manufacturers claim that their experiments show no ill effects of HHP.[6] Dr. William S. Harris, a cardiologist at the University of Illinois, responded to this claim[7] and explained that by varying the procedures and by drawing faulty conclusions the industry researchers concluded that HHPs are nontoxic.

Cardiac patients should be particularly cautious in using aerosols. Even the small amounts of propellant introduced with normal use can put an added burden on their hearts. In his experiments with animals, Du Pont's Dr. Charles F. Reinhardt found that an increase of noise in the laboratory enhanced the effect of HHP on the heart. He advises that serious consideration be given to the effects of HHP in combination with stress, exercise, caffeine, and drugs.[4]

Experiments, except for those being conducted daily in millions of homes, have yet to be done to determine the long-term effect of propellants on the heart and other organs.

Aerosol sprays have been implicated in the development of lung cancer. Dr. William Good, of Montrose, Colorado, has followed cell changes in the lung with the Pap smear technique. He designated five classes of change from normal through to precancerous. In a study of two hundred people with one thing in common—all were *heavy* users of aerosol sprays—he found precancerous lung cell changes in all two hundred.[8]

Dr. Good in conjunction with Dr. Carl Ellison and Dr. Victor E. Archer, medical director of the Western Area Occupational Health Laboratory of the Department of Health, Education, and Welfare, completed a study comparing about fifty average daily users and fifty light-to-nonusers of several sprays. All the first group had gone to Dr. Good with complaints of tiredness, irritability, and vague muscle and joint pain. In this group, cultures of sputum, collected by induced coughing, uniformly grew coliform organisms (bacteria commonly found in the intestinal tract which are disease producers when introduced into other body cavities or into wounds). Atypical cells were seen in the sputum of all regular aerosol users, whereas seven of the no/low-use group showed none. The first group had moderate or marked changes in cell form, whereas only two of the other group showed atypical, precancerous cells.[8]

Aerosol propellants can be damaging to the body surface as well. Most readers are familiar with sprays used to chill cocktail glasses. The average spray will chill your skin when directly applied and even cause frostbite. Because they dissolve fats, the HHPs diffuse into the skin and remove natural oils and cause local irritation. Spraying accidentally into the eyes is known to cause corneal irritations and freeze burns. Besides freons, other less widely used propellants for both aerosol sprays and pressurized foams can be dangerous. Nitrous oxide, used in some food products and some shaving lathers, and methylene chloride, used in some hair sprays, have an anesthetic effect. Propane, a flammable material, is also used in some hair sprays.

Store shelves contain a large variety of aerosol sprays used in the garden and home such as insect sprays, cleaning agents, and paints. Most of these products contain poisons (see Sections I and O). Since federal law requires labeling poisonous contents, toxic ingredients in aerosol bug and weed killers are now listed on the cans. This labeling has proven inadequate, however. Consumer groups urge that aerosols containing poisons be color-coded or labeled more boldly. They express deep concern about safety for children who are attracted to aerosol containers as playthings.

Hair sprays are among the most dangerous of the aerosol sprays. They are widely used in close quarters—beauty parlors and bathrooms. The mist is emitted near the face, and thus the air breathed is heavily contaminated. The ingredients are unique and have toxic effects.

Like most other aerosol products, about 60–70 per cent of a hair spray can's contents is propellant. Besides this, neutralizers, plasticizers, a solvent (usually alcohol), and often perfume are present, as are substances which coat hair strands. These coating substances differ among brands, but include shellac, starch, Gantrez, and polyvinylpyrrolidone (PVP). The plasticizers reduce the tendency of the coating materials to form flakes.

PVP was first considered to be nontoxic and nonallergenic. However, recent evidence links PVP with thesaurosis, a lung disease afflicting some users of hair spray. Victims show enlarged lymph nodes and develop small firm masses in the lung which can be detected by X-ray examination. Victims also have an accumulation of an unusual number of eosinophils (white blood cells which stain red) in the blood (eosinophilia). Victims have shown dramatic improvement after halting the use of hair spray. The FDA reported on twenty-three women who were daily users of hair spray and whose X-rays showed lung changes. Of these, fifteen recovered within six months after spraying stopped.[9]

Since eosinophilia is associated with allergy, thesaurosis could be an allergic condition. This would explain why only some hair spray users develop the disease.

Plasticizers in hair sprays can also be harmful. One of these is silicone, which is damaging to the eyes. The cleansing action of eye fluid cannot wash silicone away and thus an irritating coating of the cornea results.

Among the aerosol sprays, feminine deodorants stand out as a blatant insult to the consumer. The need for these sprays was fabricated in the minds of industry executives who then foisted a totally unnecessary chemical concoction onto the consumer market. As *Aerosol Age*, the aerosol spray trade magazine, says, "But such is the American way of advertising, suggestion and persuasion that even the best smelling ladies began to feel insecure and wonder if they were offending—and another new market was born."[10]

In the case of feminine sprays, commercial exploitation led to health problems. Many cases of vulvar irritation have been observed by gynecologists and were directly attributed to these sprays. Of course, no real benefits accrue from such sprays. On the contrary, the sprays are irritants. Some also contain talc, which is often contaminated with asbestos, a known carcinogenic agent.

"Air fresheners" and deodorants are of major concern (see Section J), as are a number of medicinal products also offered in aerosol spray form: vaporizers, nasal sprays, skin bandages, antibiotics, topical anesthetics, contraceptives, and medicines for athlete's foot, poison ivy, and burns. Pressurized aerosol vaporizers have come into wide use in the past decade for emergency treatment of bronchial spasm, particularly in asthmatic seizures. They contain propellant plus a drug which acts on the nervous system to cause dilation of the ends of the bronchial tree in the lung.

In the last decade a number of deaths in this country were directly associated with the use of isoproterenol, a drug used to control asthma. However, the situation here never became as serious as in England and Wales where death rates among asthmatics increased sevenfold between 1959 and 1966. When it was realized that the users in England were getting five times as much isoproterenol as others throughout the world, the concentrated dose was banned and the epidemic regressed.[11]

However, a closer look at the physiological effects of isoproterenol reveals that the propellant and not the drug could have contributed to the deaths. Experiments with isoproterenol showed that the small amounts which reach the heart with normal use are not damaging. With larger doses or with prolonged use there is a phenomenon which causes a worsening of the bronchoconstriction. Perhaps the asthmatic who is gasping for breath increases spraying and inhales large quantities. This could cause the same kind of cardiac death from HHP as seen with many young "sniffers." Some of the victims of the United Kingdom epidemic were found with empty vaporizers beside them.

Safety Effects

A department store fire in West Germany in the fall of 1967 caused the explosion of one thousand aerosol containers, which became jet-propelled flaming torches. The resulting panic took twenty-two lives.

There are many recorded examples of the lethal effects of exploding aerosol bombs. These "A-bombs" are presented to the consumer in metal containers with ingredients pressurized between 40- and 100-pound-per-square-inch gauge, with 60–70 per cent of the contents of the can being propellant. The mixtures in aerosol cans are not dangerous under normal conditions, but when stored where the can is exposed to high temperatures, the pressure in the can will increase, reaching bursting pressures of 210 to 400 psig. Temperatures ranging from 120–160° Fahrenheit can cause the inside pressure to rise enough to burst the container.

Furnaces, stoves, ovens, and even proximity to strong sunlight have been known to cause aerosol can explosions. A nineteen-month-old baby was seriously injured when the can of hair spray she was playing with exploded. It happened in a well-heated room during the winter. Investigators deduced that the heat was sufficient to cause the propellant gases to reach the point of explosion.[12] In another case, an aerosol paint container exploded while on the seat of a car parked facing the sun.[12]

Many cans do not carry warnings telling of the danger of explosion. Those which do are often ignored by consumers and most certainly by small children. Familiarity breeds contempt, and that certainly applies to aerosol bombs.

The aerosol industry is well aware of the explosiveness of its product. It says remedies are available to prevent explosions and that development of safety mechanisms started back in 1924. Since the aerosol boom, no fewer than sixty-three patents for safety releases have been introduced for incorporation into aerosol cans. These mechanisms would cost from one to five cents per can, which is a small price to pay for such protection.

Among some of the ideas for safety mechanisms are plugs which are released with increasing pressure, puncture devices, and scored or thinner places in the walls or seams of the cans. While they do not eliminate the hazardous chemicals emitted during use, all are designed to give way when the pressure increases to a dangerous level and, thus, prevent high-pressure build-up.[13] Corporate inertia has so far kept these from being used.

Child-proofing is another major concern. The Poison Prevention Act of 1970 of the FDA encourages work in this field. A provision states that all aerosol oven cleaners and other caustic products must have child-resistant closures. Manufacturing firms like Seaquist, Union Carbide, Knight Engineering, Molding Company, and Safety Packaging have successfully prepared closures now available for aerosols. Safety closures should be required on all pressurized containers.

Many aerosols contain flammable materials such as alcohol, a commonly used solvent, and propane, used as a propellant in some sprays. Many paints, varnishes, and petroleum distillates are flammable. A Galesburg, Illinois, three-year-old was playing with a can of flammable hair spray which ignited. He died from severe burns. A Pittsburgh woman was so severely burned from the ignition of her flammable hair spray that she died. In another case, a fifty-three-year-old woman was severely burned on her back, arm, chest, foot, and neck from the ignited ingredients of her punctured 3M spray adhesive. It had been overheated by a nearby gas burner.[12]

Aerosol sprays are also quite corrosive to steel and other metals. HHPs are known to cause damage to nonelectric furnace heat exchangers. The first documented cases occurred in 1948 in dry-cleaning plants. Since the advent of hair sprays, beauty shops have been plagued by corrosion of heating units. A direct connection has been shown between HHP concentration in the air and the degree of corrosive damage. The effect is not caused by HHP, but by the strong acids which result from the breakdown of HHP in the presence of heat. Even minute amounts as little as 1 part per million of hydrochloric acid will damage steel heating chambers and flues. These concentrations are well below the threshold for smell and thus go undetected. One beauty parlor, where about twelve propellant cans were used each week, had to replace the furnace after two years of use because of serious corrosion.[14] A Detroit city ordinance was passed in 1965 against using HHP sprays in beauty salons. Sprays could not be used unless the heating unit was far from the work area and well ventilated. Lennox Industries, a manufacturer of heat elements and exchangers, recognized the problem of acid corrosion by HHP breakdown products. Their equipment warranty does not cover furnaces operated in atmospheres contaminated by compounds of chlorine, fluorine, and other damaging chemicals frequently found in aerosol sprays.

Areas in private homes can suffer damage by prolonged use of aerosols. Air contaminated with HHPs can corrode and shorten the life span of furnaces, especially if circulating air is in a closed circuit. Interior decorations can take on a yellow-brown discoloration from aerosol spray ingredients. Aerosols sprayed into an open fire can cause the generation of corrosive gases (hydrofluoric acid, hydrochloric acid, and phosgene) which are highly toxic.

The aerosol boom has had its impact upon the environment in general. Difficulties arise in attempting to recycle aerosol cans and to dispose of the empty containers at traditional sites. Aerosol cans present a unique recycling problem because residual gases can ruin metal shredders. This is analogous to recycling problems in the scrap automobile industry, where great care is taken to remove gas tanks because of dangers of explosion from residual gases.

Billions of aerosol cans are creating a mountain of solid waste in already overburdened city and town dumps. These dangerous throwaways litter homes, yards, dumps, and recycling depots. Home incineration is blatantly dangerous. Home compactors are now being used in increasing numbers. These appliances could be ruined and people in the room could be seriously injured from an exploding aerosol can. Exploding aerosol cans can be a hazard for attendants and bystanders at open-burning disposal sites. Municipal incinerators can be damaged and cracked by the internal bombardment caused by aerosol containers.

Worker safety in aerosol manufacturing plants is also becoming a significant concern for industry. Aerosol manufacturing plants commonly suffer tragic explosions. In the month of January 1976, twenty-six employees were seriously injured and four killed in two separate plant explosions.[15]

Resource Waste

For the most part, the 3 billion aerosol sprays produced each year are unnecessary consumer items which waste vast amounts of materials, such as steel, plastic, paper, and energy. The spray valve alone has eight separate plastic parts, and the filling of these pressurized containers requires tremendous amounts of energy.

Because aerosol containers are explosive and since the separation of nonreusable container materials is difficult at best, recycling aerosol cans is next to impossible. So essentially all of the energy that goes into the production of an aerosol product is lost forever.

Another example may help clarify the enormous waste of resources and energy inherent in the aerosol spray can. Compare the cost in materials required to manufacture "disposable" aerosol cans of shaving cream with the costs of a brush, mug, and soap shaving kit that can be reused indefinitely. A simple survey of shaving habits conducted by the authors revealed that one bar of shaving soap lasted as long as four cans of aerosol shaving cream. The resource and energy savings of the soap over the aerosol can are significant and so is the money saved, over four dollars in this case.

Environmental Effects

Considerable recent scientific evidence has been mounting that indicts certain acrosol propellants, principally dichlorodifluoromethane and trichloromonofluoromethane (Freon 12 and 11) as the causative agents in the depletion of ozone in the upper atmosphere. Reduction of the ozone layer and the resulting rise in harmful ultraviolet (UV) radiation reaching the earth could result in a number of adverse biological effects in human beings including increased incidence of skin cancer, sunburning, skin aging, eye damage, and vitamin D poisoning. In addition, ecological changes could occur which have fundamental implications for the well-being of the biosphere. Recent studies postulate worldwide crop damage, increased incidence of cancer in livestock, modification of insect behavior, major alterations in aquatic and terrestrial ecosystems, and pronounced global climatic changes.

Early in 1974 Drs. F. S. Rowland and M. J. Molina at the University of California, Irvine,[16] reported that a photolytic reaction on the stratosphere, involving short wave-length UV radiation acting upon fluorocarbon gases, yielded chloride radicals, which serve as a catalyst in eroding the ozone layer at a rate now estimated to be 10,000 ozone molecules per chlorine atom.[17] The initial ozone depletion theory proposed by Rowland and Molina has since been confirmed by a number of independent research investigators[18] and a fourteen-member Interagency Federal Task Force on the Inadvertent Modification of the Stratosphere. Perhaps the most significant endorsement of the theory has come from a high-level panel of the National Academy of Sciences. The panel's report predicted that if current levels of fluorocarbons continued, the earth's ozone layer would ultimately be depleted between 2 and 20 per cent.[19] (It has been estimated that a 7 per cent reduction of the ozone layer could result in an additional 42,000 cases of skin cancer a year.)[20] Calling such a prospect "intolerable,"[19] the Food and Drug Administration subsequently joined with the Environmental Protection Agency to announce a ban on most aerosols containing fluorocarbons. Scheduled to go into effect by April 1979, the ban does not cover products still on the shelf in the store or home.

In anticipation of the fluorocarbon ban, aerosol manufacturers have been switching increasingly to hydrocarbon gas and pressurized petroleum for propellants. While the atmospheric impact of these alternatives is substantially less than their fluorocarbon counterparts, the substitute propellants will generate health hazards of their own. According to Du Pont Company's inhalation toxicologist, Dr. Henry Trochimowicz, the "alternative compounds . . . will certainly be a little more toxic than the ones we have now from a basic inhalation point of view."[21] It is also important to remember that even when the fluorocarbon threat to the ozone layer is diminished, problems of flammability, waste disposal, and resource depletion will remain.

Economic Argument

Quite often economic reasons may be more persuasive than health, safety, and environmental ones. The extra expense is subtly concealed from the consumer with fancy packaging and deceptive advertising. Uninformed by the label and unable to inspect the contents of the aerosol spray can, the consumer is forced into making choices based upon a false impression of the product's contents.

The amount of propellant in any aerosol spray is an accurate measure of the added cost of aerosol products. In comparing aerosol and nonaerosol products the price differential is directly related to the amount of propellant. The more propellant in an aerosol spray can, the less the concentration of active ingredients and the greater the cost of convenience. In a 1975 petition to the FTC, Students Resisting Aerosol Fluorcarbon Emissions (STRAFE), a Geroge Washington Law School group, identify the camouflaged costs of aerosol sprays that dupe the consumer:[22]

"Walking into his neighborhood market, a consumer approaches a shelf abundantly stocked with aerosol products. Reaching for an aerosol can of Alberto VO5 hair spray, he sees that a 16-ounce can sells for $1.99, or what seems to be 12¢ per ounce.

"Nearby he notices Alberto VO5 in another form. It is the familiar nonaerosol pump system which produces a mist when the pump is depressed. Selling for $1.99 for 8 ounces, the pump spray costs 25¢ per ounce. Comparing the two alternatives, the consumer would undoubtedly make what he perceived to be the optimal, rational purchasing decision—to buy Alberto VO5 in the aerosol can because of its convenience and lower cost. Is it really cheaper, though?

"The consumer's computation of unit price rests upon a deceptive foundation. The aerosol can consists of two elements: the hair spray (the product concentrate) and the propellant which forces the hair spray from the can into the hair. In Alberto VO5, the amount of propellant is 65% of the total net weight. Only 5.6 ounces of the total 16 ounces is actually the hair spray. The actual, as opposed to perceived, unit price of the aerosol is thus 36¢ per ounce, three times the original cost estimate and 50% more expensive than the nonaerosol package.

"This price differential is material and substantial enough that, if disclosed to the consumer, it might alter his purchasing decision, especially in light of the health, safety, and environmental costs associated with the use of aerosol cans."[22]

The ratio of propellant to active ingredient varies depending on the particular chemical characteristics of the product, but in each product class, such as deodorants or oven cleaners, there are typical formulations having only minor brand differences. These standard formulations are not trade secrets, yet few consumers are aware of the inherent waste in aerosol sprays. Examples of typical formulations are listed in Table I.

The most meaningful comparison of costs for aerosols and nonaerosols are based on the average cost per application.

New York's Public Interest Group tested various consumer products in the laboratory under conditions simulating normal usage in the home. The testing was completed in the summer of 1975, and the results clearly show that the cost per application of aerosols was significantly higher than for nonaerosols. Table II includes a sample listing.

Aerosol spray cans also have an added cost which results from the inability of the spray valve mechanism to effectively dispense all its contents. A study in 1971 showed that the spray can is never completely emptied.[23] Some product and/or propellant remains even after the can is no longer usable. Further waste results when the can has a faulty valve and must be discarded. Clogged nozzles, common among spray starches and powders, are also extremely costly and wasteful. By contrast, alternative products in solid, liquid, or pump spray form can be dispensed completely.

Table I TYPICAL AEROSOL FORMULATIONS

Product Class	% Propellant	% Product Concentrate
Underarm deodorant		
Type A	45	55
Type B	90	10
Antiperspirant		
Type A	30	70
Type B	90	10
Feminine hygiene spray	95	5
Antifogging agents	60	40
Oven cleaner		
Type A	25	75
Type B	10	90
Pre-laundry spot remover	30	70
Floor wax	50	50
Frying pan spray	45	55
Varnish	41	59
White enamel	27	73
Insect repellent	70	30

Source: J. Sciaria and L. Stoller, *The Science and Technology of Aerosol Packaging* (New York: Wiley-Interscience, 1974), p. 32.

TABLE II
COMPARATIVE COSTS OF PRODUCTS

PRODUCT	Container	Retail price $	Net wt. (oz.) from label	Usable net wt. (GM.) from lab	Average wt. per application (GM.)	Average no. of applications per container	Average cost per application	Cost per application of aerosol as % of cost per application of non-aerosol**
Solarcaine								
Spray	aerosol	2.19	4	116.04	2.75	42.2	.052	433% of bottle
Lotion	sqz. bottle	2.19	6*	156.26	.88	178.1	.012	
Mennen								
Spray Deodorant	aerosol	1.39	7	117.24	.496	236	.006	225% of pump
Pump Spray Deodorant	pump spray	1.08	3*	103.76	.251	413.1	.003	666% of roll-on
Roll-on Deodorant	roll-on	.99	2*	54.95	.048	1144.9	.0009	
Adorn								
Self-Styling Hair Spray	aerosol	2.49	13	302.43	4.950	61	.040	118% of bottle
Firm & Free Hair Spray	spray bottle	2.39	8	198.97	2.81	70.8	.034	
Lysol Cleaner								
Aerosol	aerosol	1.75	17	474.78	4.642	102.2	.017	243% of bottle
Liquid	bottle	1.89	15*	451.49	1.956	230.7	.008	
Jubilee								
Kitchen Wax	aerosol	1.49	10.5	296.94	5.94	50	.030	250% of bottle
Kitchen Liquid Wax	bottle	1.19	14*	387.04	4.03	96	.012	

*Fluid Ounces
**Calculated with unrounded numbers

"Aerosol Sprays," C.S.P.I., Washington, D.C., 1976, p. 29. Data from "A Comparative Study of the Costs of Aerosol and Non-Aerosol Products," New York Public Interest Research Group, Inc., 5 Beekman Street, New York, N.Y. 10038

Avoid Aerosol Sprays

For the most part, the use of aerosol sprays is no more effective than pouring, wiping, or dusting; it is often wasteful because the sprayed substance goes beyond the target area. When spraying is desirable to cover a surface evenly or to get into intricate surfaces, use spray guns. Despite the inconvenience of cleaning them out, they provide a safer method for painting difficult areas or waterproofing fabrics.

Other reasons already stated for avoiding aerosol sprays include safety and health effects on home dwellers, disposal problems, use of nonrenewable resources, high cost of items, and threat to environment from propellants.

There is really no proper manner of using aerosol sprays in the home. If unused or partly used spray cans are around the house, take them outdoors and empty contents into a garbage can. Don't inhale ingredients. If the can is rusted, wrap it with a cloth and release the contents while wearing gloves. Never throw the emptied containers into a fire or incinerator.

Work toward the removal of aerosol cans in your neighborhood stores and lobby for municipal, state, and federal laws to ban their use. For further suggestions see Section U.

Aerosol Spray Substitutes

The big question after one is aware of aerosol sprays is "What can I use instead?" The proliferation of aerosol sprays in drug, hardware, and grocery stores creates the impression that consumers cannot function without them. Careful shopping, however, turns up many satisfactory substitutes. For some aerosol spray products which represent a blatant abuse of merchandising practices no substitutes are necessary or recommended.

The following is a selected list of personal aerosol spray

substitutes. Before purchasing a substitute ask whether it is needed. MENTION OF A PRODUCT IN NO WAY CONSTITUTES AN ENDORSEMENT, but it does indicate the product's superiority over the alternate aerosol spray package.

BREATH FRESHENERS:

Doctors recommend warm salt-water rinse. If you prefer to buy a commercial mouthwash, many companies produce them:

Listerine, Warner-Lambert Co., Morris Plains, N.J.
Scope, Procter & Gamble, Cincinnati, Ohio
Lavoris, Vick Chemical Co., New York, N.Y.
Cepacol, Merrill National Labs., Cincinnati, Ohio
Chloraseptic Pump Spray, Norwich Pharmaceutical Co., Norwich, N.Y.

DEODORANTS AND ANTIPERSPIRANTS:

Many companies produce roll-ons, creams, sticks, or non-aerosol sprays that are displayed beside their aerosol products. A sampling would be:

Arrid, Carter Products, New York, N.Y.
Mitchum Anti-Perspirant Dab On, Mitchum Thayer, Inc., Tuckahoe, N.Y.
Fresh, Pharmacraft, Pennwalt Corp., Rochester, N.Y.
Body Guard, Bonne Bell, Lakewood, Ohio
Certain Dri, Leon Products, Inc., Jacksonville, Fla.
Revlon Hi & Dry, Revlon, New York, N.Y.
Secret, Procter & Gamble, Cincinnati, Ohio
Shaklee Spray Deodorant, Shaklee Corp., Hayward, Calif.

DEPILATORIES:

A razor won't cause the dermatitis that some chemicals can.

Neet, Whitehall Labs., Inc., New York, N.Y.
Nair, Carter Products, New York, N.Y.

FEMININE GENITAL DEODORANTS:

NOT RECOMMENDED IN ANY FORM. There is absolutely no need for this type of product. You risk rashes, itching, or more severe irritations. Use soap and water instead.

HAIR CARE PRODUCTS:

The oldest and cheapest of the products to hold hair in place are wave-setting lotions such as:

Dr. Ellis Wave Set, A. R. Winarick Inc., New York, N.Y.
Nestle Superset, Nestle LeMur, New York, N.Y.
Dippity-Do Setting Lotion, Gillette, Chicago, Ill.
Clairol Easy Comb, Easy Set, Clairol, Inc., Stamford, Conn.
Revlon Professional Setting Lotion, New York, N.Y.

Then there are nonaerosol sprays, which also claim to be hair conditioners:

L'Oreal Satine Hair Set Lotion, Cosmair, Inc., Clark, N.J.
VO 5 Protein Setting Lotion, Alberto Culver Co., Melrose Park, Ill.
Get Set, Alberto Culver Co., Melrose Park, Ill.
Flex, Nonaerosol "hair net," Revlon Co., New York, N.Y.
Hold & Hold & Hold, House of Style, Division of LaMaur, Inc., Minneapolis, Minn.
Style Hair Spray, House of Style, Division of LaMaur, Inc., Minneapolis, Minn.
Just Wonderful Hair Net, Caryl Division, Faberge, Inc., New York, N.Y.
Suave Protein Hair Setting Lotion, Helene Curtis, Chicago, Ill.
Clairol Final Net, Clairol, Inc., Stamford, Conn.
Long & Silky, Clairol, Inc., Stamford, Conn.
Flex, Revlon Co., New York, N.Y.
Breck, John H. Breck, Inc., Wayne, N.J.

Protein 21, Mennen Co., Morristown, N.J.
Alberto, Alberto Culver Co., Melrose Park, Ill.

Note: Although aerosol shampoos are appearing on the market, most brands are still sold in liquid form.

MEN'S HAIR DRESSING:

Gillette The Dry Look comes in liquid as well as aerosol.
Vitalis is a liquid.

HAND LOTIONS:

Although aerosols are creeping into the market, most of these are put out in cream or lotion form, often with a hand pump.

PERFUME AND COLOGNES:

Most perfumes and colognes still come in liquid form. A few are also available in pump sprays.

SHAVING CREAMS:

Williams Brushless, J. B. Williams Co., Cranford, N.J.
Gillette Regular or Brushless, Gillette Co., Boston, Mass.
Mennen Regular or Brushless, The Mennen Co., Morristown, N.J.
Old Spice Regular or Brushless, Shulton, Inc., Clifton, N.J.
Barbasol, Pfizer Inc., New York, N.Y.

These are some common aerosolized products. See sections in which they are discussed.

1. Air fresheners	Germicides
2. Antimister for mirrors	Aerosol sprays
3. Antirust sprays	Motor products
4. Antistatic products	Clothing supplies
5. Artificial plant gloss sprays	Yuletide supplies, etc.
6. Asthma and breathing aids	Aerosol sprays
7. Breath sweeteners	(Cos)*

8. Car starters	Motor products
9. Cheese spreads	Aerosols
10. Choke cleaners	Motor products
11. Deodorants and antiperspirants	(Cos)*
12. Deicers	Motor products
13. Dust sprays	Insecticide
14. Electric hair setting mists	(Cos)*
15. Fabric finish and stain repellents	Clothing supplies
16. Feminine deodorant sprays	(Cos)*
17. Glass cleaners	Oven cleaners, etc.
18. Hair conditioners	(Cos)*
19. Hair removers	(Cos)*
20. Hair sprays	(Cos)*
21. Insect repellents	Insecticides
22. Insulation sprays	Building materials
23. Kitchen utensil coatings	Utensil coatings
24. Medicinal and first aid sprays	Aerosol sprays
25. Mouthwash sprays	(Cos)*
26. Oven cleaners	Oven cleaners, etc.
27. Paints of all kinds	Solvents, lead, mercury
28. Perfumes and colognes	(Cos)*
29. Pesticides	Insecticides
30. Refrigerants	Emissions
31. Rug shampoos	Clothing supplies
32. Shaving creams	(Cos)*
33. Shoe polishes	Clothing supplies
34. Skin adhesives	Aerosol sprays
35. Spot removers	Clothing supplies
36. Spray snows	Yuletide supplies
37. Starches	Clothes
38. Upholstery cleaners	Clothing supplies
39. Veterinary products	Zoological wastes
40. Varnishes	Solvents
41. Waxes and furniture polishes	Furniture products
42. Weed killers	Insecticides
43. Whipped toppings and frostings	Aerosol sprays

* (Cos) refers to products which will be treated in a later book on cosmetic products.

REFERENCES

[1] G. J. Taylor and W. S. Harris, "Cardiac Toxicity of Aerosol Propellants," *Journal of the American Medical Association,* Vol. 214 (Oct. 5, 1970), pp. 81–85.

[2] N. C. Flowers and L. G. Horan, "The Electrical Sequalae of Aerosol Inhalation," *American Heart Journal,* Vol. 83 (May 1972), pp. 644–51.

[3] S. M. Kilen and W. S. Harris, "Direct Depression of Myocardial Contractility by the Aerosol Propellant Gas, Dichlorodifluoromethane," *Journal of Pharmacology and Experimental Therapeutics,* Vol. 183 (1972), pp. 245–55.

[4] D. F. Reinhardt et al., Cardiac Arrhythmias and Aerosol Sniffing," *Archives of Environmental Health,* Vol. 22 (Feb. 1971), pp. 265–79.

[5] N. C. Flowers and L. G. Horan, "Acid-Base Relationships and the Cardiac Response to Aerosol Inhalation," *Chest,* Vol. 63 (Jan. 1973), pp. 74–78.

[6] D. A. McClure, "Failure of Fluorocarbon Propellants to Alter the Electrocardiogram of Mice and Dogs," *Toxicology and Applied Pharmacology,* Vol. 22 (1972), pp. 221–30.

[7] W. S. Harris, in *Journal of the American Medical Association,* Vol. 223 (Mar. 26, 1973), pp. 1,508–9.

[8] W. O. Good, Personal communication, Oct. 11, 1973. W. O. Good, Carl Ellison, and Victor Archer, "Sputum Cytology Among Frequent Users of Pressurized Spray Cans," *Cancer Research,* Vol. 35 (Feb. 1975), pp. 316–21.

[9] J. M. Gowdy and M. J. Wagstaff, "Pulmonary Infiltration Due to Aerosol Thesaurosis," *Archives of Environmental Health,* Vol. 25 (Aug. 1972), pp. 101–8.

[10] *Aerosol Age,* Dec. 1971, p. 30.

[11] P. D. Stolley, "Asthma Mortality: Why the United States Was Spared an Epidemic of Deaths," *American Review of Respiratory Diseases,* Vol. 105 (June 1972), pp. 883–90.

[12] "Aerosol Hazard Accident Reports," National Electronic Injury Surveillance System (NEISS), Washington, D.C., Apr. 1967 through July 1972.

[13] R. Hotchkiss and M. Gulak, "The Aerosol Bomb: A Common Sense Engineering Analysis," Center for Concerned Engineering, Washington, D.C., Dec. 3, 1972.

[14] G. M. Hama and L. C. Curley, "Corrosion of Combustion Equipment by Chlorinated Hydrocarbon Vapors, *Air Engineering,* Apr. 1965.

[15] *Aerosol Age,* Feb. 1976, p. 8.

[16] M. J. Molina and F. S. Rowland, "Stratospheric Sink for Chlorofluoromethanes: Chlorine Atom Catalyzed Destruction of Ozone," *Nature,* Vol. 249 (1974), p. 810.

[17] R. J. Cicerone, R. S. Stolarski, S. Walter, "Stratosphere Ozone Destruction by Man-Made Chlorofluoromethanes," *Science,* Vol. 185 (1974), p. 1,165.

[18] P. J. Crutzen, "Estimates of Possible Future Ozone Reductions from Continued Use of Fluoro-Chloro-Methanes (CF_2Cl_2, $CFCl_3$)," *Geophysical Research Letters,* Vol. 1 (1974), p. 205. S. C. Wofsy, M. B. McElroy, and N. D. Sze, "Freon Consumption: Implications for Atmospheric Ozone," *Science,* Vol. 187 (1975), p. 535.

[19] "Deadline Is Set on Fluorocarbon Spray Can Curbs," *Wall Street Journal,* May 12, 1977, p. 3.

[20] Natural Resources Defense Council Petition to the Consumer Product Safety Commission, Dec. 22, 1975, p. 35.

[21] Transcript, Technical Review on Inhalant Abuse Conference, National Institute on Drug Abuse, Rockville, Md., Dec. 12, 1975.

[22] STRAFE Petition before the Federal Trade Commission, George Washington University Law School, Washington, D.C., 1975, p. 2

[23] "Disposal of Aerosol Cans," *Consumer Bulletin,* Vol. 54 (Feb. 1971), p. 25.

B. BUILDING MATERIALS

Many people may be surprised to learn that hazardous materials have been built into homes they have long regarded as safe and secure. Some of these products may cause problems only during construction and renovation, while others are active throughout the life of the structure.

Our purpose here is to discuss those hazardous construction materials which are not treated elsewhere in this book (see the end of this section for building supplies described under other headings). The two most important substances to consider here are asbestos and fiber glass, which are extensively used for their insulating, fireproofing, soundproofing, dielectric (nonconductive), and reinforcing properties. A wide variety of materials may contain one or the other of these two products: cement supplies, pipes, wallboard, shingles, plastics, vinyl and asphalt floor tile, glues, paint supplies, etc.

Regardless of the warnings of many scientists, the public has been until recently unconcerned or uninformed about the health risks associated with asbestos and fiber glass. The pervasiveness in our society of these materials has lulled us into a perilous feeling of security. Nevertheless, their hazardous qualities have been known for many decades by government and corporate officials, who have still been slow to protect consumers (not to mention factory workers and the residents of communities contaminated by fibrous industrial wastes). A number of asbestos and fiber glass products are now required by law to bear warning labels. Consumer hazards persist, however, because labels may not disclose the full range of health risks involved, or may be missing altogether. In the absence of an aggressive government campaign to educate the public, we must thus educate ourselves about the nature of the problem.

Asbestos

Asbestos is a generic term for a number of naturally occurring fibrous silicate minerals which are usually classified as either serpentinite (chrysolite) or amphibolite. Since 1900, world production of asbestos has grown a thousandfold.[1] Today it has over 3,000 industrial uses[2] and can be found in over three hundred consumer products (see Table I).

As in the case of many hazardous chemicals, the medical effects of asbestos were first observed among factory workers habitually exposed to the material. The most obvious problem was asbestosis, a respiratory illness caused by the grating of inhaled asbestos fibers against sensitive lung tissue. Once a certain level of fiber inhalation has been reached, the disease becomes progressive—that is, continues to scar and damage the lungs even after exposure to asbestos stops.

It is interesting to note that as early as 1918, six years before the first case of asbestos disease was reported in the medical literature, life insurance companies routinely declined to cover asbestos workers. Eventually, dust control systems were installed, and the number of asbestosis cases subsequently declined. Unfortunately, such dust control devices are still absent from many homes today where dusty renovation is taking place.

More frightening than the threat of asbestosis is the risk of lung cancer and cancer of the lung and body lining (pulmonary bronchial carcinoma, pleural and peritoneal mesothelioma) from even low-level exposure to asbestos. Like asbestosis, these forms of cancer may not become evident until twenty to forty years after initial exposure. Smokers appear to be particularly vulnerable to this threat. We know today that eventually one out of every five asbestos-insulation workers dies of lung cancer, and that one out of every ten dies of cancer of the body lining.[3] Such probabilities are obviously far above the national average. The case against this material needs no embellishment: Asbestos is deadly. Consumers should therefore become familiar with its many home uses, attempt to find substitutes, and ensure adequate protection when asbestos products must be used.

Table I CONSUMER USES OF ASBESTOS

Aprons	Filtering materials
Arm protectors	Filters
Bags	Flooring
Belting	Gaskets
Blankets	Gloves
Blocks	Hats
Boards and shingles	Helmets
Bonded pipe	Hoods
Braid	Insulated cables
Brake lining	Insulation
Caps	Lagging
Cards	Legging
Cement boards	Lining
Cement clay	Lumber
Cement machy	Mats
Cement partitions	Metallic cloth
Cement roofing	Millboards
Cement sewer pipe	Mittens
Cement tile	Overgaiters
Cements	Packed corrugated metal
Cloth	gaskets
Clothing	Packing
Coating	Pads and covers
Cords	Paints
Corrugated roofing	Panels
Corrugated sheets	Paper paste
Covered cables	Pipe and boiler coverings
Covered hose	Plastic shingles
Covered wire	Pot and pan holders
Covering	Powder
Covers	Protected metals
Curtains (theater)	Protecting roofing
Discs	Ribbons
Fabrics	Rings
Felt	Roof coatings
Fiber and cement pipe	Roof ventilators
Fillers	Rope

Scrap	Textiles
Sheathing	Thread
Sheeting	Tubing and tubes
Sheets	Twine
Siding	Wallboard
Sleeves	Washes
Sleeving	Wicking
Stove linings	Wire
Stove mats	Wood
Suits	Wool
Table padding	Working machy
Tapes	Yarns

Source: "Thomas Register of American Manufacturers," 1971, Vol. 8.

There are two basic kinds of asbestos products, distinguished by their respective types of fiber bond. The first category is often called "friable," that is, containing loosely bound fibers that readily crumble and flake. Examples of friable asbestos materials include asbestos cement, spackling, fire brick, textured materials, paints, and patching compounds. Fibers from these commonly available hardware supplies can easily become airborne and inhaled. As late as 1973, there were no government regulations requiring these friable materials to bear warning labels about the dangers of asbestos inhalation. Such cautions do appear on some of these products today, although they do not on an unknown number of others. In some cases, there is not even a notice that asbestos is an ingredient.

The second type of asbestos material has "locked-in" fibers which do not become disturbed through ordinary handling. Industry claims that the overwhelming majority of asbestos products are of this type.[4] To the extent that this is true, there is substantially less risk that the user's household will be exposed to toxic dust. It is important to note, however, that even locked-in supplies like tile and pipe can produce airborne particles when sawed, ground, or sanded in home remodeling. Exterior uses are generally not as dangerous as dusty indoor applications, which should always take place with adequate ventilation.

It is also important to point out that not all asbestos products are building materials as such. Asbestos can be found in such unlikely places as draperies, rugs, and ironing board covers (see Table I). It can come into the home through the most "innocuous" routes: in papier-mâché cement, the artificial ash in prefabricated fireplaces, and talc (which can contain asbestos fibers) in deodorant powders and sprays (see Table II). Stay on guard! When in doubt ask salesperson or manufacturer whether asbestos is present.

Fiber Glass

Fiber glass has many uses and characteristics similar to those of asbestos. It is utilized in building materials like thermal and acoustical insulation, as well as in heavy fabrics, sporting goods, and miscellaneous items.

Table II CONSUMER USES OF TALC

1. Asphalt filler
2. Carving
3. Ceramics
4. Chewing gum
5. Dressing textiles
6. Dusting foundry facings
7. Dusting rubber to prevent sticking
8. Fillers for asbestos paper
9. Fillers for rubber products
10. Fillers for scouring soaps
11. Gas burner tips
12. Glazes
13. Insecticide carrier
14. Nontransparent glass
15. Plaster products
16. Polish
17. Porcelain
18. Refractory brick
19. Roofing
20. Solid lubricants
21. Surgical gloves (discontinued in most hospitals)
22. Tailor's chalk
23. Toilet preparations: talcum powder, vaginal deodorants
24. Toy balloons

Source: Barry I. Castleman and Albert J. Fritsch, *Asbestos and You* (Washington, D.C.: Center for Science in the Public Interest, 1974).

Because of its fibrous properties, fiber glass generated some concern within the medical community as the carcinogenic potential of asbestos became evident. A few animal studies suggested that fiber glass could cause cancer. It was also hypothesized that the fibers' microscopic size, and not their chemical properties, triggered malignancy.[5] There has been some question, however, whether the implant techniques used in these experiments were themselves responsible for the results. Because this subject has yet to become a high research priority, there have not been enough studies to determine conclusively whether fiber glass is carcinogenic under ordinary conditions of exposure. Consumers should therefore treat fiber glass as they would any inadequately tested material: with extreme caution.

Even if fiber glass is ultimately exonerated of carcinogenesis, the inhalation of airborne fibers can still injure sensitive lung tissue. Those working regularly with this material have a tendency to develop such respiratory tract ailments as bronchitis, pharyngitis, rhinitis, asthma, laryngitis, sinusitis, and nosebleed.[6]

There is little disagreement that fiber glass is also a potent skin irritant. This material is by far the most important cause of mechanical contact dermatitis. Although many people suffer only minor discomfort from this disease, others may have severe reactions. Fiber glass dermatitis is no longer just an occupational hazard for insulation workers, but a significant problem for the consumer. This is because of the increasing influx of fiber glass products into our homes over the past fifteen years: curtains, draperies, tablecloths, etc. The problem does not usually arise in their use, but in their cleaning. When these items are laundered, large numbers of glass fibers may be released to contaminate other fabrics in the same (or future) wash load. Physicians have reported entire family outbreaks of dermatitis from contaminated clothes, sheets, towels, etc.

In 1968 the Federal Trade Commission finally required that fiber glass fabrics bear labels informing consumers of the dermatitis hazard. Such notices now warn the user about direct contact with these textiles and the special precautions necessary for laundering them. Unfortunately, one apparent result of this action has been increased use of laundromats for cleaning fiber glass fabrics. Obviously, this merely shifts the problem to the unsuspecting people who subsequently use the same washing machine. If it is absolutely necessary that fiber glass materials be cleaned, (a) wear gloves, (b) keep materials separate from other fabrics, and (c) clean in a special tub or basin which can be repeatedly rinsed and wiped out. Also, when doing your regular wash at the laundromat, look and feel inside the washer for fiber glass residues from other people's thoughtless actions.

For information on other building materials and supplies, see dust, emissions from heating and cooling, hobbies (glues and woodworking), lead paints, plastics, mercury products, solvents, and water pipes.

READY MIX JOINT COMPOUND
(H. Georgia-Pacific—Gypsum Div., 900 S.W. Fifth Ave., Portland, Ore.)

CAUTION:
  *Contains ASBESTOS FIBERS
  *Avoid breathing dust
  *Breathing asbestos dust may cause serious bodily harm
  *Use approved respirator when sanding

ZONOLITE PANEL FOAM
(W. R. Grace & Co., Cambridge, Mass.)

CAUTION: Do not expose package or contents to open flames, sparks, or excessive heat. Zonolite Styrene foam is an organic cellular plastic foam and, therefore, is combustible. Exposure to open flames, sparks, or excessive heat should always be avoided.

CORNING FIBERGLAS BUILDING INSULATION
(Owens Corning Fiberglas Corp., Toledo, Ohio)

CAUTION: Insulation may cause temporary skin irritation. Wash with soap and warm water after handling. Wear loose clothing. Wash work clothes separately. Fiberglas insulation is noncombustible. Kraft and standard foil facings are combustible and should not be left exposed. Special care should be taken when working close to the facing with an open flame.

NOTE: Stack in paper-wrapped rolls on floor.

Building with Safe Materials

For certain uses, fiber glass and asbestos are superior in quality to alternatives, and their hazards may be minimized. Locked-in materials like asbestos floor tiles, for example, present virtually no exposure risk to the consumer (except in sanding, sawing, etc.) and offer superior fire protection. Unfortunately, the asbestos and fiber glass workers who manufacture these goods may still be exposed to the health hazards already noted.

Consumers still remain vulnerable to airborne fibers from loosely bound products. All friable products (containing loosely bound fibers that readily crumble and flake) should be kept outdoors. The major uses which deserve special attention are:

■ Insulation. Preformed batts and blankets of fiber glass or rock wool can be easily and safely placed between uncovered ceiling joists and (in houses under construction) between wall studs. On the other hand, loose fill that is poured and raked between attic joists may become airborne during installation and drafty periods. Loose fill is also frequently machine-blown through holes in finished surfaces (attic floors, completed walls). This is a complicated, sometimes expensive process and should not be undertaken by anyone except an experienced insulation worker. Those who choose this type of insulation should receive assurances from contractors that the blowers used will not stir up fibrous dusts.

There is risk involved in using any form of sprayed asbestos insulation, particularly along air plenums, drafty halls, and other areas where rapidly moving air can erode asbestos fibers.

▪ Fireproofing. Sprayed asbestos has been used to fireproof many buildings. Substitute materials such as the following brand-name products save workers from the extremely dangerous exposure to asbestos:

Mono Kote (MK4)
Cafco (less desirable than MK4)
Sprayed-On
KDB Pyrospray[7]

▪ Wallboard. Avoid asbestos-impregnated products. Gypsum sheetrock is the preferable alternative to asbestos products for interior wall sheathing.

▪ Caulking and patching compounds. A number of these products contain friable asbestos fibers. If this information is not to be found on the label, store personnel or the manufacturer can provide a list of ingredients.[8]

▪ Corrugated and flat pipe. Despite the low initial expense, asbestos cement pipes expose workers to respiratory hazards during manufacture and pose potential pollution problems for consumers. Water lines and drains made of clay, reinforced concrete, cast iron, and copper are safer and more durable alternatives.

▪ Draperies and other heavy-duty fabrics. Because of their flame-retardant properties, modacrylics are a good substitute for asbestos and fiber glass products in the home. The flammability of materials like acetate, cotton, and blends can also be reduced by special treatment at some dry cleaners and fabric shops. Since certain flame retardants may contain caustic agents, see Section C before proceeding with this process. Remember that fiber glass draperies may contaminate other clothing in washing machines and cause dermatitis.

■ Artificial fireplace ash. When the Consumer Product Safety Commission (CPSC) formally banned asbestos fireplace "ash" in 1977, an estimated 300,000 to 500,000 homes contained this extremely hazardous substance. Once alerted to this danger, members of these households should exercise great care in removal of the ash. Recommended safeguards for this process include the use of a pump spray-type bottle, paper towels and newspapers, washable clothing, a scoop, a single-use respirator, a nose-mouth mask, and two heavy-duty plastic bags with ties. It is important to follow a set procedure to protect those doing the work, other members of the household, pets, and those removing contaminated trash. The CPSC has published a complete set of instructions (Guidelines for Asbestos Fireplace Ash Removal) that can be obtained from CPSC, 5401 Westbard Ave., Washington, D.C. 20207.

REFERENCES

[1] Barry Castleman and Albert Fritsch, *Asbestos and You* (Washington, D.C.: Center for Science in the Public Interest, 1974), p. 4.

[2] D. V. Rosato, *Asbestos—Its Industrial Applications* (New York: Reinhold, 1959).

[3] Paul Brodeur, "Annals of Industry: Casualties of the Workplace," *New Yorker*, Nov. 26, 1973, pp. 126–79.

[4] I. R. Tabershaw, in *Journal of Occupational Medicine*, Vol. 10, 32 (1968).

[5] Merl F. Stanton et al., "The Carcinogenicity of Fibrous Glass: Pleural Response in the Rat in Relation to Fiber Dimension." Unpublished paper. Laboratory of Pathology, National Cancer Institute (Bethesda, Md., 1976).

[6] Thomas Milby and Richard Wolf, "Respiratory Tract Irritation from Fibrous Glass Inhalation," *Journal of Occupational Medicine*, Vol. 11, No. 8 (Aug. 1969).

[7] Information provided by Mr. Clint Fladland, executive director of the Minnesota Lathing and Plastering Bureau, as reported in *Hazards of Asbestos to Human Health* (Minneapolis: Minnesota Public Interest Research Group, 1972), pp. 34–35.

[8] See N. Rohl et al., "Exposure to Asbestos in the Use of Consumer Spackling, Patching and Taping Compounds," *Science*, Vol. 189 (Aug. 15, 1975), pp. 551–53.

C. CLOTHING AND FABRIC CARE PRODUCTS

The purchase of clothing is a difficult task, especially for the person with an eye to fashion, economy, durability. But personal and environmental safety issues complicate selections and care even more. One must consider such factors as flammability, potential dangers of flame-retardant materials; pollutant chemicals found in cleaners and polishes; hazards to workers in the textile industry; energy costs in washing and cleaning; and nonrenewable energy used to process fabrics. Following is a description of common chemical ingredients and some associated problems found in fabrics and fabric care products. See Table I for information on their toxic effects. (Energy and conservation questions are covered in *99 Ways to a Simple Lifestyle*.[1])

Dry-cleaning Fluids and Spot Removers

Some people have their clothing cleaned at a professional establishment, while others prefer to use a coin-operated machine. In either case, some of the fluids used in the cleaning operation enter the environment or adversely affect the worker. Cleaning compounds are generally noncombustible, toxic chlorinated solvents. The original favorite solvent-cleaner was carbon tetrachloride, which is easily inhaled or absorbed in the skin. Carbon tetrachloride damages the liver and other parts of the human body. Because of its high toxicity, it has been removed from consumer products. Older bottles and containers still lingering around the home should be discarded.

A leading substitute for carbon tetrachloride is perchloroethylene (or tetrachloroethylene), which is a volatile, nonflammable solvent. About 60 per cent of the domestic consumption can be attributed to the textile industry, primarily in dry cleaning. This solvent accounts for most of the dry-cleaning market, especially the coin-operated segment. Perchloroethylene is an ingredient in many aerosol spray specialty products. Fatal in large doses, its nonlethal effects from inhalation are a major health concern today. The primary physiological effect resulting from both acute and chronic inhalation is depression of the central nervous system. Symptoms include lightheadedness, dizziness, sleepiness, nausea, tremor, loss of appetite, and disorientation. Liver damage may result from cleaning clothing in poorly ventilated areas.

Another less important dry-cleaning and fur-cleaning agent is trichloroethylene. This noncorrosive and nonflammable liquid is used principally as a degreasing agent in industrial metal fabricating plants. Again the major physiological response in human beings to both acute and chronic exposure is depression of the central nervous system. Additional effects such as damage to the liver, kidney, and heart have been reported, especially when persons are heavy consumers of alcohol. Blindness, loss of hearing and tactile senses, and death from cardiac arrest and ventricular fibrillation following acute exposure have also been reported.

Other toxic chemicals often found in spot-removing products include: 1,1,1-trichloroethane, naphtha, ammonium hydroxide, amyl, butyl, and ethyl acetate, benzene, oxalic acid, toluene, sodium hypochlorite, powdered silica, sodium silicofluoride, and sulfamic acid. Because the dry-cleaning and spot-removing processes depend upon the dissolving properties of highly volatile solvents, danger is only associated with fumes. Precaution should definitely be taken to avoid inhaling the evaporating solvent, but once garments have dried, they are safe to wear.

CARBONA SPOT REMOVER
(Carbona Products Co., Long Island City, N.Y.)

CAUTION: combustible vapor harmful
DANGER: harmful or fatal if swallowed. Use with adequate
ventilation. Avoid prolonged or repeated breathing of
vapor. Avoid prolonged contact with skin.
Ingredients: 1,1,1-trichloroethane, perchloroethylene, petroleum hydrocarbons

Rug and Upholstery Cleaners

Most popular commercial rug cleaners do not list ingredients on the label. The various brands are thought to contain
one or other of the following ingredients: turpentine, borax,
naphthalene, 1,1,1-trichloroethane, and petroleum distillates.

Fabric Finishes and Cements

Fabric finishes are chemicals applied to raincoats, sporting equipment, shoes, awnings, and camping equipment to
make them water repellent. The most popular varieties include dry silicone water-repellent and vinyl-silicone waterproofing agents. The aerosol varieties are particularly dangerous because tearing cannot wash the product out if it gets
into the eyes. Consumers Union found that the spray of some
aerosol finishes flashed alarmingly and that all liquid finishes
were combustible; they opted for using the paint brush variety
which can also be applied by a paint roller or home spray
gun.[2]
Fabric cements may include camphor and the solvents acetone and ethyl acetate. Fabric cements should be used with
proper ventilation.

Antistatic Agents and Fabric Softeners

Nylon-pile and polypropylene-pile carpets are noted for static electricity build-up. An antistatic agent improves the fiber's ability to conduct electricity by forming "an electric network" which dissipates the charge rapidly over much of the fabric surface area. Antistatic agents such as Carbona, Johnson, Glamourine, Bissel, and New Lees are generally found in stores in an aerosol spray form. The safety of these ingredients cannot be judged because of the trade secrecy surrounding their contents.

Fabric softeners are used in washing to allow easier ironing and reduce wrinkles. They may include fabric brighteners (see Section K). While the nonaerosolized forms may not be highly toxic, still some of these softeners cause the finishes of some clothing drier drums to deteriorate and rust—thereby staining clothing. Some softeners can also clog lint filters and thus reduce the drying efficiency of the appliance. The failure of the drying sensor resulting from fabric softener clogging presents a fire hazard potential.[3] *Consumer Research* gives a nonrecommended rating to aerosol fabric softeners.

Shoe-care Products

A large number of chemicals have been used in shoe preparations, some of which are quite toxic when inhaled, ingested, or touched to the skin or eyes. Some ingredients include:

Shoe Polishes:	Shoe Dyes:
aerosol freons	1,1,1-trichloroethane
methylene chloride	propylene dichloride
trichloroethylene	denatured ethanol
alcohols	o-dichlorobenzene
mineral spirits	mineral spirits
turpentine	xylene
1,1,1-trichloroethane	

Shoe Cleaners:
   methylene chloride
   nitrobenzene
   perchloroethylene
   trisodium phosphate
   trichloroethylene
   propylene dichloride

Again, with a few exceptions the toxic chemicals in these products are usually the solvents. It is very important to let shoes dry thoroughly before wearing.

Special precautions should be taken with dyes containing nitrobenzene, a fat-soluble solvent which is absorbed into the leather. This chemical is so toxic and so easily absorbed by the skin that an accidental spill can be fatal.[3] Acute effects of nitrobenzene poisoning are cyanosis (a bluing of the tissues), shallow breathing, and vomiting. The effects are multiplied by any alcohol in the system. The combined effect killed a man who was wearing shoes stained with a nitrobenzene-based shoe black within a few hours after drinking beer.[4]

Spray Starch

CONTENTS UNDER PRESSURE. DO NOT PUNC-
TURE OR INCINERATE. DO NOT STORE OVER
100° F. AVOID FREEZING. DO NOT SPRAY TO-
WARD FACE. KEEP AWAY FROM CHILDREN.

If a label of this type of warning is not enough to dissuade potential consumers, the following might: "To prevent clogging after each day's use: (a) Pull off spray button; (b) rinse button under running water; (c) replace button making sure arrow on top of button points toward red mark."

This section of the label converts a convenience item into an inconvenient one, but it does more—it allows the company to remove itself from responsibility for the frequent clogging of spray starch cans, and thus seals the consumer into bearing total blame for the purchase of a product which seldom lasts the entire lifetime of the can. And clogging does happen with this inherently sticky material. Toxicity of these products is unknown.

Flame Retardants

The drive to reduce fabric flammability is not new, but some of the chemicals used as flame retardants are. In 1820 Gay-Lussac was commissioned by the King of France to protect theater fabrics. He found ammonium salts of sulfuric, hydrochloric, or phosphoric acid to be effective, a discovery still applicable today.[5] In recent years public alarm over the high combustibility of modern fabrics and the number of children's deaths has led to an infant sleepwear standard (1972) and one for older children's sleepwear in 1975. Other regulations on carpets, rugs, and mattresses have helped spawn a mushrooming flame-retardant (FR) textile market using 300 million pounds of chemicals (1975) and reaching to one-half billion by 1980 (or 20 per cent of the textile market).

Flame-retardant chemicals are generally made from one or more of six elements: bromine, chlorine, phosphorus, nitrogen, boron, and antimony. Some have particular toxicological problems. Others are effective on only certain types of fibers. Cellulose phosphate esters are used to flame-retard cotton and other cellulose-based fibers (rayon and acetate as opposed to nylon or acrylics, which are noncellulosic fibers). However, cotton suffers a loss of strength of about 30 per cent. No economically successful FR treatment has yet been found for cotton and blends.

For synthetic fibers, tris (2,3-dibromopropyl) phosphate or "tris-BP" is the most important. It has been almost exclusively used for sleepwear made from polyester, acetate, and triacetate synthetic fibers and in acrylic carpeting. Before its wide distribution, tris-BP was studied for toxicity through oral ingestion using rats. Since then, a number of toxilogical problems have been found. Absorbed through the skin, tris-BP

Table I
TOXIC CHEMICALS FOUND IN FABRIC CARE PRODUCTS

Chemical	Disaster fire	fume	Potential explosion	Rating of Acute Effects	Cancer-causing	Mutation-causing
Acetone	dang,*	—,*	mod*	severe	under test	X*
Amyl acetate	dang,	—,	mod	mild	X	X
Benzene	—,	—,	—	severe	yes	yes
Butyl acetate	dang,	—,	mod	mild	X	X
Camphor	mod,	—,	mod	severe	produces neo-plasm	X
Carbon tetrachloride	—,	—,	—	severe	yes	yes
Dichlorobenzene	mod,	—,	—	severe	yes	X
Ethyl acetate	—,	—,	—	severe	X	X

Acute Symptoms	Chronic Symptoms	Products Containing Chemicals
eye effects, CNS,* paralysis	eyes, nose, and skin irritation, chronic respiratory tract irritation, dizziness	fabric cements
headache, fatigue, chest oppression, irritant to mucous membranes	estrus cycle disorder, liver, kidney, lung damage, hormone alteration, bone marrow hyperplasia, implicated in leukemia and sarcoma	dry-cleaning agent spot remover
blood effects, aplastic anemia, local skin irritant, narcotic action on CNS, euphoria		dry-cleaning agent spot remover
irritant to mucous membranes, eyes, and respiratory tract		dry-cleaning agent spot remover
irritant, convulsions		fabric cement
(not specified)	(not specified)	dry-cleaning agent spot remover
unspecified toxic effects	mammary, liver and bladder tumors, respiratory disorders, paraplegia and paraparesis, CNS inhibition, kidney hyperplasia	shoe dye
(not specified)	irritating to mucous surfaces, dermatitis, congestion of liver and kidneys, anemia	fabric cement

Chemical	Disaster fire	fume	Potential explosion	Rating of Acute Effects	Cancer-causing	Mutation-causing
Ethyl alcohol (ethanol)	dang,	—,	mod	mild	X	X
Freon-12 (dichlorodi-fluoromethane)	—,	dang,	—	mild	X	under test
Isopropyl alcohol	dang,	—,	mod	mild	X	X
Methyl alcohol	dang,	—,	mod	severe	X	X
Methylene chlorine	—,	dang,	minor	severe	X	X
Naphtha	dang,	—,	slight	severe	yes	X
Naphthalene	mod,	—,	mod	severe	yes	X
Nitrobenzene	mod,	mod,	mod	severe	X	X
Oxalic acid	—,	—,	—	severe	X	X
Perchloro-ethylene	—,	dang,	—	mild	X	X

Acute Symptoms	Chronic Symptoms	Products Containing Chemicals
gastrointestinal effects	irritation of eyes and mucous membranes, CNS depressant	shoe dye
narcotic in high concentrations	increase lymphocyte count, liver damage, transitory hyperemia	spray spot remover
conjunctivitis, anemia, irritant		shoe dye
eye irritant, blindness, skin drying, dermatitis	headache, dizziness, insomnia, gastric disturbances, failure of vision	shoe dye
narcosis, blood effects	dermatitis, liver damage, reduced growth size	suede renewer, spray shoe shine, shoe dye
(not specified)	(not specified)	spot remover
nausea, anemia, liver damage, convulsions, coma		rug cleaner
blood effects, cyanosis	heart, liver, and kidney damage, CNS effects, damage to embryo	fabric and shoe dyes
corrosion of mouth, esophagus and stomach, kidney and liver damage, irritation of eyes and upper respiratory tract	skin irritation	dry-cleaning agent spot remover
vomiting, drowsiness, attitude of irresponsibility, anesthetic, headache, local irritant, irritation of nose and throat		shoe water repellent suede renewer, spot remover

Chemical	Disaster Potential fire fume explosion	Rating of Acute Effects	Cancer-causing	Mutation-causing
Polyethylene glycol	mod, —, —	—	yes	X
Propylenedichloride (dichloropropane)	dang, dang, —	severe	X	X
Sodium carboxymethyl cellulose	—, —, —	—	produces neoplasm	X
Toluene	dang, mod, mod	severe	yes	X
1,1,1-trichloroethane	—, dang, —	severe	X	X
Trichloroethylene	slight, dang, —	severe	yes	X
Xylene	dang, —, mod	severe	produces neoplasm	X

Acute Symptoms	Chronic Symptoms	Products Containing Chemicals
—	—	fabric sizing
dermatitis, degeneration of liver, kidney, heart		shoe cleaner/ conditioner
—	—	fabric sizing
CNS and psychotropic effects	blood abnormalities, bone marrow chromosome damage, metabolic effects, enzymatic effects	dry-cleaning agent, spot remover
psychotropic and CNS effects	reduced growth, narcotic effects, reversible changes in kidney, liver and lungs	cleaning fluid, shoe coloring, patent leather polish, spray shoe shine
CNS effects, conjunctivitis, irritation of skin and respiratory tract	kidney, spleen, and liver damage, metabolic and enzymatic effects, hypertension, reduces antibody formation, anorexia, CNS disturbances, skin decay	shoe cleaner/ conditioner, dry-cleaning agent
(not specified)	hyperglycemia	shoe dyes

* mod – moderate   dang – dangerous   — – no information
X – not tested   CNS – central nervous system

Source: "Scoring of Organic Air Pollutants Chemistry, Production and Toxicity of Selected Synthetic Organic Chemicals" (McLean, Va.: Mitre Corp., Sept. 1976).

causes delayed hyper- and allergic sensitization in human beings.

Evidence that tris-BP is itself a carcinogen has accumulated.[6,7] In recent tests, tris-BP extracted from treated fabrics that had been laundered three times caused high mutation rates in cultures of *Salmonella* bacteria. Such activity has been highly correlated with carcinogenicity. In other tests tris-BP has been found to damage human DNA *in vitro*. All of this recent evidence points to possible serious consequences of widespread use of tris-BP. The Environmental Defense Fund has petitioned the CPSC to require warnings on clothing labels urging that clothing be washed three times before using,[8] an immediate protective measure obvious to all familiar with infants' predilection for sucking clothing. Support for a ban on tris has begun in earnest, but its fate in the courts is uncertain.

Blum and associates argue that the risk of exposure of tens of millions of children to a large amount of such a chemical must be balanced against the risk of a fire.[5] Calculation suggests that the cancer risk is higher than the risk from being burned. Burned clothing accounts for 15,000 injuries a year and about 500 deaths in the United States, of which one fifth can be associated with children's nightwear. However, the use of this untreated chemical as an FR additive may result in enormous possible risks.

Fearing that lower income groups would not choose to pay the extra 10 to 30 per cent that FR-treated fabrics cost, the CPSC implemented compulsory FR standards. Thus, by law, all children's clothing, adult sleepwear, hospital garments (including those for the newborn infant), and nylon backpack tents must be flame-retardant. Considering not only immediate physical risks involved but the environmental burdens of these chemicals in laundry wastes, the wisdom of this decision is dubious. The consumer no longer has a choice in the matter, since even such natural fire-resistant materials as wool must now be treated with FR chemicals.

Choosing Clothing Supplies Wisely

Care in choosing and using clothing supplies is necessary for human health. Some suggestions include:

■ Dry-cleaning fluids: Ventilate well when using coin-operated machines. Don't breathe fumes from dry-cleaning machines. Allow door to remain ajar for a few minutes after the operation is complete to reduce vapors. The solvent will evaporate quickly and not remain in the garments. Remove garments from machine and allow to cool before folding.

■ Spot removers: Use where there is plenty of ventilation. Wear gloves when working with chlorinated hydrocarbons. Never use carbon tetrachloride.

■ Rug and upholstery cleaners: Don't use aerosol sprays. Apply with gloves. Ventilate the room well while using.

■ Fabric finishes: Apply outdoors or where there is plenty of ventilation. Make sure there is a favorable breeze carrying vapors away from applicator.

■ Keep silicone waterproofing away from eyes.

■ Antistatic agents: A good substitute is a humidifier, since static build-up tends to dissipate readily on its own in relatively humid air.

■ Shoe preparations: Polish shoes with polishes which do not contain trichloroethylene, methylene chloride, or nitrobenzene. When unsure because of incomplete labeling, allow polish or dye to dry thoroughly before wearing.

■ Spray starches: The best substitute is the old standby—cornstarch. Mix the cornstarch with water and sprinkle on clothes before ironing. Some leave clothes in the refrigerator before ironing to prevent starch from drying out. Consider permanent-press garments as a substitute for fabrics more prone to wrinkling (see *99 Ways to a Simple Lifestyle*[1]).

■ Flame retardants: If nightwear is worn, cotton is far preferable to synthetics. Use garments which can be easily removed. For homemade nightwear or other clothing choose inherently fire-resistant fabrics such as modacrylics and wool, and avoid very flammable ones such as acetate. Many synthetics melt when on fire, which complicates the healing of a body burn. *Avoid tris-treated clothing.*

▪ Work for legislation requiring self-extinguishing cigarettes. Present cigarette formulations include additives in the paper and filter which cause them to last up to thirty minutes, a significant interval when one considers that 27 per cent of all fire deaths are cigarette-related.

REFERENCES

[1] Center for Science in the Public Interest, *99 Ways to a Simple Lifestyle* (New York: Anchor/Doubleday, 1977), #5, p. 194.

[2] "Water Repellent Finishes," *Consumer Reports,* Vol. 38, May 1973, p. 336.

[3] "Dryer Fabric Softeners," *Consumer Research Magazine,* Vol. 57, Oct. 1974, p. 30.

[4] J. Dorigan and J. Hushon, "Air Pollution Assessment of Nitrobenzene, The Mitre Corporation, McLean, Va., May 1976, pp. 15, 36.

[5] A. Blum and B. Ames, "Flame Retardant Additives as Possible Cancer Hazards," *Science,* Vol. 195 (1977), p. 17.

[6] J. McCann et al., *Proceedings of the National Academy of Science USA,* Vol. 72 (1975), p. 5,135.

[7] M. J. Prival et al., "Tris (2,3-Dibromopropyl) Phosphate: Mutagenicity of a Widely Used Flame Retardant," *Science,* Vol. 195 (1977), p. 77.

[8] J. E. Bishop, "Flame Retardant in Children's Sleepwear Is Suspect as Potential Cause of Cancer," *Wall Street Journal,* Jan. 4, 1977.

D. DUST

Dust is a general term for the millions of varieties of tiny particles which ride our air. These ghostly minutiae respect no boundaries—even the most fastidious housekeeper must partake of our communal refuse with every breath.

The human body (and especially the respiratory system) evolved in the presence of soil and volcanic dust. The labyrinthine trachea with its cilia filters protects the delicate alveoli from moderate quantities of particles of "earth dust" size (1 to 5 microns) and composition. But our respiratory systems are not adapted to the novel forms of dust which have accompanied our technological advances. Aerosolized chemical products (0.3 microns in diameter) are led directly into the blood system, where they are absorbed along with oxygen. Not only are such small particles taken in more deeply and easily but there is no mechanism for their removal.

In many polluted areas, urban and rural, discharge of wastes into the air have increased the filtering load upon the human breathing apparatus to a point of strain. Studies have revealed that high rates of respiratory disease are associated with areas of heavy industry, such as Donora, Pennsylvania; London; the Meuse Valley; and the Kanto Plain in Japan. In New Orleans the spontaneous burnings of an abandoned underground incinerator were highly correlated over a period of years with emergency room admissions for wheezing.[1]

Another problem of modern dust is its novel composition. A number of toxic chemicals are contained in either the nuclei or outer layers of dust particles. Auto emissions from leaded gasoline have resulted in city dirt which contains a lead count higher than the Environmental Protection Agency standard for lead in paint.[2] Every aerosol product adds new toxic layers to existing dust.

The contents of these particles combine in a variety of ways with each other and with the tissues within our bodies. Some cause a sensitization of the body to other chemicals. Three main types of reactions to different features of particulate matter can be defined: allergic reaction, irritation, and chemical reaction.

Many bodies develop allergic reactions to organic matter in the air. The air is a teeming biological environment, house air being especially enriched. The damp warmth of air-conditioning systems promotes great flourishings of mold drawn in from outside and circulated about the house in spore form. A favorite breeding place of the allergy-activating organism *Thermophilia actionycetes* is the home furnace.[1]

The organism most strongly associated with allergic reactions is *Dermato phagoides,* the microscopic house mite.[3] In a survey of the major geographic areas of the United States, house mites were found in 60 per cent of the house dust samples. Ninety per cent of the samples taken from bedrooms of persons with allergy problems included this mite, with mattress samples showing the highest concentrations. Colonization by this tiny insect is probably responsible for a phenomenon which has baffled allergy researchers for years—that old samples of furniture and bedding materials often produce allergies while new samples do not.

Drifting organic matter resulting from the breaking down of larger organisms also plays a major role in allergy activation. Many allergies have been specifically related to human and animal danders—the flaked scales from skin, feathers, and hair.[4] An occupational hazard in the baking industry, and a problem to some home breadmakers, is rhinitis, a sensitivity to fine wheat powder.[5]

Allergic reactions are primarily respiratory but also include urticaria (skin welts)[4] and Ménière's disease (the allergy-produced impairment of the nerve of the inner ear).[6]

A second type of reaction to dust is irritation, which results from the physical properties of the particles. Irritation often leads to permanent scarring, especially with particles sized between .05 and 5 microns. Pneumoconiosis is the family name for lung damage of this type, of which the coal miner's "black lung" is a member. Silicosis, another disease of this family, has been found among residents neighboring dusty quarry and strip mine sites and among abrasive-cleaner workers. Extreme irritation and scarring is also the body's reaction to asbestos, as discussed in Section B.

A third bodily response to the presence of foreign substances in breathing passages is chemical reaction. Obvious examples of this category are aerosolized chemicals and pesticide-coated particles. Perhaps less obvious are the potential reactions of what have been termed "carbonized house dust" and the associated gaseous by-products.[5] According to Casimir M. Nikel,[6] house dust burns into charcoal at 325° F. (well below the average furnace temperature) releasing minute quantities of such toxic gases as phosgene and cyanide. The reactions of such particles and gases in the lungs may reduce access to the available oxygen supply.

As pointed out by R. Kane at the American Academy of Science Conference on indoor air pollution, it is children who suffer most from the poor quality of our air.[2] Because children breathe more air per unit body weight and have respiration rates of up to ten times adult rates, their systems must handle greater quantities of air impurities. In addition, their air supply comes from lower, denser air that is highest in concentrations of pollutants. Toxic ozone concentrations at three feet have been measured to be four times the concentrations at six feet.

The range of hazardous dusts to which both children and adults are exposed will, of course, depend greatly upon a variety of environmental factors in the home: proximity to heavy industry, household appliances and chemicals present, type of heating system, etc. Since it is impossible to anticipate all the possible sources of dust problems, the following general guidelines should be observed.

Table I COMMON CONTAMINANTS OF HOUSEHOLD DUST

Type	Source	Dangers
Asbestos	street dust (brake linings of cars) insulation in buildings	see section on Building Materials
Carbon monoxide, nitrogen oxides, hydrocarbons, oxidants	attaches onto dust from the exterior or enters as a gaseous pollutant and attaches onto household dust	see section on Emissions see section on Motor Products
Household chemicals aerosol sprays powdered detergents	from ordinary cleaning operations in the home	see section on Aerosol, Kitchen Soaps, Oven Cleaners, Furniture Polishes, Utensil Cleaners
Lead mercury cadmium, etc	from auto emissions or from burning of coal or factory wastes	see section on Lead see section on Quicksilver
Lint	originates principally from clothing and home furnishings indoors and from failure to properly ventilate dryers	in large amounts may cause "brown lung" disease
Pollen	from outdoor or possibly some indoor vegetation	causes allergies see section on Vegetation
Silicone particles	enter from exterior, especially from quarry and strip mine operations	causes silicosis
Smoke	attaches onto dust particles within tobacco smoking environment	see section on Tobacco Smoke

Type	Source	Dangers
Soil, dirt, earth	carried in from outdoors	can bear toxic materials
Solvents, resins	from home hobbies and repair	see section on Solvents see section on Hobbies
Sulfur dioxide	attaches to exterior of indoor particulates, coming from lead processing plants, paper mills, steel plants, coal-fired furnaces	respiratory diseases
Vinyl chloride plastic chemicals	from occluded vinyl chloride in PVC	see section on Plastics
Bacteria	grow in house humidifiers, ventilation systems, heating and cooling systems	cause infection

How to Deal with Dust

No single solution to the dust problem exists. However, both individual and community steps can be taken to reduce dust levels in the home:

■ Reduce the use of spray chemicals (aerosols, insecticides, paint, and motor products).

■ Clean and vacuum regularly. A clean, reasonably powerful vacuum will remove about 80 per cent of the dust around the house. Mattresses, sills, radiators, and the floor under furniture are dust reservoirs that are a key to dust control.

■ Clean air system filters and vents regularly. The value of electronic air cleaners has been debated because they require regular attention to avoid efficiency reduction, ozone emissions, and fire hazards. Good forced-air heating systems, which have proven to reduce airborne dust, are probably more effective.

▪ Keep humidifying systems free from sediment and bacteria build-up.

▪ Reroute children out of areas of the house or neighborhood associated with high levels of air contamination— hobby rooms, houses under construction or refurbishment, roadways, incinerators.

▪ Place non-PVC plastic (see Section P) covers on mattresses and pillows as well as over the open bottoms of chairs and sofas to lighten the dust load for an allergy-prone housemate. Fabrics can be coated with emulsified oil compounds which serve as dust seals.

▪ Cover or store outside any work clothes that are contaminated by chemicals or toxic dusts.

▪ Vent stoves directly to the outside.

▪ Make the most of the body's own air-cleaning systems by breathing through the nose, especially during heavy exercise.

▪ Support environmentally conscious candidates for political office.

▪ Complain to polluters and regulatory agencies and praise nonpolluters.

▪ Join the National Clean Air Coalition (620 C Street S.E., Washington, D.C. 20003) or local citizen action groups fighting for cleaner air.

REFERENCES

[1] "New Orleans Asthma," *Journal of Allergy,* Vol. 39 (Apr. 1964), pp. 27–33.

[2] Michael Clark, "Home Brewed Pollution Hurts the Little Ones," *Prevention,* July 1976, pp. 165–71.

[3] G. W. Wharton, "Mites and Commercial Extracts of House Dust," *Science,* Vol. 167, No. 2923 (Mar. 6, 1970), pp. 1,382–83.

[4] "Dust Allergy," report from the National Institute on Allergy and Infectious Diseases, Department of Health, Education, and Welfare publication #75-440, Bethesda, Md.

[5] Herman Hirschfield, *The Whole Truth About Allergy* (New York: Arc Books, Inc., 1969).

[6] Casimir M. Nikel, *Breathing for Survival: A Case of Slow Suffocation* (Hicksville, N.Y.: Exposition Press, 1975).

E. EMISSIONS FROM HEATING AND COOLING DEVICES

All the heating and cooling methods used in the home are associated with some form of pollutants. Electrical methods are far from being pollution free even though the fossil and nuclear pollutants may be at power plants miles from the home. Even materials used in essentially pollution-free solar devices are not without some—albeit small—environmental costs, for the copper and aluminum solar collectors require energy to produce and the metal processing has accompanying pollutants. Granting some emissions from all heating and cooling of homes, the goal should be to minimize environmental impact. Greater concern should be given to home fossil-fueled heating.

Few studies have been conducted to determine the extent to which gas stoves, furnaces, and refrigeration units degrade the quality of air in the home. One study commissioned by the EPA and conducted by the Research Corporation of New England states that gas stove emissions do substantially degrade the quality of indoor environment.[1] These stoves produce various kinds of noxious gases such as carbon monoxide and nitrogen oxides. Carbon monoxide is a colorless, odorless gas created through the incomplete combustion of fuel. It combines with blood hemoglobin and impairs the normal oxygen-carrying capacity of the blood. Carbon monoxide levels in the blood create increased stress on the heart and impair reflex co-ordination. When inhaled in large quantities, this is fatal.

Nitrogen oxides are extremely irritating to the eyes and

upper linings of the respiratory tract. High doses cause coughing and chest pains immediately; lower concentrations may produce only mild discomfort. The most dangerous of these nitrogen oxides is nitrogen dioxide. Acute high doses cause pulmonary edema, and chronic low doses may cause chronic bronchitis.

Gas Stoves

The Research Corporation has found that the amount of noxious fumes produced by gas stoves was related directly to the number of burners that were operating and the amount of gas consumed. Furthermore, in some instances levels of nitrogen dioxide and carbon monoxide in the kitchen exceeded the outdoor air-quality standard for these pollutants.[1] Gas stoves produce these fumes both when used for cooking and when only the pilot light is on. Pilot lights are a significant source of nitrogen oxide emissions, and the average kitchen equipped with a gas stove has concentrations two to four times that of the outdoor ambient air level. The highest concentrations occur during the winter when the house is closed.

Air quality tends to differ according to heating equipment operation and location. For gas stoves and gas space heaters emissions are highest during warm-up. The kitchen concentrations are higher than other rooms of the house, though as mentioned, all indoor areas using these devices show higher concentrations than outdoors. Concentration levels directly over a stove are much higher than a few feet away in the kitchen. This suggests the desirability of a good exhaust hood or fan.[2] But properly vented stove hoods capture and exhaust only about half the pollutants generated; even recirculating hoods with charcoal filters do not prevent contaminated air from circulating about the household.

Houses using gas often show slightly higher incidences of illness. However, the results may not be significant because of small sample size. An eye opener is the effect of gas usage on asthma sufferers, heavy smokers, and those whose occupations expose them to higher pollutant concentrations. In each case the incidence of illness is significantly higher in gas-using homes.[3]

Grills

Many tribes and peoples have cooked indoors with charcoal (generally small amounts) for centuries. They have found through sad experience that smoldering charcoal can kill. Most Americans use sizable portions of charcoal in outdoor grills. While cooking over smoldering charcoal is no major hazard in well-ventilated situations (the outdoors or well-equipped restaurants), a summer shower may tempt an amateur to move a grill to the back porch or indoors. This can be dangerous.

One family in the state of Washington learned through tragedy that smoldering charcoal can build up lethal concentrations of carbon monoxide in minutes.[4] This family of three was camping in a thirteen-foot camper in the early fall. Using a charcoal brazier for overnight warmth, they left a roof vent and a lower window partly open in the camper for fresh air. During the night, as a result of the cold night air, the lower window was closed. Upon waking at dawn the mother found their twelve-year-old daughter dead of carbon monoxide poisoning. The parents were hospitalized with symptoms of nausea, vomiting, and exhaustion.

What levels of carbon monoxide are harmful? The Federal Air Quality Standards set the outdoor safety level of 9 parts per million (ppm) of carbon monoxide. In industry the limit is 50 ppm of carbon monoxide but efforts are being made to lower this limit to 25 ppm. Tests by the University of Washington with carbon monoxide in the camper found that with the window closed and the roof vent partly open the level of carbon monoxide rose to 1,100 ppm in the trailer within 10 minutes. At that concentration death can occur within 90 to 120 minutes. With the windows half open the carbon monoxide level reached 650 ppm in 11 minutes.

Refrigerants in Refrigerators and Air-conditioners

Refrigerators or air-conditioning units are not perfect. They can spring leaks or be damaged and result in the emission of freon refrigerants used in the thermal system.

Two kinds of systems are used in refrigerators and air-conditioners: an open and a closed system. Fifty-two per cent of air-conditioners and refrigerators are constructed with prefabricated closed refrigerant systems. The fluorocarbon refrigerant is put into a vacuum-sealed system at the factory and the units need only be delivered and installed as such in the home. The other 48 per cent are large central air-conditioning units assembled on site by a building contractor. The refrigerant is injected into the system at the site.

A refrigerant acts as a heat transfer agent through the absorption of heat by the fluid and its vaporization and condensation in the refrigeration system. Refrigerants most commonly used today are the fluorocarbon compounds already mentioned as aerosol spray propellants. Estimates are that 14 per cent (204 million pounds) of the world-wide releases of F-11 and F-22 are from cooling devices[1] (see Table I). Thus environmental problems involving depletion of atmospheric ozone involve refrigerants as well as aerosol sprays.

Up until the 1940s ammonia, sulfur dioxide, and methyl chloride were used as primary refrigerants, but since that time they have been exclusively replaced by fluorocarbons because of their high toxicity, flammability, and corrosiveness. The fluorocarbon compounds are less corrosive and not flammable and were thought to be less toxic. Health and environmental concerns associated with fluorocarbon use are mentioned in Section A.

Prefabricated cooling units (closed systems) hold twelve to eighteen ounces of fluorocarbons; a 12,000 BTU room air-conditioning unit contains about two pounds of fluorocarbons. These products generally last for about ten years before requiring recharging. A central air-conditioning unit system with about six pounds of refrigerant requires recharging about every five years. Thus fluorocarbon refrigerants normally leak out at a very slow rate until there is no longer sufficient fluid left to accomplish heat exchange. Can this be harmful to us in the home environment? Prudence dictates an urgent search for safer refrigerants or the design of new cooling methods.

Table I
ESTIMATED 1975 WORLDWIDE RELEASES OF F-11 AND F-12

Cooling	Millions of pounds
Vehicle air-conditioners	90
Building cooling	43
Food and beverages	39
Home refrigerators and freezers	6
Misc. air-conditioners/ refrigerators	27

Source: "Halocarbons: Environmental Effects of Chlorofluoromethane Release" (Washington, D.C.: National Academy of Sciences, 1976), pp. 1–18.

Draining cooling systems during repair operations emits fluorocarbons in large amounts. Severe leakage of refrigerants from a damaged system presents further dangers. One victim suffered fluorocarbon inhalation by breaking a cooling coil in a refrigerator while defrosting. Another, perhaps more potentially dangerous hazard, is fluorocarbon leakage from a central air-conditioning unit. The cooling coil of such units is usually installed next to the home furnace. If fluorocarbons leak from the unit cooling coil, decomposition into highly toxic chemicals (hydrochloric acid, hydrofluoric acid, and phosgene) can occur on contact with a heated surface, sparks, or flames of a furnace or fireplace.

Because fluorocarbons are invisible and odorless, it is almost impossible for a homeowner to detect whether or not a leak exists. It is uncertain whether a small leak in a refrigerator or

central air-conditioning unit can adversely affect the quality
of air of an average home. However, the possibility of jeopard-
izing human health by a severely damaged refrigeration or
air-conditioning unit is significant. Using an ice pick to hur-
riedly defrost a refrigerator will both damage the appliance
and very likely expose one to a toxic gas.

Eliminating Harmful Emissions

Some of the ways of reducing or eliminating noxious emissions and possible harmful health effects are:

■ Use a proper venting system if the home is equipped with
a gas stove.

■ If purchasing a gas stove, buy one with an electric igniter
and thus eliminate the pilot light pollution.

■ Look into whether one's existing gas stove can be converted to an electric igniter system.

■ If uncertain as to whether carbon monoxide levels are
high near a gas or oil furnace, have the furnace checked.

■ Never take smoldering charcoal indoors unless a good
ventilating system is provided.

■ Use care when defrosting a refrigerator. Do not use a
sharp instrument.

■ Have the refrigerating and air-conditioning system checked
if a major leak is suspected.

REFERENCES

[1] W. A. Wade III et al., "A Study of Indoor Air Quality," *Journal of the Air Pollution Control Association*, Sept. 1975, pp. 933–39.
[2] W. A. Wade, "Indoor Sources," in *Improving Indoor Air Quality Conferences*, summary edited by J. B. Chaddock, EPA.
[3] R. Chapman, "Indoor Sources and Health Effects," ibid.
[4] *Consumer Reports*, June 1972, p. 337.

Additional Source

W. A. Cote et al., "A Study of Indoor Air Quality," EPA Research, Triangle Park, N.C., Sept. 1974.

F. FURNITURE AND FLOOR POLISHES

Homemakers enjoy keeping the house "spic and span." A good floor polish or wax both prolongs the life of the wood and brings out the beauty of the wood grain. The entire home becomes more comfortable and warmer when there is a gloss to wood and metal.

The age of convenience and comfort has encouraged the development of home products which save time. Cleaners, polishes, and waxes have widespread use; a plethora of specialized metal polish and tarnish-preventing agents bedazzle the consumer.

Besides being generally more costly than old-fashioned polishes and waxes, the health of the homemaker and members of the family may be threatened by some of these time-saving products. There is a lack of knowledge about the contents of polishes and wax formulations, and the effects of different exposure periods on the lungs and skin. Vapors from the products pose real hazards in the closed atmosphere of the home where fresh air is lacking. Most homemakers don't know that petroleum distillates cause local skin irritation (see Section S), naphtha can induce cardiac death, nitrobenzene is highly poisonous when ingested, and oil of cedar wood is a nervous stimulant. Yet the television commercials of sparkling furniture which please both guests and family members do not mention the chemicals found in furniture polishes, nor that the application may have to be made with special care.

Furniture Polishes

There are three general types of commercial furniture polish formulations: solvents, emulsions, and aerosol sprays. The essential ingredients in these polishes are oil and wax. Each is a slightly different approach to applying the oil or wax to the furniture surface, and each contains specific chemicals which enhance its method of application.

The solvent product formulation dissolves the oil (conditioner) or wax (protector) ingredients into a solution by use of a chemical solvent. For oil or wax polish a petroleum or mineral spirits solvent is used. After application, the solvent dries, leaving behind the protective surface coating of oil or wax on the various items of furniture. This method coats with a certain amount of evenness and ease.

The emulsion product type does not dissolve the two essential ingredients into solution as does the solvent variety. It provides rather only a physical means of application, wherein the active ingredients are suspended in a liquid medium. In addition to this agent, many other chemicals are used to aid in applying the oil or wax more evenly onto the furniture surface.

The aerosol spray delivery package is the more modern method. It is far faster to apply, does not require elbow grease and cloths, and requires little cleanup afterward. But the aerosol sprays have the disadvantages of higher cost, health hazards, environmental dangers, and the likelihood of spreading the wax or oil on undesired surfaces in the vicinity of furniture.

The health dangers that most often occur with furniture polishes are poisoning, acute ingestion of the liquid solvent or emulsion type by children, and inhalation of fumes and vapors, especially from the aerosol spray variety. Furniture polish spray propellants may decompose to harmful gases when in contact with a heated surface.

ENDUST AEROSOL SPRAY
(The Drackett Products Company, Cincinnati, Ohio)

CAUTION: Contents under pressure. Temperatures over 120° F. may cause bursting. Do not puncture, incinerate, or use near fire or flame. Use only as directed. Intentional misuse by deliberately concentrating and inhaling the contents can be harmful or fatal. Keep out of reach of children.

NOTE: Use on: furniture, floors, window sills, baseboards, books, blinds, lamp shades . . . everywhere. Spray Endust directly on furnace and air-conditioning filters to keep your home more dust-free.

Another common danger in application is the polishes getting into the sensitive parts of the body, especially the eyes. Most polishes are flammable and can ignite when applied by active smokers. The petroleum distillates and petroleum naphtha (mineral spirits) found in many polishes can easily produce local skin irritation and among certain individuals can cause skin photosensitization (sensitivity to light).

Nitrobenzene and dinitrobenzene found in some polishes are highly toxic if ingested, inhaled, or absorbed by skin. Oil of cedarwood, a common oil used for polishes, has been used to induce abortions, and is, as mentioned, a nervous system stimulant.

If the conscientious consumer takes the time to read ingredient labels, it may come as a surprise that furniture polishes generally do not have such warnings listed. Nor do many mention any ingredients other than the petroleum distillates.

OLD ENGLISH LEMON OIL FURNITURE POLISH
(Boyle-Midway, Inc., New York)

DANGER: Harmful or fatal if swallowed. Keep out of reach of children. Contains petroleum distillates. If swallowed, do not induce vomiting. Call a doctor at once.

CAUTION: Combustible mixture N.Y.F.D.C. of A. No. 1617. Do not use near fire or flame.

DIRECTIONS: Pour a small quantity of polish on a clean, damp cloth. Apply to surface to remove dust, grease, or stain. Polish to a high luster with a soft, dry cloth. Brings out the beautiful wood finish on pianos, fine furniture, and woodwork. Excellent for renewing oil mops.

In a letter to the Consumer Product Safety Commission regarding Lemon Pledge, an S. C. Johnson and Sons, Inc., product, a consumer complained of symptomatic effects from the use of the aerosol spray product. She could not find the ingredient listing on the product label. The commission apologetically responded that when attempting to obtain information from the manufacturer it was informed that trade secrets were involved. CPSC admitted being unable to take additional action other than to continue to watch for similar complaints.

A manufacturer is not required by law to submit product formulation information to any regulatory authority or to obtain any prior approval from CPSC before a product is marketed. Only if a product contains a hazardous substance as defined by the Federal Hazardous Substances Act must the product bear a cautionary warning. However, be cautious about an incompletely labeled product. It does not mean that there is a tacit endorsement of product safety by a regulatory agency. Vigorous reassurances from the manufacturer are not to be regarded as convincing.

Liquid polishes, especially "lemon oil" polishes, present a definite poisoning hazard to youngsters. Manufacturers make these products more appealing by using attractive colors and fragrances in their formulations and putting them in enticing containers. Often liquid polishes resembling soft drinks are especially attractive to children. Old English Red Oil and Scratch Cover resembles strawberry soda and has frequently been involved with children's poisonings. O'Cedar Cream Polish looks like milk, and Old English Lemon Oil looks and smells remotely like apple juice.

Clancy Emert, of Peoria, Illinois, drank approximately three tablespoons of Old English Furniture and Scratch Cover Polish. His father got him to the hospital in ten minutes; the emergency room had already been alerted. But Old English polish consists primarily of a kerosenelike substance that, when ingested, enters and saturates the lungs so that they cannot function. There is no way to rid the body of the poison or to reverse its effect. Clancy was dead in forty hours.[1]

The danger is the ready accessibility of the product to the child. The pattern is a familiar one to attending physicians in hospital emergency treatment rooms. The product is stored at floor level and the child tries to taste it when unattended. A two-year-old picks up the bottle, opens the lid, and swallows the polish, and the results can be fatal. While furniture polishes of more than 10 per cent petroleum distillates must now have child-proof lids, a large number of older containers are still present in the homes, and the danger will be very real for a number of years. Estimates are that 1 to 2 million children swallow harmful household substances each year and hundreds die. Generally, it is the younger ones who injure themselves with nonedible products, while the older ones suffer from ingesting medicines.

Floor Polishes

Many of the same wood polishes for furniture can be used for floors also. The same cautions must be taken. The distinction has become less important by the use of multipurpose cleaners and polishes. Many of the active agents (the polishing ingredients) are not notably toxic, but again, as in the case of furniture polish, the solvents used to emulsify or liquefy the polish may very well be. These solvents are often combustible as well.

WOOD PREEN: Wood floors, cabinets, paneling

Other uses for Wood Preen: paneling, countertops, slate, hearthstones, venetian blinds, sticking windows, drawers, and doors.

Will protect all outdoor wood, aluminum storm sash and doors, garden tools, and leather.

CAUTION: Combustible mixture. Do not use near fire or flame. Contains petroleum naphtha. If swallowed, do not induce vomiting. Call physician immediately.

Furniture and Floor Polish Safety Hints

If the urge is to buy commercial products, follow these hints:

▪ Avoid aerosol spray products. Use either the solvent or emulsion variety.

▪ KEEP OUT OF REACH OF CHILDREN. Think twice before purchasing polishes with fruity smells. If children are present, replace old furniture polish containers with a childproof variety. This measure of safety is worth the extra cost.

▪ Use furniture polish sparingly, and only with enough ventilation so that fumes do not accumulate in the room. Wax and polish build-up is symptomatic of overuse. Usually a clean cloth with some mineral oil applied to it will do as good a job as a reapplication of commercial varieties, and saves money as well.

▪ Avoid products containing the highly toxic ingredients nitrobenzene and dinitrobenzene. Be careful with less toxic ones like oil of cedar.

▪ It is always wise to wear rubber gloves when applying furniture or floor polish with a cloth.

Furniture and Floor Polish Substitutes

There are several alternatives to using commercial polish:

▪ Use soapy water or a clean cloth for furniture and floors.

▪ To make furniture and floor polish, melt carnauba wax into mineral oil (1 tablespoon of wax in 2 cups of oil).[2] Other more volatile petroleum distillates such as mineral spirits can be dangerous when inhaled or when absorbed through the skin.

▪ For lemon oil polish, dissolve 1 teaspoon of lemon oil into 1 pint of mineral oil. Don't try making a thin film polish by use of benzene. It is quite toxic.

REFERENCES

[1] "Furniture Polishes," *Consumer Reports*, Vol. 39, 748 (Oct. 1974).
[2] N. Stark, *The Formula Book* (Kansas City: Sheed and Ward, Inc., 1975), p. 25.

G. GARBAGE AND SOLID WASTES

All consumers are familiar with garbage and trash, because all—even the most resource-conscious people—produce wastes. The amount of materials thrown away from each home is a gauge of lifestyle and consumerism. We are what we waste, and Americans are conspicuous in the world for wasting precious resources. Solid wastes now amount to over half a ton of material per American per year. And abatement efforts never seem to make much difference.

Solid Waste Problem

Garbage and trash are both pollutants around the home and the cause of solid waste environmental pollution in the neighborhood. The disagreeable odors, the unsightliness, and the sanitation problems associated with household garbage prompt us to "get that stuff out of the house." But what is discarded from numerous residences soon becomes a major problem for the community. What can be done with the mountain of materials which come forth damp, unsorted, and smelly? No one wants another's garbage in the back yard or in a land fill near the home. Land prices depress as a result of smells and the fear of attracting rats and other rodents. Strong breezes leave paper and other litter all over the countryside. Truly trash and garbage may continue to pollute long after first generated in the home.

We know more what garbage is than what to do about it. Stuffing garbage down a disposal flushed with water does not solve the problem. The ground-up materials find their way to treatment plants where costly energy-requiring operations remove water and condense the sludge. Disposal of this sludge is still a problem. New York and Philadelphia for years dumped their sludge off the Jersey coast until it began to reappear on the beaches. Now time is running out for these and other municipal areas.

"Trash" usually refers to paper refuse. Some paper can be recycled and some should never have been used in the first place. One paper plague of the average home is junk mail. Letter carriers have estimated that between half and two thirds of what they carry is junk mail—the bulk of which will very shortly be thrown into the trash heap.

While food wastes and paper account for over half the solid waste load (see Table I), still a number of other materials add to the burden. Glass, especially nonreturnable bottles are bulky and costly from a total environmental viewpoint. The same may be said for unrecycled cans and metal products. Plastics, which along with rubber are less likely to be recycled, are a source of potentially dangerous fumes and chemicals (see Section P). Wood and yard wastes, if not composted, add another burden to the waste load.

Increasingly it will become necessary for our society to put aside and utilize this abundant and valuable resource of garbage. Garbage can be converted into valuable fertilizer through composting. Ground garbage can be transported to water treatment plants via sewer effluent and condensed into a sludge that can be returned to agricultural land. Combustible materials can be burned to generate steam for electricity. Food wastes can be treated and fed to livestock.

Guidelines for Household Garbage Disposal and Reduction

Regardless of all our care, there are still some wastes which must be removed. Pollution near the household occurs through improper storage of this garbage. Improperly stored garbage provides a prolific breeding ground for flies, other insects, and rodents. Studies have shown that garbage as a breeding site is responsible for half of all indoor larval infestations. Bottles or cans which collect moisture create an attractive breeding area for mosquitoes. Spilled or uncovered garbage attract mice and rats.

Table I

ESTIMATE OF RESIDENTIAL AND COMMERCIAL SOLID WASTE (1973)

Material	Pounds per capita per day	Per cent
Paper	1.36	38.9%
Glass	0.36	10.3
Metals	0.35	9.9
Plastics	0.14	4.1
Rubber and plastics	0.10	2.7
Textiles	0.06	1.6
Wood	0.13	3.6
*Total nonfood product waste	2.50	71.1%
Food waste	0.47	13.3
*Total product waste	2.97	84.4%
Yard waste	0.50	14.1
Misc. inorganic	0.50	1.5
*Total	3.97	
		100.0%

Source: "Resource Plant Implementation Technologies" (U. S. Environmental Protection Agency, 1976), p. 15.

Note: Because of the recession the 1974 and 1975 data were unrepresentative of solid waste generation, and incomplete 1976 data more closely resemble the above figures for 1973.

The first step to reduce the inevitable home garbage pollution problem is to use proper storage techniques. Drain and wrap wet garbage, and use cans lined with paper sacks or plastic bags and containing tightly fitting lids. Sprinkle baking soda inside the can to help reduce odors, and clean and allow to dry often. Remove garbage from the kitchen to these cans after each meal.

The second step for reducing household garbage is to reduce the use of materials—and thus generation of wastes. Coupled with this is the reuse or recycling of otherwise wasted materials.

The less solid waste we make, the less we have to contend with. Every person generates wastes, but the amounts vary considerably. Some hints for curtailing generation of solid wastes include:

■ Refrain from purchasing nonreturnable bottled beverages.[1]

■ Shop at food co-ops and purchase fresh produce which require little or no packaging.[2] When doing the shopping at such places, bring along old sacks, bags, and egg cartons from home.

■ Reduce junk mail by (a) writing individually to any organization using your name to remove it from their trading lists; (b) considering junk mail as pandering and filling out Form 2150 at the local post office (the Postal Service also has a form to block the delivery of pornographic mail); (c) writing to Direct Mail/Marketing Association, Inc., 6 East 43rd St., New York, N.Y. 10017. This will block about 70 per cent of all consumer third-class junk mail.[3]

■ Use handkerchiefs and cotton towels for paper tissues and towels; china, glass, and ceramics instead of paper plates and cups; washable cups in the bathroom instead of paper ones; and cloth instead of disposable diapers.[4]

■ Ask to take purchased materials without the wrapping.

■ Refuse to purchase overly wrapped personal items.

Some hints for reusing and recycling "waste" or trashable materials include:[5]

■ Newspapers—tie in bundles and take to recycling centers; use in rolled form as logs for the fireplace; have shredded and fireproofed for insulation.

■ Glass jars—use for storage of food; recycle.

■ Plastic bags—use for garbage and storage of nonedible items.

■ Paper bags—use for lining trash cans.

- Magazines—give to friends and neighbors to read.
- Cardboard boxes—use for toys and games; reuse for food; recycle.
- Used envelopes—reuse in mailing or for making filing folders.
- Blank pages—use for scratch paper.
- Aluminum cans and foil—crush and recycle.
- Steel cans—wash, remove labels and ends, flatten, and recycle.
- Old clothing—make into dustcloths or reuse as clothing.
- Yard wastes—compost and mulch.[6]
- Food wastes—compost and mulch.

REFERENCES

[1] Center for Science in the Public Interest, *99 Ways to a Simple Lifestyle* (Garden City, N.Y.: Anchor/Doubleday, 1977), ¶48, p. 183.

[2] Ibid., ¶47, p. 180.

[3] "Junk Mail," *Consumer Reports,* Sept. 1976, p. 540.

[4] *99 Ways to a Simple Lifestyle,* ¶46, p. 179.

[5] Ibid., ¶49, p. 185.

[6] Ibid., ¶44, p. 169.

H. HOBBIES, ARTS AND CRAFTS

In an age of mass production, arts and crafts provide millions of people an outlet for creative self-expression and personal fulfillment. Hobbyists can participate in the shaping of their physical environment instead of passively consuming the output of machines.

On the other hand, certain avocations may be the cause of serious pollution problems within the home. In fact, some of these hobbies require many of the potentially harmful chemicals regulated for industry use by the occupational safety law. While we have come to demand that large manufacturers eliminate worker, consumer, and environmental hazards, hobbyists do not always give comparable consideration to themselves and their families. Before undertaking any craft project, the hobbyist should reflect on the following questions:

- How many toxic substances are required?
- Is special safety equipment necessary?
- Is the work area properly ventilated?
- Will others be exposed to hazardous fumes, solvents, dusts, noise?
- Is this done with their knowledge and consent?
- Will others be exposed to toxic residues after the project is complete?
- To what extent is the work environment separate from living quarters?
- Are materials used which produce serious outdoor pollution in their extraction, manufacture, or disposal?

Such questions are not meant to discourage or overwhelm the

hobbyist, but merely to call attention to the serious nature of working with toxic substances.

Following are the basic modes of exposure to dangerous chemicals.

Inhalation

One major area of medical concern with arts and crafts is human respiration. A number of hobbies (metalwork, pottery, plasticrafts, jewelry making, lapidary work, sculpture, and woodworking) generate dust through sanding, grinding, sawing, and other machining. Moving about chemicals in powder form, such as lye, hydrosulfite, and asbestos dust (used for papier-mâché products), also sends noxious particles aloft. Similar dangers are posed by careless handling of paint pigments containing such toxic components as lead, cadmium, mercury, and selenium. Breathing these particles may lead to scarred lung tissue, impaired respiration, and eventually to chronic respiratory diseases like bronchitis, emphysema, or pulmonary fibrosis.

In addition to dust, there are fumes from volatile toxic chemicals. Inhalation of solvents used in photography, printing or furniture refinishing, for example, can cause headaches, drowsiness, chemical intoxification, impaired motor response, and eventually death (see Section S). Lead vapors and carbon monoxide are often produced in soldering, welding, and the firing of glazed pottery. Likewise, in modern metalworking, blowtorches operating at very high temperatures can give off noxious nitrogen oxides and metallic vapors. When plastics are heated directly or incidentally in machining, toxic gases can be set free.

Such respiratory hazards are compounded by the absence of adequate safeguards in many homes. Workshops are usually not equipped with protective devices such as lab hoods and dust attachments for power tools, and adequate ventilation is frequently lacking. This is especially serious for amateur photographers who do one-step color processing in their homes.

As mentioned in other sections, the home generally has recirculating air systems which easily allow rapid build-up of airborne particles and fumes. If work areas and clothes are not cleaned after daily use, dusts can be tracked or carried into other parts of the house. Hobbyists should note, however, that broom sweeping may aggravate more than abate the workshop dust problem.

Skin Contact

Another major area of toxic exposure for the craftsperson is the skin. Many frequently used chemicals, such as acids, lye, and other alkalies can cause severe burns and eye damage. Dangerous solvents used in adhesive, varnishes, lacquers, oil paints, and paint thinners can irritate exposed parts of the body and penetrate the skin by dissolving natural oils (see Section S). Some of these, like the benzoil in Red Devil Paint and Varnish Remover, probably cause cancer.

The eyes are particularly vulnerable to toxic substances when goggles are not used. Welders should protect themselves from ultraviolet radiation. Wearers of contact lenses should take special note that the same absorbency that allows soft contact lenses to retain medication may prove dangerous in the presence of strong vapors. These contaminants can be held against the eye until the lenses are removed, rather than being quickly washed away be tears.

Despite the appeal of their fast-drying properties, the instant glues and cyanoacrylate adhesives marketed in variety stores like Woolworth's can pose severe hazards in the home. Instant Krazy Glue and Permabond International 102 Contact Cement can bond so rapidly and strongly that the least sloppiness can be very dangerous. A child (or even adult) who spills a drop on a finger and then touches an eye can end up with "a permanent finger in the eye."[1]

Ingestion

While it is unlikely that hobbyists will inadvertently swallow large amounts of craft-related chemicals, some substances are so toxic that even minuscule amounts can be quite poisonous. Perhaps the most frequent manifestation of this problem is eating in the workshop, where food can be contaminated by dusts, filings, vapors, and spilled chemicals. Mealtime hazards are created outside the workshop as well by toxic residues on clothes, beards, hands, and fingernails. Hand-to-mouth contamination is in fact a problem inside and outside the workshop, particularly for smokers.

Craftspersons should always remember that ingestive hazards may continue to exist after a product is made. Eating utensils, pipes, flutes, whistles, etc., should obviously be free of contaminants. Beware of using toxic glues in laminated cutting boards and bowls, leaded solder in metal food and beverage containers, and certain poisonous species of wood (e.g., cocobolo) in objects that will come into contact with food or mouth.

Table I

HAZARDS POSED BY COMMON HOBBY SUPPLIES

Materials/ Supplies	Health Hazards	Recommended Precautions
Clay, Stone modeling clay, dolomite, sandstone, limestone, plaster, marble, diabase, flint, travertine, gemstones,	Inhalation of clay and rock dusts is the main danger. Respiratory tract problems, including silicosis, may result. Soapstone	proper ventilation, prompt cleanup of chips and dusts, venting of kilns to the outdoors, use of respirators for grinding, avoidance

Materials/ Supplies	Health Hazards	Recommended Precautions
granite, soapstone*, serpentine*	and serpentine(*) contain asbestos, a cause of asbestosis and cancer of the lungs and body lining.	of asbestos-containing materials
Wood cocobolo, redwood, birch, beech, boxwood, myrtle, pine, satinwood, dogwood, mahogany	Sawdust inhalation can eventually lead to respiratory problems and an increased susceptibility to nasal cancer. Cocobolo can produce dermatitis. Other woods may be allergenic for some people.	dust attachments on power tools, regular cleanup of dust and shavings, proper ventilation, personal inquiry into the application of fire retardants and fungicides by local lumber dealers (such additives could be toxic)
Solvents, Solutions (e.g., Painting Vehicles, Finishing Materials, Photographic Supplies) turpentine**, ethanol**, methanol**, benzene**, xylol**, toluol**, ketones**, methylene chloride**, lacquer solvents**, acetates**, hydrochloric acid, acetic acid,	Many of these chemicals are quite flammable(**). All have the potential to irritate the lungs, skin, and eyes and may cause severe internal poisoning if ingested. Bases(†) and acids in particular are caustic, capable of	gloves, goggles, careful handling of chemicals, good ventilation, tight lids on containers, storage of flammable supplies in unbreakable containers away from heat, storage of acids and bases in durable nonmetal containers, proper mixing of

Materials/ Supplies	Health Hazards	Recommended Precautions
sulfuric acid, sodium hydroxide†, potassium hydroxide†, sodium carbonate†, lime†	producing severe burns and blindness. Methylene chloride is a narcotic, as is benzene, which also causes cancer.	acids and water (acid is added to water, not water to acid), flushing of eyes and skin with water immediately after contact with caustic agents, avoidance of any products containing benzene
Pigments, Dyes, Glazes, Inks compounds containing lead, chromium, antimony, uranium, arsenic, manganese, vanadium, cadmium, mercury	While some of these, such as chromium, arsenic, and antimony, are skin irritants, all are dangerous if ingested or inhaled, either as dusts or as fumes from the firing of glazed articles	careful handling of powders, scrubbing hands and changing clothes after leaving studio, keeping food and beverages out of the work area, using only lead-free glazes on eating utensils
Metals (Soldering, Welding) cadmium (in silver solder), nickel (in stainless steel), zinc, lead, copper, iron, beryllium, manganese, magnesium, and alloys containing the above	Inhalation of toxic fumes from heated metals and alloys is the major danger. Episodes of fume fever can result from inhalation of such gases. Metals such as lead are also sources of severe chronic poisoning. The nickel in stainless	proper ventilation, goggles, gloves, workshop free from solvents and other potential explosives, exhaust hoods for welding operations

Materials/ Supplies	Health Hazards	Recommended Precautions
	steel is converted during heating to nickel carbonyl, an extreme hazard to the respiratory and nervous systems. The welding process itself produces ultraviolet light (associated with eye disorders and skin cancer), ozone (lung irritant), and nitrogen oxides (eye and respiratory tract hazard).	
Miscellaneous glues (epoxy, instant, urethane, etc.)	Many are flammable, some are skin and lung irritants and allergic sensitizers, and a number have narcotic (possibly fatal) effects when inhaled.	careful reading of labels before use, storage away from children and heat, gloves as directed, proper ventilation, use of dust mask when sanding glued materials
auto body repair compounds	These are essentially glue products; see preceding comments.	same as for glues
lead came (stained-glass work)	Heating lead (soldering iron, etc.) poses an inhalation hazard.	proper ventilation

Materials/ Supplies	Health Hazards	Precautions Recommended
papier-mâché	Asbestos is contained in some papier-mâché supplies; this fibrous material can cause asbestosis and cancer.	avoidance of products where asbestos is listed or where label is absent

Table II

DANGERS ASSOCIATED WITH THE USE OF PLASTICS

Plastics	Chemical Ingredients			Dangerous Practices	Illnesses
	Monomers Used to Make Plastics	Catalysts	Solvents/Other Chemicals		
1. *Acrylics* sheets: Plexiglas a) blocks: Lucite b) paints (see c) solvents)	methyl methacrylate (MMA)	benzoyl peroxide	cements contain dichloromethane, ethylene dichloride, and trichloroethane	inhalation of dusts, heat decomposition products, use of acrylic glues and cements	MMA: strong skin sensitizer and irritant, vapors cause nausea, loss of appetite, headaches, and lowering of blood pressure
2. *Epoxy resins* for: a) laminating b) casting c) glues d) lacquer coatings	uncured epoxy resins	hardener (amines) strong sensitizer and irritant		overheating of cured resins during sawing, sanding, etc.	skin irritant and sensitizer, suspected cancer-causing agent, peroxides (see below: vinyl polymers, illnesses)
3. *Fluorocarbons:* Teflon, TPFE				cigarette smoking, heating to decomposition	polymer fume fever

| Plastics | Monomers Used to Make Plastics | Chemical Ingredients | | Dangerous Practices | Illnesses |
		Catalysts	Solvents/Other Chemicals		
4. *Polyesters, resins* variety of types	polyester plus styrene monomer, methacrylate monomer, vinyl toluene	methyl ethyl ketone peroxide; benzol peroxide		casting and laminating require excellent ventilation	irritant to eyes, respiratory tract and acute dermatitis
5. *Polystyrenes* a) sheets, molding pellets b) Styrofoam	styrene occluded especially in cements			open flames cause combustion, cutting and sawing release methyl chloride	(see section on Solvents)
6. *Polyurethanes* a) urethane rubber b) urethane foam	isocyanate, polyol	catalysts and additives, fluorocarbon blowing agents (see section on Aerosol Spray)		casting or sculpturing, spraying polyurethane foams (highly toxic)	disabling illness, bronchitis, coughing spasms, skin and eye problems, allergic reactions in the lungs

Plastics	Monomers Used to Make Plastics	Catalysts	Chemical Ingredients Solvents/Other Chemicals	Dangerous Practices	Illnesses (See Section S)
7. Silicone rubber a) cement b) molding	nonoccluded	catalysts	petroleum distillates	inhalation of solvents (see Section on Solvents)	
8. Vinyl polymers a) polyvinyl chloride (PVC) b) polyvinyl acetate (PVA) c) PVC/PVA copolymers d) polyvinyl alcohol	vinyl chloride (occluded VC)	peroxides	solvents can be toxic	release of hydrogen chloride into heat welding at 390° F. (see section on Plastics)	Peroxides: flammable, explosive, skin irritant and sensitizer (see section on Plastics)

Other materials found in many plastics: fillers, colorants, stabilizers, plasticizers (see Section P), fiber glass, asbestos (see Section B).

CHARCOAL FIXATIVE VARNISH
(Grumbacher, Inc., New York)

CONTAINS xylene and ethylene, glycol monoethyl ether
acetate.

CAUTION: Harmful if swallowed or vapor or spray mist
inhaled. Keep from heat and flame. Spray in ventilated areas
and never toward you. Do not get in eyes. Always keep bottle closed tightly.

CYANOACRYLATE SUPER GLUE 3
(Woodhill Chemical Sales Corp., Cleveland, Ohio)

WARNING: Eye irritant. Bonds skin in seconds. Contains
cyanoacrylate ester. Avoid contact with skin and eyes. In
case of eye or mouth contact, hold eyelid or mouth open
and flush with water. Call physician immediately. If fingers
become bonded, apply solvent (acetone or nail polish remover) to contact area and carefully pry skin apart. Avoid
prolonged breathing of vapors. Use with adequate ventilation. Keep out of reach of children.

Precautions

■ Identify any toxic materials that may be involved in the
hobby or craft; learn any special precautionary measures required.

■ Wear protective clothing when required—goggles, gloves,
and work apron.

■ Change clothing and thoroughly wash immediately after
leaving workshop.

■ Set work area apart from living space and physically separate as much as possible.

▪ Properly ventilate work area when indoors. Make sure exhaust fans do not send fumes into residential intake ventilation systems.

▪ Work outside if equipment and weather permit. Keep kilns outdoors or in outbuildings away from residential structures.

▪ Keep lids tight on solvents. See Section S for further solvent precautions. When using oil-based paints or acrylics, remember to keep solvent fumes at a minimum. Water-based paints are generally preferable.

▪ Don't allow unaccompanied small children in the work area.

▪ Keep food and beverages out of workshop.

▪ Use dust attachments on power tools. Clean up dusts and filings with vacuum sweeper when indoors.

▪ Become familiar with OSHA standards for industries related to hobby and crafts; follow guidelines for these related occupations.

▪ Be particularly careful about chemicals used in photographic work.

Hobby Substitutes

A large number of relatively safe, low-pollution options are available to the hobbyist. These include:

▪ Collecting: stamps, coins, letters, antiques, barbed wire, beer cans, autographs, books, sea shells, rocks, trinkets, pictures, postcards, maps, etc.

▪ Dramatic arts: play writing and acting, dancing, ballet, set design, production. (Here, fabrication of sets could involve use of materials which have some potential pollutants. However, the time of use is generally short and the places where sets are constructed are generally well ventilated.)

▪ Musical arts: playing instruments, singing, choral arts, etc.

▪ Organic gardening: raising one's own vegetables and

fruits; indoor plants and herb gardening (provided no pesticides and other chemicals are used).

- Food preparation and preserving: cooking, canning, drying, freezing, and salting foods.
- Carving relatively harmless materials: wood, soap, ivory.
- Clothes-making: weaving, embroidering, darning, sewing, tailoring, knitting.
- Home decorating: using flowers, rugs, pictures, and curtains (provided poisonous and dangerous materials are not used).
- Game playing.
- Creative writing: poetry, fiction, personal letters.
- Collect genealogical information.

REFERENCE

[1] "An Instant Glue Equals an Instant Hazard," *Consumer Reports,* Vol. 38, 663, (Nov. 1973).

Additional Sources

Art Hazards Resource Center*   Michael McCann
    220 Fifth Ave.   *Health Hazards Manual for*
    New York, N.Y. 10001   *Artists*
                                   (above address)

Michael McCann   Bertram Carnow, M.D.
    Art Hazard News   *Health Hazards in the Arts and*
    Art Workers News   *Crafts*
    (above address)   5340 North Magnolia
                                    Chicago, Ill. 60640

Jeanne Stellman and Susan Daum, *Work Is Dangerous to Your Health* (New York: Vintage Books, 1973).
"The Hobby Sickness," Washington *Post,* Dec. 16, 1976.
Michael McCann, Testimony on Control of Toxic Substances in the Workplace, U. S. Government Operations Committee, House of Representatives, May 11, 1976, p. 169.

* Established by the Foundation for the Community of Artists in an attempt to inform artists and craftspeople about occupational health problems.

I. INSECTICIDES AND OTHER CHEMICAL PESTICIDES

Pesticide Dangers

Chemical pesticides are a convenient way to get rid of or control unwanted insects, small mammals, plants, fungus growths, soil nematodes, and other pests. But, as already noted, convenience sometimes comes at a high price. This price was realized by an 8½-month-old infant who had been suffering from a cough for a few weeks and then died five days after her room had been sprayed by an exterminator. The high cost of convenience is realized as well by the ten thousand children who are treated in hospital emergency rooms each year for pesticide poisoning.

Chemical pesticide manufacture is a major business in this country. About 1.3 billion pounds of pesticide active ingredient is produced annually. Of the over 1 billion pounds consumed in this country, 55 per cent is used in the agricultural sector, 30 per cent in industrial or institutional applications, and a surprising 15 per cent by home and garden users (or over two pounds per year per American household). Thus it is not surprising that the sharp rise in pesticide consumption in recent years has been accompanied by an increase in hazards and risks both to farm workers and to home dwellers.

The growing use of organic pesticides following World War II has been credited with saving tens of thousands of potential victims from malaria, typhus, and other deadly diseases, and with augmenting production of food and fiber. Regardless of these benefits, a number of potential hazards have

been imposed upon both human beings and the environment
as the result of improper or careless pesticide use. As was first
brought to the public's attention in 1962 by Rachel Carson
in *The Silent Spring,* certain pesticides can harm plants,
birds, fish, squirrels, or other wildlife. Likewise pesticides
can injure the user if consumed, absorbed through the
skin, or inhaled. Pesticides are biological poisons seldom
specific in time, place, or target of chemical activity. Some
of them may remain in the environment for long periods of
time, and resist natural means of breakdown and decomposition. Some pesticides have "broad-spectrum effects" and
thus may destroy beneficial as well as harmful insects. Pesticide biological activity is not fully understood and what *is
not* presently known may in the long run prove more important than what *is* known. Furthermore, as in the case
of other aerosol sprays, dangerous synergistic effects may
result from the mixing of chemical pesticides with spray propellant and solvents in the environment under specific conditions.

Congress acted on the growing problem of pesticides by
amending the Federal Insecticide, Fungicide, and Rodenticide
Act in late 1972. The act extends federal control to pesticide
application by all users and regulates both intrastate and in-
terstate marketing of products. The primary method of control is through registration of pesticides by EPA. As of
October 1977 all chemical pesticide formulations must be
registered. The burden of proof of this registration rests with
industry, but EPA must depend on industry to furnish information which in some cases may not be totally reliable.

Yet federal pesticide regulation is far from perfect. Note
the tragedy at a Kepone plant in Hopewell, Virginia, in 1976
when both workers and residents were contaminated by large
doses of a highly toxic pesticide. Testifying under oath in
April 1976 at a Senate hearing, twelve present or former
EPA scientists challenged the reliability of animal tests for
safety done by pesticide manufacturers and by contract
laboratories. They called into question EPA's determination
to protect the public health.[1] Despite the reported "nega-

tive" findings, in at least one study the pesticide appeared to cause cancer in the test animals. Concerning pesticide safety, a Senate subcommittee report in early 1977 accused EPA of striking "an incorrect and dangerous balance between the sometimes conflicting demands of limited resources, bureaucratic efficiency, and public health."[2]

Potential pesticide risks and failures in regulating pesticides by the federal government necessitates extremely prudent action by the homemaker. Under present circumstances, the most reasonable recourse appears to be to keep chemical pesticides out of the home whenever possible. Approximately 70 per cent of the pesticide case reports received in poison control centers across the country involved not farm workers but children under five years of age.[3] Children account for over half of pesticide-related deaths.

Other notable dangerous pesticide practices of which the homemaker must be aware include:

- Spraying of trees and shrubs near the home. Vapors and dusts may enter the home through open windows or ventilation systems. Researchers have found that Reyes syndrome, a rare but often fatal children's disease, may be linked to petrochemical solvents used in pesticide forest and roadside spraying programs. The solvent interacts with common viruses to cause the disease.
- Fumigation of homes for roaches, which are not innocent insects and which have been implicated in outbreaks of asthma and skin allergies and in the spread of polio, hepatitis, and food poisoning. People often do not vacate rooms which have been fumigated.
- Sale of chemicals in stores where food is stored. The dangers of accidental spillage and release of these pesticides in supermarkets and drugstores are always present.
- Food contamination from garden or agricultural spraying. Often insecticides are not removed in commercial washing practices.

The varieties and different formulations of pesticides are in the thousands and increasing every year. Such listings are

not necessary here but some basic classifications may help
the reader. Insecticides are the most predominant type of
pesticide. Other types include acaricides (mite killers), nema-
tocides (worm killers), fungicides, herbicides (weed and brush
killers, defoliants and desiccants), molluscides, repellents,
algaecides, and rodenticides. (For bacteriacides, see Section
J.) Nematodes (worms) and acrids (mites) are not insects but
behave in a similar manner and generally are controlled by
similar means.

Protective insecticides are chemicals which are dispersed
over the surface of plants which insects eat. These are stomach poisons and include such inorganic chemicals as lead ar-
senate, Paris green, and cryolite. Less common ones are arsenic trioxide, sodium arsenite, and other compounds used
in baits to control ants, grasshoppers, and other insects.

Contact insecticides are toxic sprays and dusts applied
directly to the body of the insect or to the surface areas
where the insect will walk or into the air the insect breathes
(fumigation). Another though more rare type of insecticide
is a "systematic" one which is taken up by plants and then
eaten by a feeding insect. Examples of contact insecticides
which are directly applied include nicotine, petroleum oils,
pyrethrum, and parathion.

Surface or residual applications kill insects which come in
contact for extended lengths of time and include DDT,
chlordane, methoxychlor, and aldrin. Fumigants which are
used in enclosed spaces include such chemicals as hydro-
cyanic acid gas, methyl bromide, paradichlorobenzene, and
carbon disulfide.

Shell No-Pest Strip is a popular insecticide product used in
the home which emits a nerve poison, DDVP, twenty-four
hours a day throughout the house. Over 12 million such strips
are sold annually in the United States. Furthermore, 32
million dogs and 22 million cats wear flea collars containing
DDVP. EPA consultant, Dr. Melvin Rueber has warned that
DDVP testing suggests that the chemical has cancer-causing
properties. Dr. Lawrence Valeovic of NIEHS told EPA that
there is sufficient evidence from nonmammalian systems to

indicate that DDVP has the intrinsic potential for inducing genetic alteration. He recommended that human exposure be avoided.

Homemakers use a variety of herbicides, most of which could easily be replaced by a good pair of hands and a hoe or clippers. Many formulations have either 2,4-D (2,4-dichlorophenoxyacetic acid) or 2,4,5-T (2,4,5-trichlorophenoxyacetic acid), the second of which is known as "agent orange" —a defoliant used by the U. S. Air Force in Vietnam. Apart from possible environmental hazards, 2,4,5-T may contain a chemical dioxin impurity called TCDD, which is an extremely toxic chemical.

Nitrosamines, which are potent cancer-causing agents in animals, have been found to contaminate routinely a number of herbicides including three household weed killers: Unico Turf Treater "T," supplied by Universal Cooperatives, Inc., Black Leaf Lawn Weed Killer, supplied by Black Leaf Products, and Sears Broadleaf Weed Killer.[4]

BLACK FLAG TRIPLE ACTION BUG KILLER
(Boyle-Midway, Inc., New York)

Active Ingredients: Pyrethrins 0.30%, Technical Piperonyl Butoxide 1.5% (equivalent to 1.20% (butyl carbitol) (6 propyl-piperonyl) ether and 0.30% related compounds) Petroleum Distillates 4.20%

Inert Ingredients: 94.00%

CAUTION: Keep out of reach of children. Do not spray to ward face. Do not spray on humans or pets. Cover or re move exposed foods when spraying. Do not contaminate fish ponds. Spray ornamentals from 4–6 feet away.

The toxicity of rodenticides such as strychnine is often general enough to be of danger to a variety of animals. Red squill, which is obtained from bulbs of a member of the lily family, will cause convulsions and death from respiratory fail ure within about twelve hours when fed in significant dosage to rats. It is also a natural emetic for men and animals. Preferable to such extermination methods are community prevention measures including the proper disposal of garbage and the sealing of grain stores after use. Mechanical traps are a safe and effective last resort.

Insecticide Safety Hints

If total abstinence from the use of organic pesticides is impossible, the following considerations are important:

▪ Read the label before buying or using pesticides. Use pesticides only for the purpose(s) listed and in the manner directed.

▪ Do not apply more than the specified amount of pesticide. Overdoses can harm you and the environment.

▪ Keep pesticides away from food and dishes.

▪ Keep children and pets away from pesticides and sprayed areas.

▪ Do not smoke while spraying.

▪ Avoid inhalation of pesticides.

▪ Do not spray outdoors on a windy day.

▪ Pesticides that require special protective clothing or equipment should be used only by trained, experienced applicators.

▪ Avoid splashing when mixing pesticides.

▪ Avoid spills and breakage of pesticide containers.

▪ If a pesticide is spilled on skin or clothing, wash with soap and water and change clothing immediately.

▪ Store pesticides under lock in the original containers with proper labels. Never transfer a pesticide to a container such as soft-drink bottle that would attract children.

▪ Dispose of empty container safely. Wrap single containers of home-use products in several layers of newspaper, tie securely, and place in a covered trash can. Never burn boxes or sacks. In case of farm or ranch use, single containers may be buried where water supplies will not be contaminated. Dispose of large quantities in special incinerators or special landfills.

■ Wash with soap and water after using pesticides, and launder clothes before wearing again.

■ If a pesticide is swallowed, check the label for first-aid treatment. Call or go to the doctor or hospital immediately keeping the pesticide label with you.[5]

■ Check out fumigators to make sure they are dependable

■ Don't use the house when fumigated. The need to keep the house closed means that the inhabitants will not have enough fresh air. Airing out will simply reduce the effectiveness of the operation.

■ Try to discourage general use of fogging devices by neighbors or municipal authorities, and if this can't be helped, protect the home by closing doors and intake fans.

■ To report bird kills, problems with pesticide residues, or other environmental mishaps, call 800 424-1173.

Safe Pesticide Practices
Excerpted from "Urban Gardening II"[6]

What is defined as pests to some may be very beneficial creatures to others, so make sure the definition really fits the circumstance. We may take a rather militarist approach to insects and wish to wipe them out before learning about them. Black snakes, owls, crickets, katydids and ladybugs are no pests. Some unusual-looking creatures such as the praying mantis are really friends, and should be protected.

Some pests should indeed be killed; others should be controlled; and some should be discouraged from coming into our midst. Don't overkill with chemicals. The poisons might stay around and do harm to people and environment. Ways exist for discouraging the presence of pests. Screens on windows and doors and rat screens over drain pipes are protections against certain pests. Garbage cans with proper covers, prompt removal of discarded food, and house cats will discourage rodents. Proper fencing will usually keep out rabbits

If they do eat some carrots, beans, and lettuce, why not plant a little more? Flypaper and modern electrical nets are efficient insect killers. Plant pests can be effectively controlled by a number of biological controls: predators, parasitoids, diseases, and mixed or companion crops.

a) *Predators:* These include certain lady beetles, ground beetles, tiger beetles and soldier beetles; lacewing larva; larva of syrphid ("hover") flies and robber flies; spiders and some birds (domestic and wild). Lady beetles can be purchased, but "imported" varieties offer little help in pest control. They are collected from mountain aggregations while they are in a dormant stage and heavy with stored body fat. If released into the garden in the spring, they tend to fly away. If released in the summer, they remain but feed on their fat supply rather than on aphids and other pests. Instead, nurture those already in your garden.

The larvae of lacewings (aphis lions) are one of the most effective insect predators, eating aphids, mealy bugs, scale, mites, and small caterpillars. They can be purchased from insect houses or raised easily at home.

b) *Parasitoids:* Many insects lay their eggs near or on the bodies of other insects so that emerging larvae can easily locate the insects and eat them. Others lay eggs within the bodies of insects (eggs, larvae, or pupae) by means of a sharp ovipositor. Upon hatching, the larvae feed inside the body of the host. The larva works first as a parasite, being careful not to kill its host; later when it hatches out, it becomes a predator and destroys it. Since true parasites do not kill their hosts, the term "parasitoid" has been adapted for these beneficial insects.

Most parasitoids are tiny wasps or flies. Wasps include ichneumid wasps (braconids), chalcid wasps (*Trichogramma*), and many others. Flies include bee flies, big-headed flies, tachinid flies, and many others. A large variety of parasitoids can be purchased from commercial insectaries. Often they come as eggs already parasitized inside other insect eggs which are glued onto squares of paper (like the popular *Trichogramma*).

c) *Diseases:* Predators and parasites are disease micro-organisms (viruses, bacteria, and fungi). For the urban grower the easiest disease control to obtain is the bacteria *Bacillus thuriengensis*. It is lethal to many caterpillars, but harmless to other life forms. It is sold as a liquid spray (Thuricide) or powder (Biotrol and Dipel). To be effective, *Bacillus* must be taken into the insect with its food. Hence, the *Bacillus* spray should be applied to crop leaves when caterpillars are small and vulnerable. *Bacillus* is less effective when a caterpillar feeds mostly *within* a plant tissue as do the coddling moth, European corn borer, and corn-ear worm.

d) *Mixed or Companion Crops:* Many beneficial insects are nurtured in the garden by plants. For example, the pollen and nectar of some flowers (Compositae, *Umbelliferae*) provide food for insect predators and parasitoids. Other plants can be used to attract pests away from the main crop and, with careful monitoring, these "trap crops" can literally grow pest foods for beneficial insect predators. Hedgerows and perennial stands of herbaceous borders can provide alternative food and refuge habitats for a variety of natural enemies. An ecologically stable food garden has perennial stands as well as vegetable beds.

Hints for Integrated Pest Control

■ Learn to identify garden pests and their natural enemies especially insects. Although there are thousands of species of insects, only a few are potential pests in any one locale.

■ Keep a log of insect activities in the garden. Try to pick plants at random for observation. Most insects are small so inspect carefully under leaves and around the base of plant looking for pests. Flowers often serve as feeding stations for a variety of insects. Make observations at regular interval and recall changes in numbers of the resident "populations." Wander over the entire garden and learn to think in terms of life stages and population cycles rather than individuals.

▪ Identify the specific pest that is causing the problem. Millepedes are not wireworms; pill bugs will often seek refuge in fruit holes made by slugs; leaf hoppers, although abundant, are not serious pests; tomato hornworms rarely eat tomato fruit. Place the blame correctly.

▪ BE PATIENT! Remember that all animals are kept from overrunning the countryside by their natural enemies. The process goes on all around us, although we usually take it for granted. Beneficial insects are small, uncommon, and don't kill bugs immediately like pesticides. Instead, there is a lag between peak numbers of the pest and the time when their enemies can respond and bring numbers down. Very often the best thing to do for a pest problem is wait.

▪ Release predators and parasitoids *before* there is a big pest population problem (at least two weeks). Biological controls are preventions, not remedies. Consider them as seeds since it is their children and grandchildren that will do most of the control. Soft-bodied insects and caterpillars are easier to manage with bio-controls than are beetles which are handled best with traps, cultural methods and botanicals.

▪ Keep a diversity of plantings in the garden including perennial borders and beds. A variety of crops and permanent stands give beneficial insects more chances for survival.

▪ Learn to tolerate a moderate amount of pest damage. Certain numbers of pests are necessary to the balance of the garden.

REFERENCES

[1] Morton Mintz, "EPA Aides Fault Pesticides Studies," Washington *Post*, Apr. 10, 1976.

[2] "EPA Charged with Poor Handling of Pesticides," *Chemical and Engineering News*, Jan. 17, 1977.

[3] "Safe Pesticides Use Around the Home" (A-107), U. S. Environmental Protection Agency, Washington, D.C. 20460, Sept. 1974.

[4] Morton Mintz, "7 Herbicides Found Tainted by Nitrosamines," Washington *Post*, Sept. 3, 1976.

[5] "Pesticide Safety Tips" (A-107), U. S. Environmental Protection Agency, Washington, D.C. 20460.

[6] Richard Merrill, "Urban Gardening II," *Simple Living*, Winter 1977.

Additional Sources

Richard Merrill, *Radical Agriculture* (New York: Harper Colophon Books, 1976).

Helga and William Olkowski, "Insect Population Management in Agro-Ecosystems," R. Merrill, ed., *Radical Agriculture* (New York: Harper & Row, 1976).

Helen and John Philbrick, *The Bug Book, Harmless Insect Controls* (Charlotte, Vt.: Garden May Publishing, 1974).

R. B. Yepsen, Jr., ed., *Organic Plant Protection* (Emmaus, Pa: Rodale Press, Inc., 1976).

Donald Borror and R. White, *A Field Guide to the Insects of America North of Mexico* (Boston: Houghton Mifflin Co. 1970).

C. W. Metcalf et al., *Destructive and Useful Insects: Their Habit and Control* (New York: McGraw-Hill, 1962).

H. H. Ross, *How to Collect and Preserve Insects*, Natural History Survey Division, State of Illinois, Urbana, Ill., Circular 39.

Craig Dremann, *Vegetable Seed Production in the San Francisco Bay Area and Other Warm-Winter Areas of the United States* (Redwood City Seed Co., Calif., 1974).

Reginald Painter, *Insect Resistance in Crop Plants* (University Press of Kansas, 1951).

Brooklyn Botanic Garden Record, *Handbook on Biological Control of Plant Pests* (Brooklyn Botanic Garden, 1966).

J. GERMICIDES AND DISINFECTANTS

The average American homemaker has a disdain of unfamiliar odors and germs. This is due in part to the barrage of commercial advertisements which extol the blessings of the germ-free, odor-free American home. This well-cultivated horror of germs and odors does not take into account the toxicities of some of the very agents used to arrest germ growth or "freshen the air." The disinfectants and air fresheners can be toxic chemicals and may do more harm than the germs which we have to live with and the odors which may have good or bad effects on our psyche. The average homemaker works under the added misconception that deodorizing means disinfecting and that disinfecting means sterilizing.

Odor Fighting

Odors arise from any number of sources in the home—people, pets, cooking materials, the bathroom, the outdoors, furnace emissions, and tobacco smoke. Many people try to remove these odors by "freshening the air." All air fresheners (sprays, wicks, cakes) act in one of four ways: (a) by masking or counteracting one odor with another; (b) by coating the nasal passages with an oil film; (c) by diminishing the sense of smell with a nerve-deadening agent; (d) by deactivating the unwanted odor. The last mentioned—true deodorizing—is the rarest mode of action by commonly found air fresheners or deodorizing agents.[1] Some medical experts advise against the use of air fresheners in any form. Instead, ventilation with fresh air is the preferred method. Tampering with the sense of smell can be quite dangerous because olfaction is one of our best human defenses against fire, toxic gases, and decayed and spoiled foods.[1]

Many air fresheners simply contaminate the air with another foreign substance and have no freshening effect at all. Many times they have no disinfecting properties, and when they do, it might not be wise to use them. One air freshener advertised for use in the nursery contains carbolic acid, a toxic chemical that can cause serious burns and tissue destruction when allowed to come in contact with the skin.[1]

Monsanto Company has found a group of chemicals (counteractants) which produce the sensation of a "fresh air" smell. These could almost instantly eliminate from a room perception of certain malodors such as lower carboxylic acids in perspiration and rancid substances, thiols, phenols, amines in fish odors, and tobacco smoke. They will also spoil a good bleu cheese odor. The company plans to use them in home air fresheners, shampoos, and cosmetic creams.

BACTINE
(Miles Laboratories, Elkhart, Ind.)

CONTAINS: alcohol, methylbenzethonium chloride, chlorothymol, trichlorofluoromethane, and dichlorodifluoromethane as propellants, and contains iso-octylphenoxypolyethoxyethanol

WARNING: Avoid spraying in eyes. Contents under pressure. Do not puncture or incinerate. Do not store above 120 degrees F. Keep out of reach of children. Intentional misuse by deliberately concentrating and inhaling contents can be harmful or fatal. Avoid eyes, mouth, ears, and sensitive areas of the body.

Medical warning: Discontinue use with infection type complications.

Often what one regards as an undesirable odor is really something which could be lived with and liked. What is liked by some is regarded as repulsive by others. In some countries body odors are "sexy." Margaret Mead postulates that the custom of masking natural odors could have detrimental effects on the human psyche. Learning to find many cooking odors—even fish odors—appetizing is possible. One gourmet tried to mask the smell of squid he was preparing by saturating the eating area with air freshener. Ironically, this action served to paralyze the sensors of his guests rather than enhance the flavor of his carefully prepared dish.

Germ Fighting

Disinfecting is often confused with sterilizing. A true disinfectant reduces but does not kill all germs present. Sterilizing means killing or removing all microbial life by use of an autoclave (high steam temperature and pressure) or some other drastic method. Disinfecting is a temporary measure at best. Some time after application, the disinfected areas will contain large numbers of unwanted organisms again.

True disinfectants are generally toxic chemicals, and any spraying in areas where children play or where the family eats may be dangerous. The most frequently used germicide and bactericide in homes and swimming pools is cresol—usually in its crude and unpurified form. There is also a wide variety of other chemicals used in these products. A recent store survey indicates the following active ingredients in some commercially available germicides and disinfectants:

Brand	Active Ingredient[2]
Lysol cleaner	5.5% soap, 2.8% o-benzyl-p-chlorophenol, 1.1% isopropanol
Lysol Disinfectant	16.5% soap, 2.8% o-phenylphenol, 2.7% o-benzyl-p-chlorophenol, 1.8% alcohol, 0.9% isopropyl alcohol, 0.9% tetrasodium ethylenediamine tetraacetate, 1.5% xylenols
Chloraseptic	1.4% phenol

Brand	Active Ingredient[2]
White Magic	0.31% sodium salt of o-phenylphenol 2.82% tetrasodium salt of ethylenediamine tetraacetic acid, 1.63% sodium xylenesulfonate, 0.24% essential oils
409 Disinfectant Bathroom Cleaner I	1.06% tetrasodium ethylenediamine tetraacetate, 0.9% alkyl dimethylbenzyl ammonium chloride, 0.9% alkyl dimethylethylbenzyl ammonium chlorate

Although it may serve as a substrate for certain yeasts and metabolites of certain fungi, cresol is toxic to both flora and fauna. It affects the central nervous system, liver, and kidneys and may also injure the lungs, pancreas, and spleen of human beings. Cresol may be absorbed through the skin and mucous membranes of the respiratory tract. In general, cresol is caustic to tissue upon contact. Repeated exposure may cause dermatitis. Ingestion of cresol has resulted in at least one fatality. Jouglard et al. reported that at the Marseilles Poison Center during the years 1968–70 the frequency of cresol poisoning was slightly more than 1 in every 1,000 poison victims with a frequency of 1 in every 2,000 for serious cases.[3]

According to the Mitre Report on cresol, the greatest risk to the general population is that presented by the commercial cresol solutions which are used in many households as disinfectants. There is danger of accidental or intentional ingestion of cresol and of accidental poisoning by inhalation.[4] Open and/or leaking bottles of cresol could contribute significant quantities of cresol vapor to the air in closed rooms over a period of time.

Unfortunately, there has been little inhalation research done on cresol. The U. S. Occupational Standard, a maximum time-weighted average concentration that is based on a forty-hour work week, is 5 parts per million for total cresol. It should be noted that the Federal Republic of Germany has a basic standard of only 0.05 parts per million for a thirty-minute averaging time and a permissible standard (not to be exceeded more than once in any four hours) of 0.15 parts per million. Thus the United States time-weighted average for cresol is tenfold the concentration permitted in Germany.

The toxic effects of cresol ingestion have been more thoroughly documented. Cresol is present in tobacco (cigarette, pipe, cigar) and marijuana smoke. The three isomers of cresol in tobacco smoke are all active tumor-promoting agents.[5,6] Chronic poisoning from oral or percutaneous absorption (through the skin) may produce digestive disturbances, nervous disorders with faintness, vertigo, mental changes, and skin eruptions.

Besides germicides, cresol is found in a variety of consumer products. Paracresol is found in a score of essential oils and has been used in fragrances since the 1930s. These fragrances are, in turn, used in soaps, detergents, creams, lotions, and perfumes.[7] There may be health dangers involved. In Europe paracresol has been declared "not admissible" in such products. Cresol has been used as a vaporizing liquid to treat whooping cough and bronchial asthma and is used for wound dressings and douches. Cresol is used in the manufacture of fungicides, herbicides, dyes and pigments, antioxidants, surfactants, resins, plasticizers, and tricresyl phosphate.

Disinfectants should only be used through a doctor's advice. When conditions such as contagious disease require drastic germicidal action, the use of strong chemicals may be warranted. However, normal usage of large amounts of cresol-containing materials in the home should be discouraged.

A final word should be made about a common bacteriacide, which acts much in the manner of germicides. Benzalkonium chloride is used as a preservative and as a bacteriacide in many over-the-counter products such as contact lens solution. It is the most commonly used eyedropper preservative in the United States. But there is strong suspicion that such compounds as benzalkonium chloride may produce damage to the cellular components of the cornea.[8]

Reasonable Odor and Germ Fighting

Some sound rules for odor-fighting include the following:

- Open the window or use an exhaust fan as a natural air freshener. Make a habit to sleep with a partly open window. In urban areas wait until the traffic is at a low ebb for a good airing out of the house.
- Take a sane and wholesome attitude about household odors. Learn to regard cooking odors as appetizing.
- A dish of hot vinegar can displace pronounced fish odors.
- A box of baking soda in the refrigerator and a light sprinkling of this powder in a garbage can will reduce odors.
- Never use aerosol spray "air fresheners."
- Avoid products containing cresol and related chemicals.
- For a mild scent in the home, try freshly cut flowers (if no one is allergic). There's no need to deaden the smelling sense by desensitizing the chemical receptors in the nose.
- For more drastic needs try burning incense, scented candles, or leaving a bowl of ammonia in the room (out of the reach of children).
- Use wick and cake chemical deodorizing methods sparingly.

Some healthy rules for the germ-conscious include:

- Never use aerosol spray disinfectants.
- Don't buy disinfectants unless advised to do so by a physician. When treating a sick member of the family, boil objects used by the patient. The use of disposable eating ware is a small environmental price for the good health of other members of the family and can certainly be justified in such circumstances.
- Don't buy disinfectants for the sake of a germ-free environment. Good cleaning methods with soap and detergent are far better.
- Keep any necessary germicides and bacteriacides out of reach of children.

REFERENCES

[1] F. Silver, "Housing for Healthy Living," *Herald of Health,* Feb. 1967, p. 18.

[2] The active ingredients were compiled in a CSPI market survey in July, 1976. It should be noted that cresol does not appear on these products. However, over 10 million pounds of cresols were used in 1973 for cleaning and disinfecting compounds. Likewise it must be noted that the common name "lysol" or "lysitol" means crude cresol mixed with a soft soap solution. Gardener & Cook, *Chemical Synonyms and Trade Names,* CRC Press, 7th Ed., 1971, p. 392.

[3] J. Jouglard et al., "Intoxications aiguës par un antiseptique ménager: le 'crécyl,' " *Marseilles Medical,* Vol. 108 (1971), pp. 425–531.

[4] J. Gordon, "Air Pollution Assessment of Cresols," The Mitre Corporation, MTR-7227 (June 1975).

[5] R. K. Boutwell and D. K. Bosch, in *Cancer Research,* Vol. 19 (1959), pp. 413–24.

[6] G. Zamfir, "Air Pollution and Bronchopulmonary Cancer," *Revista Medico—Chirvrgicala a Societatii di Medici si Naturalisti din Iasi,* Vol. 76 (1972), pp. 273–80.

[7] D. L. J. Opdyke, "Fragance Raw Materials Monographs: p-cresol," *Food and Cosmetics Toxicology,* Vol. 12 (1974), pp. 389–90.

[8] Gasset et al., "Cytotoxicity of Ophthalmic Preservatives," *American Journal of Ophthalmology,* Vol. 78 (July 1974), pp. 98–105.

K. KITCHEN AND LAUNDRY SOAPS AND DETERGENTS

To the daytime television viewer there is a constant reminder of our need for soap through the constant barrage of kitchen and laundry soap and detergent advertisements. They overwhelm the viewer with brand names and claims, all of which are hard to evaluate.

Procter & Gamble is the number-one supermarket advertiser, spending almost $300 million a year to buy large blocks of advertising space and time.[1] Supermarket sales reflect this fact: Soaps and detergents represent 39 per cent of a supermarket's household supplies gross profits and about 52 per cent of their sales;[2] detergents and soaps are the number-one most bought and used item—far ahead of milk (ranking number 77) or butter (number 86)[3] (see Table I).

Billion-dollar advertising blitzes hawk gimmicks—"whiter than white," "easy to use," "cheaper," "soft on hands," "perfect for cold water"—which hardly tell the entire story. Information on safety cautions, optimum cleaning amounts, chemical contents, are seldom aired. In fact, one TV ad shows someone with a heaping cupful of detergent, implying far more is needed than what is stated in the fine print on the box.

All these bits of information are more important than adding an attractive blue color or a yellow box. Informed readers need to know about soaps and detergents: what they do, the controversies associated with various chemical ingredients, especially environmental and human health ones, and the dangers products present.

Detergents are substances that have cleaning action due to a combination of properties: lowering of surface tension, wetting action, emulsifying and dispersing action, and foam formation.

The ingredients used in detergents enhance either the cleansing power or the consumer's notion of product effectiveness and appeal (perfumes). Ordinary soap which has been made for thousands of years is the best known example of a detergent cleaner. Today, however, the word "detergent" is increasingly associated with the synthetic variety of soaps rather than natural soap, which is a water-soluble mixture of the sodium or potassium salts of fatty acids (Ivory, for instance).

Detergents cause more poisoning than any other household product. Small children are particularly at risk. Detergents are kept in low places; their beautifully colored boxes are ready temptations to the young exploring mind. The preponderant majority of the 1,629 poisonings in 1969 were among children under five years of age. In 1975 NEISS estimates are that over 1,300 laundry soap detergent and 776 dishwasher product poisonings occurred.

Part of the problem is that consumers do not recognize the serious difference between synthetic chemical laundry and dishwashing detergents and ordinary soap. They are aware that ordinary soap is not very harmful and have heard of its use to wash the mouths of the naughty. They extend their lack of caution, however, to synthetic detergents. A glance at most detergent containers might reveal the following:

DANGER: In case of eye contact, flush with water for 15 minutes. Get prompt medical attention. Keep out of reach of children.

Detergent Ingredients

The ordinary laundry detergent soap has seven kinds of ingredients: surface active agents or surfactants, cleaning agents or builders, optical brighteners, fillers, foam boosters, perfumes, and enzymes. Solid and liquid kitchen detergents have the same kinds of ingredients. It is important to note that formulations of a single brand are subject to frequent change and regional differences.

WHITE MAGIC LIQUID DETERGENT (Safeway)

Ingredients: water; surfactants: linear alkylate sulfonate, alkyl ethoxylate sulfate; formulation aids: aryl sulfonate, ethanol, sodium citrate; suds regulator: alkyl diethanolamide; plus small amounts of inorganic sulfates, opaquing agent and perfume

---

a) *Surface active agents* (surfactants) contain water-soluble and oil-soluble chemical groups which are essentially responsible for the detergent's cleaning action. The surfactant reduces the surface tension of the washwater, permits the fabric to be wetted properly, and facilitates loosening and removal of fabric soil. Surfactants generally amount to 14 to 20 per cent of a typical synthetic laundry detergent. The most extensively used surfactant today is LAS (linear alkylate sulfonate) (possible human health risk of LAS will be discussed later).

ERA (Procter & Gamble) Laundry Detergent

Ingredients: ERA consists of an aqueous solution of ingredients to lift soils from clothes (anionic and non-ionic surfactants). There is also an ingredient to provide for convenient dispensing (ethyl alcohol) plus small quantities of soil suspending and stabilizing agents, fabric whiteners, colorant and perfume

---

b) *Builders* are actual cleaning agents. They consist of sequestering agents like sodium tripolyphosphate, phosphate detergents, sodium carboxylate, and nonphosphate detergents which keep calcium and magnesium ions from interfering with the surfactant and from hardening the water. Builders also consist of antisoil redisposition ingredients and anticaking ingredients like sodium silicate, which preserve the enamel on the inside of washing machines from corrosion. A typical laundry detergent is 40 to 60 per cent sequestering agent, 0.5 to 0.9 per cent antiredisposition agent, and 5 to 7 per cent anticaking agent.

c) *Optical brighteners* make the fabrics washed appear whiter or brighter. They compensate for the naturally yellowing effects of impurities in fabrics by converting some invisible ultraviolet sunlight into visible blue light. A typical synthetic laundry detergent is 0.3 to 0.75 per cent optical brightener.

d) *Fillers* are inert additives which provide bulk and alkalinity.

e) *Foam boosters* add sudsiness for satisfaction but do not actually effect or enhance the cleaning action.

f) *Perfumes* add a cosmetic fresh smell to the washed goods to further enhance the consumer's notion of a clean wash.

g) *Enzymes* attack protein and carbohydrate grime, soil, and stains. Enzymes convert insoluble proteins and carbohydrates into soluble compounds which can be removed by detergent action. Until recently, about 0.2 to 0.75 per cent of a typical synthetic laundry detergent's content was enzyme, either protease (a protein-dissolving enzyme) or amylase (a starch-digesting enzyme). They are presently being abandoned because of questions that have been raised about their safety.

Keeping Both Environment and Health in Mind

The controversial issues surrounding the impact of detergent soaps on environment and health revolve around the particular kinds of chemicals used in each of the ingredient categories. The most widely acknowledged conflict has been with the use of phosphate chemical builders (trisodium phosphate or TSP, sodium metaphosphate, etc.).

Phosphates pollute our waterways when present in large amounts. The phosphates from detergents encourage extensive algal growth. With a limited volume of water present in lakes and rivers, the added burden of prolific growth rapidly depletes available oxygen from the water, causing fish losses and premature aging or death (eutrophication) of the water body.

The source of the phosphate problem is not laundry detergent alone. Phosphates are one of the major categories of commercial fertilizers. Fertilizer runoff has some effect and so do machine dishwashing detergents. Laundry detergents generally contain under 8.7 per cent phosphates, but dishwashing detergents contain as high as 50 per cent or more phosphates. Still laundry detergents are of much greater concern since their volume greatly exceeds that of dishwashing detergents.

As in many environmental problems, the substitute may be as bad as, if not worse than, the original culprit. There is concern about accepting nonphosphate substitutes, especially certain highly caustic materials. Detergent formulations are already caustic, and the introduction of nonphosphate builders as a result of the phosphate controversy in the late 1960s caused an increase in their already high alkalinity. Here an indoor environmental problem is substituted for an exterior one. Phosphate detergents have an alkaline measure between a pH of 9.8 and 10.2 (pH of 7 is neutral). Nonphosphate detergents have a pH between 10.5 and 12.0. This means that the nonphosphate detergents are 100, to 1,000 times more caustic than are the phosphate ones.

A person who rubs a few grains of synthetic detergent into the eye can receive corneal burns which if left untreated could result in severe eye damage.[4] Ingestion of these chemical formulations, particularly hazardous with liquid products, can severely damage the upper digestive tract through chemical burns. In 1971 United States Surgeon General Dr. Jesse Steinfield found the danger of nonphosphate detergents sufficient and disturbing enough to advise homemakers to use phosphate detergents in spite of the known environmental repercussions. He advised that they are the safest thing in terms of human health.

Citrates, polyelectrolytes, and NTA (nitrotriacetic acid) alternatives to phosphate chemicals, which might have proved safer and less caustic than other nonphosphate replacements, were discredited for several reasons. Citrates and citric acid were determined to be poor cleaning agents, expensive, and insufficient in supply. Polyelectrolytes were rejected as unacceptable because they were not biodegradable. NTA was never marketed because it was believed to be a cancer-inducing agent. Initial concern was later discounted.

One further concern surfaced in Japan in 1973 involving toxicity of the surfactant LAS. In 1965 the detergent industry switched from one surfactant, alkyl benzenesulfonate (ABS), to LAS, linear alkylate sulfonate. LAS breaks down more readily in the environment. Without an adequate supply of oxygen present (as in eutrophying organically enriched bodies of water), LAS, however, can build up and is known to be lethal to oysters in concentrations as low as 1 milligram per liter.[5] Furthermore Japanese scientists reported evidence that LAS caused liver ailments in mice when absorbed through the skin. They have applied 0.5 milligrams per day for roughly two weeks on three-month old mice. As a 0.1 solution the equivalent dose concentration for humans would be 0.015 mg per kilogram, which is ¹⁄₂₀,₀₀₀ the oral toxicity level set as allowable by the Japanese health and welfare minister. This raises suspicions that prolonged exposure to LAS in detergents would perhaps present some danger to human beings through absorption of the compound.

Optical brighteners, which are sulfonated aminostilbenes similar to such cancer-causing chemicals as DES, were at one time suspected of analogous harm to that done by LAS. The suspicions have since been withdrawn.

Table I

HOME TESTING INSTITUTE CONSUMER SURVEY
(Partial Listing)

Rank	Item	% Usage
1	Soaps and detergents	97.0
13	Household cleaners	91.7
22	Scouring powder	89.0
25	Furniture polish	87.9
30	Scouring pads	86.4
33	Dishwashing soap	85.4
34	Window cleaner	85.3
35	Bleach	84.4
45	Air fresheners and deodorizers	80.2
57	Bathroom cleaners	79.3
61	Oven cleaners	72.0
64	Insecticides	68.9
67	Drain cleaners	66.5
77	Milk	63.5
78	Soaps for fine fabrics	61.9
79	Fabric softeners	61.4
81	Floor wax	59.3
86	Butter	52.5
84	Rug cleaners	51.2
90	Beer	49.4
105	Kitchen cleaners	43.3
112	Starch	37.4
119	Laundry presoaks	35.3
120	Metal polish	35.2
122	Flea and tick	33.0
131	Aerosol—Pam	29.4
133	Dishwashing (auto detergent)	27.1
147	Household dye	17.7
148	Laundry additives	17.5
162	Meat extenders	6.3

Source: "170 Most Used Products," published in *Progressive Grocer Magazine,* July 1976.

These statistics come from the output of TGI (Target Group Index), a national product and media survey. TGI is produced by Axiom Market Research Bureau, Inc., allowing readers of this magazine to look at the demographics of popular food store products. Location of headquarters of Axiom is 420 Lexington Ave., New York, N.Y. 10017.

Health problems with enzyme detergents and presoaks are threefold:

a. Increase in number of cases of dermatitis.
b. Creation of flulike and asthmatic conditions from breathing air with enzyme detergent dust in it.
c. Possibility of some enzyme detergents containing arsenic.[6]

The record shows that massive use of detergents containing many complex chemicals in our current American lifestyle can be harmful both to the environment and to the health and safety of householders. Chemicals demand respect and care; this certainly applies to laundry and kitchen detergents.

Curbing Detergent Use

A civilized society has no substitute for soap but an environmentally conscious society can strive to reduce the use of cleaning materials and thus save both energy and water resources. Some hints include:

■ Curb the use of phosphates especially if living in areas where increased phosphate emissions threaten rivers or lakes. In some regions—especially near oceans—this is not a problem. Check with local environmental groups if uncertain.
■ Never use enzyme detergents.
■ Bathe less frequently in winter; it's easier on the skin.
■ Rinse dishes immediately after the meal. It requires far less cleaning material.
■ Follow directions and don't overuse kitchen and laundry soap and detergent. A Consumers Union survey showed most people use at least twice as much liquid dish detergent as needed. Wait for a full load before washing clothing.
■ Don't use overly caustic soaps.
■ Where possible detergents should be replaced by soap. The advantages of soaps include: an excellent cleaning agent in soft water, relatively "nontoxic," and biodegradeable.

Soap is more difficult to use in hard-water areas. Follow directions on the box. Hard water requires addition of washing soda to soften the water and permit soap to function at full efficiency. The local water commission will tell whether water is hard or soft (anything under 50 parts per million calcium carbonate is considered soft).

Detergents, on the other hand, require scarce petrochemicals, are less biodegradable, and are more expensive than ordinary soaps. Moreover, detergents leave residues in clothes which require fabric softeners to mask. These softeners may affect the skin. Detergents are also toxic in themselves. Over half the hospital injuries from cleaning products among infants are detergent-induced.

▪ To wash out yellowish residues from detergents, prewash clothes in one-fourth cup of washing soda and then wash with soap.

REFERENCES

[1] "Top 50 Supermarket Product Advertisers," *Progressive Grocer*, Dec., 1976.
[2] "Household Supplies: 1975 Performance, $1 Million Supermarkets," *Chain Store Age Supermarkets*, July 1976.
[3] "170 Most Used Products," *Progressive Grocer*, July 1976.
[4] "Dry Detergent Soap Effects on the Rabbit Eye," *Journal of the American Medical Association*, Vol. 221 (Aug. 28, 1972), p. 1,055.
[5] "Effects of 'Soft' Detergents on Embryos and Larvae of the American Oyster," *Proceedings of the National Shellfisheries Association*, Vol. 57 (June 1967).
[6] "Enzyme Pre-soaks, Enzyme Detergents, and Soaps," *Consumer Research Magazine*, Vol. 56, 18 (Aug. 1973).

L. LEAD

Lead Exposure in the Home

A major indoor pollution problem facing many urban residential areas of this country is that of lead. The problem affects all inhabitants, especially the very young children.

Two-year-old Andy was a lively, adventurous child. However, his parents noticed that he was gradually becoming less active and was complaining of frequent stomach-aches for no apparent reason. One day Andy was caught chewing on paint peelings from the dining room window sill. The child's parents suspected lead poisoning and thus rushed him to the hospital emergency room. Tests taken there indicated Andy did indeed have an unusually high level of lead in his blood. Fortunately, with treatment and after a week's stay, Andy was able to be sent home.[1]

This case is a typical one because so many of the older homes in our country have lead paint on their walls. Children from about one to six are out to discover things. They are mobile enough to get to all parts of the house, and they always want to taste whatever strikes their fancy. The flake of peeling paint from a door or window sill doesn't taste too bad so they take another and another piece. Or they may just suck a finger or hand which has picked up some of the lead paint dust. Children not only are prone to ingest lead but also are susceptible to permanent physical damage from lead poisoning.

The concern with detecting lead exposure and poisoning in children early lies in the possibility of irreversible brain damage or even death. Children who have some amount of lead poisoning may show initial symptoms of unusual irritability, poor appetite, stomach pains or vomiting, persistent constipation, sluggishness or drowsiness. More blatant clinical symptoms include anemia, cramps, or convulsions.

The Department of Health, Education, and Welfare estimates that 100 children die each year of lead poisoning and many more suffer from apparent symptoms of lead poisoning. The National Bureau of Standards estimates that 400,000 children nationwide have abnormally high levels of lead in their blood.[1] A 1973 National Academy of Science report estimated that 200 children die each year from lead poisoning, 30,000 children demonstrate obvious symptoms of lead poisoning, another 80,000 with no demonstrable symptoms should receive treatment, and as many as 600,000 children nationwide may have abnormally high lead blood levels.[2]

Children do not shoulder the lead burden alone. During restoration or repair of lead painted houses, adults are exposed to lead dust which can be inhaled in sufficient amounts to harm their health. Likewise, adults drinking from lead-containing pottery and those working with lead products have been known to get lead poisoning.

Lead compounds have been used in paints principally for pigments, as driers, and as preservatives for the driers. In pre-1940 interior paints, lead in the form of lead carbonate (white lead) was also used as a pigment with the total lead content of those paints being on the average 50 per cent. After World War II lead contents of paints decreased significantly. Titanium dioxide, the white pigment used in many current paints, replaced lead pigments for economic reasons. However, lead drying agents were continued until the recognition of the health danger of leaded paints.

Health effects of leaded paints were beginning to be recognized as early as 1955 when the American Standards Institute suggested that a maximum of 1 per cent lead be used for any paint applied to furniture, toys, or other items used by children. The cases of lead poisoning, especially among children, touched the national conscience. Thus, in 1971, a concerned Congress passed the Lead Based Paint Poisoning Prevention

Act, which restricted the content of lead in paint to a 1 per cent maximum. However, concerned citizens thought the restrictions were still not adequate to assure safety. They sought a 0.06 per cent level which was needed to safeguard public health. The 1971 act was amended to reduce the allowable lead content to 0.5 per cent.

The paint industry contended that the 0.06 per cent sought by certain citizen groups was not necessary to safeguard health, citing the uncertainty of medical literature as to the detrimental health effects below 1.0 per cent. Furthermore the industry argued that lower lead levels would be an economic burden in the reformulation of paint mixtures and would be an inconvenience to consumers desiring faster drying paint. Still, a survey included in the amended law found that paint makers were already making paint with very little lead. Some 96 per cent of latex paint and 71 per cent of oil paints already had contents of lead below the 0.06 per cent. The classic battle of economics and health was raging.

Modern paints do not have much lead in them. A rule of thumb is that the older the paint the higher the lead content level. Old paint generally gets covered up by successive layers of lower leaded paints, so that the current coat of paint on the walls of old homes may not be highly leaded. But quite often a piece of flaked paint will contain any number of these layers, so the danger to many children is still present.

Lead screening programs have been undertaken in many inner cities through moneys made available by the above-mentioned legislation. In 1973 a lead screening program in New York City identified 941 children as "cases" (blood lead levels exceeding what the Surgeon General defined as lead intoxication). Of these 210 lived in housing where the lead content of deteriorating painted surfaces exceeded 1 per cent; 172 cases came from housing where crumbling paint contained less than 1 per cent lead content; 59 cases were found in homes with no chipping or deterioration. Programs to remove lead paints have not always been successful, because it must include vigorous governmental encouragement and community support.

The long battle over the safety of using leaded gasoline (see Section M) has included a number of studies showing that some of the leaded dust and dirt penetrating roadside and inner city homes comes from automobile tail pipe emissions. It is quite hard to determine the actual source of the lead even though the Environmental Protection Agency has shown that about 90 per cent of all the lead emitted into the environment comes from the manufacture, transportation, spillage, or combustion of leaded gasoline. Samples of dirt and dust in playgrounds and near homes were found to exceed 1,000 parts per million (0.1 per cent) in numerous circumstances. With the general phase-out of lead from gasoline, due partly to public interest litigation, the lead levels in urban dirt and dust should decline.

Other possible sources of lead exposure in the home include the following:

■ Use of heated solder in metalworking (see Section H) may pose hazards.

■ Use of lead glazes to finish pottery exposes potters to lead vapors when firing and to lead dust from dried glazes.

■ Use of unfired glazed homemade pottery for acid drinks (coffee, tea, citrus fruit juices, etc.) has caused severe lead poisoning in a number of cases.

■ Tobacco smoke contains lead in small amounts.

■ Leaded water pipes in regions where water is slightly acid have resulted in higher concentrations of dissolved lead in drinking water (see Section W).

■ Use of leaded dinnerware (quite rare today) over a period of time adds to the total body burden.

■ Leaded candle wicks cause some vapors to enter the home atmosphere. The Consumer Product Safety Commission identified Queens Braidworks, Inc., of Middle Village, Queens, New York, and American Wick Company of North Bergen, New Jersey, as two companies which continue to make lead-based wicks.

■ Yellow lacquer in pencils may aggravate a case of lead poisoning for pencil chewers. The New York state attorney general found the following five companies with paint in excess of 1 per cent lead:[3]

General Pencil Co., Jersey City, N.J.
Rueve Pencil Co., Greenwich, Conn.
Richard Best Pencil Co., Springfield, N.J.
Musgrave Pencil Co., Inc., Shelbyville, Tenn.
J. R. Moon Pencil Co., Inc., Lewisburg, Tenn.

Each source of lead exposure increases the cumulative burden of lead in the human body, which is not able to discharge all of this metal. Thus the need to identify sources and to eliminate them is necessary for a quality indoor environment.

Precautions

Protecting your home and family from excessive lead exposure is part of being a conscientious indoor environmentalist. This is not easy, especially in an urban environment where dusts and emissions from burning batteries, scrap lead reprocessing, and automobiles can enter the home. Individual resourcefulness and vigilance must be coupled with social action so that lead emissions are minimized. The following measures may help:

- Dispose of all old unused leaded paint.
- For families living in an older home with peeling paint, have small children checked for blood lead content.
- When removing peeling paint from the interior of a home, simply move out while refurbishing is taking place. Air out the house and allow time for dust to clear before reoccupying it. Wear a mask when scraping and sanding lead painted areas. Never eat in the work area. Sweep up and use a wet mop after refurbishing the older home.
- Panel over painted walls when paint removal is difficult. Some government funds are available for this type of repair work through many local housing development offices.
- If pottery is suspected of not being properly fired, send a

piece to a local analyst for checking. Make the favorite coffee
or tea cup a glazed one.

- Don't heat solder within the house.
- Refrain from buying candles with leaded wicks.
- Don't use leaded dinnerware. They are good antiques and
decorations.
- Pressure the local health department to stop battery burn-
ing and lead emissions from industrial sources.
- Support the drive to reduce and remove lead from gaso-
line.

REFERENCES

[1] "Lead Paint Poisoning," *Fact Sheet ⌗14*, CPSP, Washington, D.C. 20207.

[2] "Report of the Ad Hoc Committee to Evaluate the Hazard of Lead in Paint," Natural Academy of Science, Nov. 1973, prepared for the Consumer Product Safety Commission.

[3] "Lead in Pencil Coatings Brings New York Ban," *Consumer Reports*, Vol. 38, 459 (July 1973).

Additional Sources

"A Report to Congress in Compliance with the Lead Base Paint Poisoning," Consumer Product Safety Commission, Dec. 23, 1974.

"Lead-based Paint and Certain Consumer Products Bearing Lead-based Paint," *Federal Register*, Vol. 41, No. 155 (Aug. 10, 1976), pp. 33,636–40.

M. MOTOR VEHICLE PRODUCTS

The majority of American households have members with automobiles. Some of these autos are parked in attached garages, some in carports and parking lots, and some on the street. The products used to keep auto and other household motors (pumps, lawn mowers, appliance motors, etc.) in good working order are often stored around the house. Many of these motor products pose health and environmental problems. The warning against storing gasoline in the home is well known but often ignored. Volatile emissions can seep into the living quarters; motor oil can be spilled or drunk by infants; aerosolized lubricating products can be inhaled. In our highly motorized society it is nearly impossible to avoid pollutants because of motor vehicles.

Gasoline

Perhaps the adage "familiarity breeds contempt" is best exemplified in our handling of gasoline. America consumes about 100 billion gallons of gasoline per year or about half the total distilled petroleum used in this country. But few of us know that gasoline is highly toxic. Some people breathe gasoline and even admit liking the smell; they use leaded gasoline to remove paint from their hands and arms; they spill gasoline carelessly on the driveway or basement floor.

Gasoline consists of hundreds of hydrocarbons, some naturally found in crude petroleum, but many others formed by chemical treatment and distillation processes which help enhance the gasoline fraction and raise the octane rating. The environmental drive for no-lead gasoline has caused a shift to toxic higher octane components such as benzene. Current gasoline is not necessarily more toxic; rather, one toxic material (lead) is being replaced by another which must be treated with equal caution.

Although lead is the best known fuel additive, gasoline contains many others which are harmful to human health and the environment.

Some types of currently used gasoline additives include:

Antiknock agents (tetraethyl lead [TEL] and tetramethyl lead) are negative catalysts which prevent the type of explosive combustion known as knocking. Ingestion or tactile intake of small amounts can be fatal.[1]

Scavengers (ethylene dichloride and ethylene dibromide) remove lead oxides in the form of volatile lead halides and are severe irritants, cause liver damage, and may be cancer-causing agents.

Antirust agents (fatty acid amines, sulfonates, alkyl phosphates, or amine phosphates) keep small amounts of water from the surface of metal containers and pipelines. The toxicity is unknown.

Antioxidants (generally amines or alkylated phenols) are added to gasoline in storage to keep it from decomposing and forming resinous gums. Certain antioxidants cause burns to eyes and skin and may cause certain types of dermatitis, or skin irritation.

Metal deactivators (usually amine derivatives) counter the oxidizing effect of small amounts of metals, usually copper, found in gasoline. Like many amines these are probably quite toxic. The specific types of these compounds are trade secrets and unknown to the public.

Deposit modifiers (usually organic phosphorus compounds) change lead oxides and halide deposits into phosphates. The deposits tend to make the engine more knock-prone and raise the effective compression ratios. Some of these compounds are extremely toxic.

Dyes are inserted to indicate the presence of TEL. One gasoline dye (DAB) is a highly selective carcinogen inducing tumors in the liver of rats. Because of its selectivity it is one of the most popular agents for inducing cancer for research purposes.

Deicers (alcohols, glycols, and formamides) are added in small quantities to mix with water present and lower the freezing point. Two principal deicers, methyl and isopropyl alcohol, are well known for their toxic properties.

Detergents (usually trade secret compounds) are inserted to dissolve gum deposited by fuel oxidation. The toxicity is unknown.

Extrinsic additives. A number of additives can be purchased at filling stations or stores and added directly to fuel tanks, oil spouts, crankcase, carburetor, or fuel line. No auto manufacturer admits to the beneficial claims made by additive producers. Some simply thicken oil or have the same cleaning effects as intrinsic multifunctional additives. For safety's sake keep as few around the home as possible.

The toxicity of some of these additives is unknown, yet they are produced in massive amounts to meet gasoline needs. Newer cars containing catalytic devices, while not using leaded gasoline, may contain other harmful ingredients. For instance, an estimated 40 per cent of unleaded gasoline contains MMT,[1] a manganese additive which increases hydrocarbon emissions from the engine, plugs up some catalytic devices, and is extremely toxic to human health. Chronic manganese poisoning causes a multitude of neurological symptoms, among others, parkinsonism.[2]

Emissions from Motor Vehicles

Indoor pollutants include both those generated in or near the home and those coming from a polluted exterior. Unfortunately, no building is free of the pollutants which contaminate the exterior atmosphere. Mobile sources, mainly autos, have been a major cause of external pollution. Automotive pollution contains highly toxic nitrogen oxides, ozone, hydrocarbons, and carbon monoxide (see Section E). Being a major focus of early environmental concerns, these pollutants became the prime targets of regulations under the Clean Air Act of 1970. In that year, autos and trucks poured 90 million tons of pollutants into the American atmosphere. Of this, 59 million tons were carbon monoxide and 17 million tons were hydrocarbons.

Congress mandated that carbon monoxide be reduced to 10 per cent of the 1970 levels by 1975 and nitrogen oxides to 10 per cent of 1971 levels by 1976. Though these targets were not met, much progress in cleaning up the air did occur. Some credit goes to transportation controls which discouraged auto use and encouraged car pools, and some to mass transit. However, the major credit goes to the development of cleaner burning engines and catalytic converters. Furthermore, fuel economies helped by stricter conservation legislation is reducing gasoline consumption in newer cars and should reduce overall auto pollution levels still further. The target set by the 1975 Energy Policy and Conservation Act of 1978 model cars averaging 18 miles per gallon (mpg) was reached in 1977. The 1979 model cars should average 19 mpg, the 1980 ones, 20 mpg, and the efficiency standards are to reach an average of 27.5 mpg by 1985.

Motor Oils

Motor oil toxicity is even less recognized by the average consumer than is gasoline's. While motor oil may be less toxic than gasoline, it can still harm human health. Over a billion gallons of motor oil are used each year in the United States, much being changed and stored at home. Unused motor oil contains toxic additives. Tricresyl phosphate (TCP) is a motor oil additive of major health concern. In 1959 over 10,000 cases of paralysis were reported in Morocco due to black marketers' adulteration of cooking oil with surplus engine oil containing highly toxic TCP. In 1930 minute amounts of oil additives in containers used for Jamaica ginger extract (a moonshine ingredient) caused ginger paralysis or "jake paralysis" among thousands of persons in this country.

Waste oil is also a major environmental problem—a dilemma to the person who, though aware of potential pollution dangers, has nowhere to take the oil. An estimated 3.4 million pounds of barium, 4.2 million pounds of zinc, 59 million pounds of lead, and 21 million pounds of phosphorus compounds are annually dumped as motor oil wastes into the environment. Modern motor oils last longer because of motor oil detergents. However, traditional oil recyclers have been unable to regenerate a high-quality recycled motor oil, since many of the impurities remain after traditional oil purification. Thus far recycling industries which hope to make a profit off of recycled oil are not faring well financially.

To remove the waste oil from the home and filling station a national waste collection scheme is needed. Perhaps this could be modeled after European systems where taxes and deposits help finance an otherwise money-losing collection system. In countries like Sweden and Germany used motor oil is not returned to motor use but burned as fuel or used as petroleum feed stock. Those who are among the one third of motor oil consumers who change oil at home are caught in an environmental dilemma. To throw oil into the drain or sewer is highly irresponsible. To burn it is even more so. Those living in congested areas cannot pour it on a dirt road to allay dust or coat farm implements with it. Only regional and national environmental measures will remove this dilemma.

Other Ingredients

A number of motor products such as greases, brake fluid, and antifreeze are often found around the home (see Table I). Treat each with caution and keep out of the reach of children. Make sure antifreeze (ethylene glycol) containers are child-proofed. Once a motor product container is opened, seal properly to retard evaporation.

The caution against aerosol spray use extends to auto and motor product areas. Liquid Wrench contains petroleum distillates which can be easily inhaled. Other antirust aerosol sprays do not even list toxic products on the label or bear the proper warning. Deicer sprays are not economical and some-times freeze when the temperature gets too low.

SNAP—THE PROFESSIONAL SILICONE SPRAY
(Nationwide Industries, Inc., Huntington Valley, Pa.)

DANGER: Harmful or fatal if swallowed. Vapor harmful, extremely flammable. Contents under pressure. Read pre-cautions on back panel.

CAUTION: Harmful or fatal if swallowed. If swallowed, do not induce vomiting. Call physician immediately. Vapor harmful. Do not spray near face.

CAUTION: Flammable mixture. Do not use near fire or flame. Cannot be made nonpoisonous. Keep out of reach of children.

Table I   MOTOR PRODUCTS AROUND THE HOME

Vinyl and fabric repair kit
    (vinyl cleanser and finish)
Vinyl latex caulk
Vinyl cleaner, restorer, and
    finish
Upholstery finish
Fabric mend
Plastic rear window renewer
Simulated weather car top
Rubber-to-metal cement
Rust preventative
Metal tone
Rust remover
Zinc Rich Cold Galvanizing
    Compound (aerosol spray)
Heatproof seal for muffler
    (asbestos tape)
Ceramic coating
Aluminum muffler coat
    (plastic silicone coating)
High-temperature enamel for
    exhaust system (aerosol
    spray)
Battery additive
Engine overhaul
Gasoline catalyst
Rear main bearing sealer
Instant silicone rubber gaskets
Gasket shellac
Liquid metal (molybdenum
    disulfide plus "acid-barrier"
    magnesium, add to crankcase
    oil for coating motor parts)
Transmission lubrication
Automatic transmission sealer
Air-conditioner oil
Tire dressing
Whitewall tire paint
Polyurethane foam filler
Rustproof coating
Spray-on expansion chamber
    paint
Tire inflator sealer (aerosol
    spray)
Tire sealant
Smell-NU (aerosol spray,
    deodorizes completely)
Engine paint
Gear oil

Source: Automotive Parts and Accessories (J. C. Whitney & Co., 1976).

Maintaining Proper Motor Product Storage

Our American motorized society cannot easily provide low-pollution substitutes for petroleum distillate products. Ethanol, for example, requires vast quantities of grain, a complex fermentation and processing industry, and specially designed vehicles. The electric car, while not using petroleum distillates, does require fossil fuel to stoke the power plants which generate electricity for recharging batteries. Electric cars are less direct but still very real polluters in their own right. Besides, they are not yet mass-produced.

It is better to change the mode of passenger transportation than merely to substitute indirect polluters for petroleum fuels. Mass transport systems are far more efficient than the individualized auto, despite the inconvenience of increased travel time for some trips. For short-haul travel, the bicycle is most efficient, costs little, and can be easily parked. If these bikes must compete with autos on congested highways, they expose the biker to extra danger. Walking is the best means for traveling a few blocks for a newspaper or personal visit.

Granting that we are unable to demotorize our lives at this time, and that we will have enough petroleum through this century, problems with motor vehicles and vehicle products will persist. The following steps may reduce dangers from these products:

- Never store gasoline or other flammable and volatile petroleum distillates in the living quarters of the home. Minimize the storage of any such distillates. Keep in safety cans in a garage or outbuilding where the ventilation is good.
- Never use leaded gasoline for camp fuel or to clean off oil-based paint from the body.
- While a gasoline can should be kept in the car, don't store gasoline in it. In case of a violent accident it might explode and be fatal.

- Keep gasoline and all motor products out of reach of children, and don't let children play with empty motor product containers.

- Avoid motor vehicle fumes. Sometimes this is impossible, and merely closing doors and windows is not sufficient. In cases of severe respiratory disease, it may be best to transfer victims to a relatively pollution-free region, especially during a pollution alert season.

- Bikers, strollers, and joggers should avoid heavily polluted routes and peak-hour traffic. If living near heavy traffic, persons should not strenuously exercise during heavy pollution periods.

- Don't let youngsters play around operating or abandoned service stations. Additives often do not evaporate easily and contaminate the premises. Teen-agers often like to sniff fumes at gasoline stations and should be warned of the dangers.

- Use high-quality motor oil and thus generate less waste oil.

- If one cannot dispose of waste oil properly, the oil should be changed at a service station. Don't pour waste oil down the drain or into a water system. Pour it around the foundation of the house to discourage termites, or bury it where it will not enter a water system. In drier climates the use of waste oil to allay dust may be used.

- Never use aerosolized motor or automotive products around the home.

- Pressure congresspersons to become concerned about the unsolved waste oil problem.

- Make sure the antifreeze and deicing agents used in the winter season have child-proof container caps.

- Denatured alcohol from the medicine cabinet is a good substitute for anti-ice sprays. However, a window scraper or a heated key (for a frozen lock) will do a better job.

REFERENCES

[1] "The Latest Gasoline Additive Backfires," *Consumer Reports*, Vol. 42, 191 (Apr. 1977).
[2] Bernheimer et al., *Handbook of Neurochemistry*, Vol. 7, pp. 487–88.

Additional Source

A. Fritsch, "Gasoline Additives," CSPI Report to Consumers Union, 1972.

N. NOISE POLLUTION

The Noise Problem

Noise is a pervasive part of our lives. Some experts estimate that unwanted sound is a "significant" problem for 80 million Americans. It has been further suggested that 22 to 44 million people in the United States are exposed to chronic noise aggravation in their homes from aircraft and transportation disruptions.[1] A sign of the times, the San Diego Opera flashes a red "plane coming" light to stop the show when an aircraft approaches. In our homes, we need only think of the multiplicity of sounds that drift in from outside: the roar of motorcycles and trucks, the chatter of jackhammers, and the howl of sirens. Indoors there are sounds of TVs, stereos, blenders, air-conditioners, telephones, vacuum cleaners, dishwashers, etc. In fact, over 90 per cent of our household noise comes from appliances.[2] The manufacturers of some cleaning products admit that noise-free cleaners are poor sellers—which says something about becoming conditioned to certain noises.

It is commonly known that extremely loud noises damage the hair cells of the inner ear—producing hearing loss and, in extreme cases, deafness. The type and extent of auditory impairment varies according to the volume, frequency (pitch), and duration of the sound. While lost hearing can frequently be recovered following acute noise exposure (e.g., an explosion), repeated exposure can lead to permanent impairment, particularly in the perception of high-frequency sounds.

Noise can also affect the neurological, cardiovascular, and endocrine systems—which are typically active in a general stress reaction. Laboratory studies have revealed that rodents exposed to high noise levels developed intestinal ailments, liver and kidney damage, reproductive failures, and decreased resistance to disease.[3] Studies of the nonauditory effects of noise in humans are more difficult to conduct. Workers in loud factories, for example, may exhibit various symptoms of the general stress syndrome, but researchers may have trouble pinpointing the factor(s) responsible (e.g., noise, industrial chemicals, labor conditions, etc.). Nevertheless, some scientists have been able to isolate the effects of loud noise enough to conclude that it "causes effects which the recipient cannot control. The blood vessels constrict, the skin pales, the voluntary and involuntary muscles tense, and adrenalin is suddenly injected into the bloodstream, which increases neuromuscular tension, nervousness, irritability, and anxiety."[4] A number of job performance studies, moreover, have shown that mistakes and accidents are more likely to occur when workers are exposed to intense sounds.[5]

There is also mounting evidence that noise pollution is undermining the well-being of people outside the factory. Numerous newspaper accounts have recorded incidents where frustrated apartment dwellers have been driven to violence against noisy neighbors. Less extreme manifestations of frustration are commonplace, particularly where sleep or a tedious task is interrupted by noise. These kinds of problems have prompted the National Research Council/National Academy of Sciences to undertake more research in several areas of growing concern, including the general impacts of noise, its detrimental potential for fetal development, its disruption of the learning process in schools, and its interference with sleep.

The impact of noise on us is affected by mood, weather, loudness, frequency, and distance. Thus a universal definition for what is "noisy" is difficult to construct. A common, though incomplete, definition is that noise is any unwanted sound. However, even a wanted or desired sound may cause damage to our ears. It is really noise, because it goes contrary to our physical and psychic health needs. Generally, when any noise makes a telephone conversation difficult, hearing is being harmed.

The loudness of sound really depends on the power or pressure with which a sound comes into our ears. It is measured in units of "decibels" (after Alexander Graham bell).[6] The scale of 0 to 200 goes from the threshold on hearing of a young adult to one which would burst the eardrum. If the faintest sound that a normal ear can detect is compared to the weight of a one-ounce letter, the sound that would burst eardrums would be equivalent to a quarter of a million tons (roughly 4 times the weight of the Queen Elizabeth 2). As a rule of thumb an increase of 6 dB doubles sound loudness, and an increase of 20 dB represents a sound 10 times as loud.

Table I shows typical noise levels of common things around us. As can be seen, a rock-and-roll band is more than twice as loud as a jackhammer, and 100 times as loud as a truck at 50 feet.

Noises are cumulative. For instance, two low noises inside the house can combine to give an even louder noise.[7] Thus the little sounds in the house contribute to over-all sound levels. Table II lists possible noise sources in the home. Some can be easily remedied, others only with expense—but most can be eliminated with planning. Poor home design and cheap, lightweight construction materials do little to contain the adding, spreading sounds. How many times have we gone to another room of the house to escape a noise and had to generate noise (loud radio, etc.) in order to drown out the original distraction? The design of the modern home is often more like a kettledrum than a place of privacy.

Table III lists outdoor noise sources, which remain a significant part of the noise problem in America. In West Germany basic guidelines were set in 1968, limiting the decibel count to which a citizen could be exposed, day and night, in commercial and residential areas.[8] As a result plastic containers were substituted for metal garbage cans, and compressors at construction sites were redesigned.

Table I TYPICAL SOUND LEVELS

dB-A Scale (measures sounds in human hearing range)

195	Saturn V rocket—instant deafness
140	Ear pain
120	Rock band—ear discomfort
115	Jet overhead (at 500 feet)
113	Jackhammer drill
100	Kitchen with blender, dishwasher, mixer operating
95	Power mower
90	Outboard 10 horsepower motor
80	Truck (at 50 feet), blender, hair dryer
75	Car (at 20 feet), vacuum cleaner
70	Washing machine, noisy restaurant
65	Air-conditioner (at 20 feet)
50	Dense traffic (one mile away)
40	Office noise
0	Softest whisper

Table II INDOOR NOISES

Take an inventory of the noises in the home. Are any of the following heard from the next room?

KITCHEN
1. Dishwasher
2. Blender-processor
3. Electric knife
4. Mixer
5. Garbage disposal
6. Water hammer—pounding pipes
7. Refrigerator freezer
8. Oven or stove vent fan
9. Trash compactor
10. Electric can opener

BASEMENT OR UTILITY ROOM
1. Furnace or central A.C. blower
2. Hot-water heater
3. Washer dryer
4. Noisy belts, gears on pumps or fans
5. Electric garage door openers
6. Power tools: drill, saw, grinder, sander

BATHROOM
1. Hair dryer
2. Vent fan
3. Toilet
4. Electric toothbrush
5. Electric shaver

(Table II cont.)

LIVING—FAMILY ROOM
1. TV
2. Radio
3. Telephone conversation
4. Vacuum cleaner
5. Humidifier or dehumidifier
6. Stereo
7. Whine of slide projector blower
8. Piano

BEDROOM
1. Window air-conditioner
2. Typewriter
3. Children's noisy toys
4. Buzz of fluorescent fixtures
5. Sewing machine
6. Electric shoe polishers

Table III OUTDOOR NOISES

AROUND THE HOUSE
1. Lawn mowers
2. Lawn vacuums
3. Chain saws
4. Hedge trimmers
5. Minibikes
6. Rototillers
7. Grass and leaf choppers

GENERAL
1. Construction work
2. Roadwork, jackhammers
3. Sirens, horns
4. Trucks, buses
5. Cars, motors, and squealing tires
6. Motorcycles and motor bikes
7. Airplanes and train engines
8. Boat whistles, garbage cans
9. Firecrackers, gunfire
10. Noisy people
11. Barking dogs
12. Neighboring house noises

In the United States the Federal Noise Control Act of 1972 and the Model Noise Control Ordinance of 1975 are only a first step in the abatement of outdoor noise pollution. Permissible nighttime noise levels are fully 10 decibels higher in the United States than in Germany. Much has to be done to reduce our domestic noise problem.

Noise Reduction

Reduce noise in the home by the following methods:

- Buy only necessary appliances and check for noise levels

before purchase. Remember hair driers and can openers are energy wasters.

■ Place pads under vibrating machinery and appliances such as washing machines and typewriters.

■ Lower the loudness adjustment of the telephone and door-bell. Turn off when napping.

■ Place extra insulation between utility rooms and living quarters. Remember some members of the family need more silence and have a lower reserve of psychic energy.

■ Be considerate in the use of the television and radio when others are sleeping or talking.

■ Be aware of the need to close doors and windows when operating noisy appliances.

■ Practice with musical instruments in areas removed from others. Consider the aesthetic and economic advantages of using unamplified instruments.

■ Install extra carpets, rugs, curtains, and drapes of heavy material to reduce home noises. Allow curtains to hang loose and a small distance from the walls. The air space helps reduce noise.

■ Check basement for banging steam pipes. Place insulation around pipes where they go through walls. Add supports and dividing materials where needed.

■ Adjust and place stops on doors.

■ Oil squeaky hinges and joints.

Take joint community action to reduce neighborhood noises which infiltrate into the inner sanctum of the home:

■ See that city ordinances related to external noises such as motorcycles, motorboats, and fireworks be drawn up and/or strictly enforced. Likewise make sure that there are curfews on use of chain saws, lawn mowers, recreation centers, and other noisy spots after certain night hours.

■ Make sure that home building codes are enforced to deal with the penetration of noises through apartment floors and walls.

■ Petition regulatory agencies to set noise standards for individual appliances and equipment.

■ Check into reducing excessive use of sirens and bells in the community.

■ Organize the neighborhood for reducing local noises. Here is a place where one might preserve the health of sick and elderly friends and neighbors by affording them peace and quiet.

■ Encourage high school discussion groups to talk about the need to reduce noise pollution from musical instruments, especially electric guitars and amplifying equipment.

The Remedy of Silence

Noises are best substituted by silence and quiet places. Not all noises can be eliminated, so it is necessary that a quiet retreat be established both within the home and in our lives. We should be able to escape to restful mountains or a tranquil seashore. Take a retreat where silence is valued. Find time to take a quiet walk in the park or woods. Biking, backpacking, and jogging afford the precious moments when people can find themselves. Learn to take time out during the day for a few moments of recollection, in a quiet environment.

REFERENCES

[1] Noise Control Act of 1972, Model Noise Control Ordinance of 1975.

[2] Henry Still, *In Quest of Quiet: A Call to Citizen Action* (Harrisburg, Pa.: Stackpole Books, 1970).

[3] A. Anthony and E. Acherman, "Stress Effects of Noise in Vertebrate Animals," *WAC Tech Report*, 58-662, Wright Patterson Air Force Base, Ohio, 1959. Also see B. Zondek and I. Tomari, "Effect of Audiogenic Stimulations on Genetic Function and Reproduction," *American Journal of Obstetrics and Gynecology*, Vol. 80 (1960), pp. 1,041–48. Also see M. M. Jensen and A. F. Rasmussen, Jr., *Audiogenic Stress and Susceptibility to Infection in Physiological Effects of Noise*, B. Welch and A. Welch, eds. (New York: Plenum Press, 1970), pp. 7–17.

[4] Dr. Samuel Rogen, Columbia University, as quoted by Still, *In Quest of Quiet*, p. 192.

[5] U. S. Department of Health, Education, and Welfare—NIOSH, *Criteria for a Recommended Standard: Occupational Exposure to Noise*, 1972, pp. IV-13–IV-16.

[6] Several different noise reporting scales exist depending on which parts (frequencies) of the sound are measured. Many times "dBA" are reported—indicating the frequencies close to those the human ear detects were measured. An ultrasonic animal whistle would not significantly register on the dBA scale, whereas it would on a straight "dB" scale which measures almost all frequencies. Aircraft noise is usually reported on a perceived noise decibel scale, "PNdB." An increase of 10 PNdB represents a doubling of noisiness, but only an increase of 6 on the dB scale would be doubling. Thus a 115 PNdB sound is twice as loud as a 105 PNdB sound. (Ref. 4)

[7] "About Sound," May 1976, USEPA, Washington, D.C. 20460.

[8] Gunter Haaf, "America, the Land of Perpetual Noise," Washington *Post*, Jan. 16, 1977.

Additional Sources

Criteria for a Recommended Standard: Occupational Exposure to Noise, HSM 73-1101, U. S. Department of Health, Education, and Welfare, 1972.

"Occupational Noise Exposure Regulation," *Federal Register*, Vol. 39, No. 244 (Dec. 18, 1974).

B. F. Day, R. D. Ford, and P. Lord, eds., *Building Acoustics* (London: Elsevier Pub. Co., Ltd., 1969).

Theodore Berland, *The Fight for Quiet* (Englewood Cliffs, N.J.: Prentice-Hall, 1970).

Irving N. Sax, *Dangerous Properties of Industrial Materials,* 4th ed. (New York: Van Nostrand Reinhold Co.).

R. A. Baron, *A Tyranny of Noise* (New York: Harper & Row, 1971).

"Noise as a Public Health Hazard," *Proceedings of the American Speech and Hearing Association, National Conference,* Washington, D.C., June 13–14, 1968.

J. Stataloff, *Occupational Hearing Loss* (Philadelphia: J. B. Lippincott, "EPA Noise Control Program, Progress to Date," USEPA, May 1976).

D. M. Lupscomb, *Noise; the Unwanted Sounds* (Chicago: Nelson-Hall Co., 1974).

O. OVEN AND OTHER CLEANERS

Ovens, according to the advertising media, are caves of stonelike encrustations impervious to all but a chemical blitzkrieg. The soldier is the homemaker, the enemy, dirt, and the weapon, a chemical arsenal. But ovens are only some of the battle zones of the home. Add to them the toilets, drains, coffeepots, upholstery, and the glass windows. The chemicals involved command respect from chemists who are aware of their powerful properties, but most consumers have had at best only a very elementary course in chemistry.

The pressure to use these products is enormous. Toilets and drains are portrayed as centers of plaguelike contagion, or as invitations for a ring-around-the-bowl accusation by an observant visitor. Cleaning agents prescribed for grime found in ovens, drains, and toilets fill supermarket shelves in alluring containers. Their labels, if ingredients are properly annotated, read like a chemistry text. Myriad "special" varieties exist to clean bathroom tile and tubs, tires, countertops, windows, and sinks. Think of a home cleaning operation and some manufacturer has found a product which is supposed to do the specific job.

Chemical Household Cleaners

This section, more than almost any other, deals with some of the most chemically reactive and physically harmful household substances. Moreover, accidental mixing of some of these common materials can produce dangerous substances through vigorous chemical reactions. The description of these reactions is better handled in a chemistry course. Thus only a summary of representative and significant compounds are listed in Table I, with the remainder to be found in other references.

Oven Cleaners

Oven cleaning need not be a complicated affair if proper preventative measures such as proper-sized containers and sheets for spill-overs are used. Normal splattering, if promptly cleaned up "overnight," can be accomplished simply and without dangerous chemicals. Overkill using lye (sodium and potassium hydroxide) is seldom necessary. While lye does attack organic matter with vigor, it can also attack skin, eyes, or internal organs. About 3,000 people were wounded by it in 1973.

Oven cleaners come in four different forms, all of which contain lye: aerosol sprays, liquids, pastes, and powders.

Aerosol sprays are by far the most dangerous and popular products. Brands like Easy Off, Mr. Muscle, and White Magic conveniently dispense powerful chemicals requiring great care in use. Moreover, the aerosol spray containers dispense them in small droplets that drift throughout the room and land on skin, eyes, and, worse yet, sensitive lung surfaces. While skin constantly regenerates itself and has a protective layer of dead cells, this is not true of the lungs. We do have built-in defenses—these chemicals emit unpleasant, irritating vapors which we naturally avoid. However, companies perfume them to smell like a spring day, a lemon orchard, an aftershave lotion. Furthermore, aerosol cans explode, are difficult to dispose of, are environmental threats, and are costly (see Section A).

Table I TYPICAL COMPOUNDS FOUND IN CLEANING AGENTS

Name	Where Found	Purpose	Dangers
(Lye), potassium hydroxide, sodium hydroxide	oven and drain cleaners	chemically attack and dissolve organic matter	extremely dangerous to all parts of body, especially eyes
Ammonia	oven and window cleaners, wax removers	chemically attack and dissolve organic matter	strong concentrations attack skin, eyes, lungs
Sodium tripolyphosphate	coffeepot cleaners	water softener and building agent	strong concentrations attack skin, eyes, lungs
Sodium phosphate	cleaners, scouring powders	water softener and building agent	strong concentrations attack skin, eyes, lungs
Sodium silicate	dishwashing detergent	water softener and building agent	strong concentrations attack skin, eyes, lungs
Sodium metasilicate	dishwashing detergent	water softener and building agent	strong concentrations attack skin, eyes, lungs
Sulfuric acid	commercial drain cleaners	chemically attack and dissolve organic matter	extremely dangerous to entire body
Hydrochloric acid	drain cleaners, toilet cleaners	remove stains and deposits	extremely dangerous to entire body

Name	Where Found	Purpose	Dangers
Phosphoric acid	denture cleaners, metal cleaners and polish	remove stains, dissolve rust	extremely dangerous to entire body
Sodium hypochlorite	bleach chlorine	remove color, disinfect	dangerous to entire body; never mix with anything other than soap or water
Calcium hypochlorite	bleach chlorine	remove color, disinfect	dangerous to entire body; never mix with anything other than soap or water
Sodium perborate	oxygen bleach, denture cleaners	remove color, disinfect	dangerous to entire body; mildly toxic
Sodium dodecylbenzene sulfonate	detergent	dissolve grease and oil	continued contact removes protective oil from skin

EASY OFF OVEN CLEANER
(Boyle-Midway, Inc., New York)

DANGER: May cause burns to skin and eyes. Irritant to mucous membranes. Contents under pressure. Danger: contains lye. Keep out of reach of children. Recommended for use only on porcelain, enamel, iron, stainless steel, ceramic, and glass surfaces. Do not get on exterior oven surfaces such as aluminum and chrome trim, baked enamel, copper tone, or painted areas or on linoleum or plastics. For gas ovens avoid spraying on pilot light. Keep spray off electrical connections such as door operated light switch, heating element, thermostat, bulb, receptacles etc.
Contents under pressure. If taken internally or sprayed in eyes call physician. Antidote—drink diluted vinegar or juice of lemon or grapefruit followed by milk or egg whites beaten with H_2O.

Liquids, usually dissolved lye, spill, flow easily, and react immediately. Because of this they can severely injure people in a number of ways: Children drink them; users accidentally spill them and allow drops to splash onto skin and into eyes; homemakers often store and dispose of them improperly. Again, as in the case of aerosol sprays, these liquids are pleasant-smelling, sometimes colorless, and quite difficult to identify—once spilled or stored in an improperly marked container. Moreover, proper labeling of these dangerous components is hardly sufficient. Toxicologists and other medical experts recognize that warning labels are no adequate solution to the problem of accidental poisoning. Consumers disregard labels and children can't read them.

Pastes, at least 7 per cent lye mixed with cornstarch to thicken, are perhaps less dangerous when applying than both aerosol sprays and liquids simply because they are less mobile. There is less of a proneness to accidental spilling, though caution must still be taken.

Powder oven cleaner also exists although it is not widely used. Designed to release ammonia vapors when water is added, it is somewhat safer to handle than the other forms. However, the fumes are noxious and are dangerous if large amounts are inhaled. Fortunately ammonia is difficult to perfume and thus can alert users when present in high concentrations.

Drain Cleaners

Drain cleaners are similar in composition to the oven cleaners. They exist in liquid or crystal form and are composed of up to 90 per cent lye. They are designed to attack organic matter such as grease and food waste build-up in drains. The dangers are mainly to children (over 60 per cent of accidents) and involve chemical burns to mouth, face, esophagus, and upper digestive pathways. Drain and toilet cleaners account for about 10,000 injuries per year in this country.

Crystal forms of drain cleaner are safer than liquid types. Liquids are already dissolved and immediately attack the skin, whereas crystals falling on dry skin can be brushed off before much damage is done. Crystals can cause splattering in the presence of liquids, however. Homemakers are often unaware of the inherent dangers of drain cleaners, even with detailed instructions. What directions don't tell is that if the chemicals don't work, the drain is in worse condition. It is now full of a dangerous caustic solution.[1]

Bleaches

Bleaching agents such as Clorox, White Magic, and Miracle White are designed to break down color-containing substances and are usually chlorinated oxidizing chemicals. Bleaches quite often kill germs (see Section J) but must never be mixed with drain or oven cleaners. The temptation is great especially when the other agents are not doing the job; the homemaker chemical warrior thinks that two powerful agents are better than one.

In November 1975 a sixty-eight-year-old Portland, Maine, woman mixed ammonia and chlorine bleach in a pail to wash away eggs splattered on her windows by a Halloween prankster. When bringing the pail indoors the toxic fumes being generated killed her. The woman's niece tried to revive her by mouth-to-mouth resuscitation and she too was overcome and died by the fumes. The mixing of the chlorine bleach and ammonia produce deadly chloramine fumes. Mixing chlorine bleach with vinegar or certain toilet bowl cleaners will also produce poisonous chlorine gas.

Another case has been reported of a fourteen-month-old child who was repeatedly hospitalized with a pattern of vomiting and abdominal discomfort. It was discovered that the child had been sucking on socks which had been strongly bleached and not properly rinsed.

Chlorine bleach is not necessarily the best stain remover. While effective in normal water, where high concentrations of iron are present, the chlorine will combine to form yellow and brown stains which are difficult to remove. Likewise strong chlorine bleach can weaken the fibers and shorten the garment lifetime. To find out put a piece of fabric in some undiluted chlorine bleach. On the other hand, dry bleaches, which usually release oxygen when placed in wash water, are safer and less destructive than chlorine varieties. They all require care in handling.

Toilet Bowl Cleaners

Toilet bowl cleaners come in either the in-bowl or the in-tank (turning water blue) variety. In-bowl cleaners are strong acids which are effective in removing materials and stains. *Consumer Reports* judges in-tank cleaners to have poor cleaning and deodorizing ability.[2]

Window Cleaners

Window cleaners are a specialized variety which can be simply replaced by common ingredients found in the kitchen: water, detergents, and ammonia. The only difference between a quickly mixed homemade and commercial varieties cleaner is the blue dye found in the latter.

Scouring Powders

Scouring powders contain a bleaching agent along with a coarse polishing agent such as silica. These may severely scratch the surface of porcelain or vitreous-enameled sinks or toilet bowls, creating irreversible damage and greater susceptibility to staining.[3]

Nine parts fine-grade whiting from a paint store and one part heavy-duty powered laundry detergent will do as good a job and have low abrasive action. In fact, this home concoction is a safe cleaner for porcelain-enamel surfaces.

More than 22,000 people[4] received hospital treatment in 1973 for injuries associated with cleaning agents, solvent-based cleaning and sanitizing compounds, caustics, drain cleaners, and household ammonia.

Opting for Good Household Cleaners

Commercial materials supposedly present myriad choices for the knowledgeable person. The fact is that there is really little choice when all end results are considered. The choices become even more restrictive when recognizing dangers associated with use of certain cleaning chemicals (see Table I).

The plethora of cleaning chemicals could be replaced by six simple, inexpensive but effective substances: soap, baking soda (sodium bicarbonate), vinegar (dilute acetic acid), ammonia, washing soda, and borax. Soap has already been discussed in Section K. These cleaning substances are universally available and are adequate for most household sanitizing, laundering, softening, bleaching, dry cleaning, and disinfecting needs in the home.

General Surface Cleaning: Any surface where spots show (e.g., glass or marble) can be cleaned with several tablespoons of vinegar in a bucket of water. The vinegar quickly evaporates (soap would leave a residue) and freshens the air as well as removes the spots. The "salad" smell does not linger. Hazards are virtually nil with diluted vinegar.

Baking soda, which is often used for upset stomachs, straight or dissolved, works well on all other areas, particularly greasy ones. Coffeepots, chrome, copper, and tile are effectively cleaned by baking soda.

Bleaching: Replace with borax. Bleach chemically attacks fabrics as well as stains. Borax whitens clothes without destroying the fabric and can be used with all fabrics and colors.

Scouring: Commercial cleansers and scouring powders normally contain abrasives for removing food and materials adhering to surfaces. Over the long run the surface may be scratched and ruined. Moreover the chlorine bleach that many powders contain irritates hands, eyes, and nose. Normal bathroom cleaning can be done with baking soda, used just like commercial products.

Utensil Cleaning: Stainless-steel or enamel-coated steel or aluminum utensils are better than pure aluminum. Since many foods are acidic, minute amounts of aluminum are dissolved in the prepared food. This dissolved aluminum adds a foreign element which is unneeded and of questionable health value. The life of the utensil is shortened in the process. Vinegar and baking soda will gradually dissolve or discolor aluminum pots. If they are really greasy, try a diluted solution of ammonia and go purchase good cookery utensils.

Oven Cleaning: Most ovens can be cleaned with either baking soda or ammonia. Baking soda is advised for normal cleaning since it is safe and easy to use. A water solution of soda will remove grease. More stubborn spots require sprinkling of dry baking soda for five minutes, followed by scrubbing with a damp rag. Severe spots can be scraped off. Even commercial cleaners probably wouldn't get them either.

To use ammonia, place one-fourth cup in a nonaluminum shallow dish and fill with water. Set this bowl in the middle of the oven overnight. In the morning the stains can be removed with a damp rag. Ammonia requires more care than baking soda since it gives off irritating vapors which can be toxic in high concentrations.

Drain Cleaning: Commercial drain cleaners should be avoided in all cases. The strong acids and basis used are extremely dangerous to personal health and plumbing. If drains are kept free of grease, food scraps, and hair, clogging would never occur.

Slow drains can be opened by pouring hot water down them, adding one-fourth to one-half cup washing soda, and waiting a minute or so before flushing again with hot water. In the case of blockage, a plumber's helper (mechanical plunger) should open the drain. A small plumber's snake can also be used by sliding it through the pipe. Follow this up with the slow drain treatment.

CLOROX
(Clorox Company, Oakland, Calif.)

Keep out of Reach of Children

Active ingredient, sodium hypochlorite 5.25%, inert ingredients 94.75%.

Use clorox on all these fabrics (white and colorfast): cotton, linen, rayon, acrylic, acetate, nylon, polyester, modacrylic, triacetate and blends of these fibres. —Do not use on silk, wool, mohair, leather, spandex, or non-fast colors. Retardant sleepwear may cause loss of flame retardancy.

REFERENCES

[1] "Drain Cleaners," *Consumer Reports,* Vol. 41, 592 (Oct. 1976).
[2] "Toilet Bowl Cleaners," *Consumer Reports,* Vol. 40, 156 (Mar. 1975).
[3] "Scouring Powders," *Consumer Bulletin,* Vol. 56, 27 (Feb. 1973).
[4] *Neiss News,* U. S. Consumer Product Safety Commission, Mar. 1974.

Additional Sources

"Oven Cleaners," *Consumer Reports,* Vol. 41, 400 (July 1976).
"General Household Cleaners," *Consumer Reports,* Vol. 39, 676 (Sept. 1974).
"Toilet Bowl Cleaners," *Consumer Reports,* Vol. 40, 156 (Mar. 1975).
"Glass Cleaners, *Consumer Reports,* Vol. 40, 30 (Jan. 1975).
"Oven Cleaners," *Fact Sheet No. 67,* U. S. Consumer Product Safety Commission, May 1975.
"Poisonous Household Substances," *Fact Sheet No. 21,* U. S. Consumer Product Safety Commission, Washington, D.C.

P. PLASTICS AND PLASTICIZERS

Most homemakers are familiar with plastic toys, light fixtures, bottles, sheet and upholstery covers, Plexiglas blocks, Styrofoam cushions, and numerous other household items and building materials. They know that the modern petrochemical industry has produced this multitude of synthetic textile, resin, and rubber products, all of which bear the generic name "plastics." They are perhaps less familiar with the ingredients which go into making plastics, the method of manufacture, the amounts of each being produced (see Table Ia), and the dangers associated with these materials.

Chemically, plastics refer to a large group of materials of high molecular weight. Plastics are not necessarily new, for many of the natural tars, gums, and resins were regarded as "plastic" before the dawn of modern chemistry. What is new is the use of petrochemicals and other semisynthetic organic substances to make synthetic plastics through a complex system of polymerization or condensation reactions. The resulting condensed or polymerized products are then shaped generally by heat into a variety of solid or nearly solid items. These processes may or may not involve fillers, plasticizers, reinforcing agents, and other chemical ingredients, which add to the complexity of the final product.

Notwithstanding all the advantages of plastics, there are a number of health and environmental dangers due to the use or decomposition of these plastic materials. Some are more home-related and some have to do with occupational health and outdoor pollution.

Fumes from Burning Plastics

Fire can produce large quantities of very dangerous fumes, some of which are far more deadly than the home fire itself. This is especially acute when dealing with mobile homes, which have larger amounts of plastic building materials present than do permanent dwellings.

Table Ia TYPES OF PLASTICS AND AMOUNT USED
(1,000 pounds)

Thermoplastic Resins Consumed

1. Cellulosic	124,632
2. Acrylic	280,612
3. Polyamide (nylon)	79,695
4. Polyethylene	4,045,493
5. Polypropylene	652,893
6. Styrene and copolymer	2,252,025
7. Vinyl and vinyl copolymer	2,642,513
8. All other thermoplastics and n.s.k. (not specified by kind)	694,955
Total	10,772,818

Thermoset Resins Consumed

1. Melamine	90,206
2. Phenolics and other low acid resins	322,022
3. Polyester resins (including diallylphthalate)	359,371
4. Urea	39,730
5. Diiocyanate and polyurethane	681,512
6. All other and n.s.k.	129,984
Total	1,622,825

Source: U. S. Department of Commerce, Bureau of Census, "Shipments of Selected Plastic Products," Series: MA-30D(74)-1 December 1975 (Washington, D.C., 1974 data), p. 2.

Table Ib VALUE OF PLASTIC SHIPMENTS

Categories	Millions of Dollars
1. Unsupported plastic film, sheets, sheeting, rods, tubes, and other stock shapes	2,694.7
2. Framed plastic products	1,149.0
3. Laminated sheets, rods, and tubes	710.7
4. Plastic packaging and shipping containers	1,784.9
5. Industrial plastic products	2,426.6
6. Construction plastic products	1,661.7
7. Plastic dinnerware, tableware, and kitchenware	543.9
8. Consumer and commercial plastic products	665.5
9. Custom compound purchased resins	365.1
10. Plastic products, not specified by kind	3,532.3
Total	15,534.3

Source: U. S. Department of Commerce, Bureau of Census, "Shipments of Selected Plastic Products," Series: MA-30D(74)-1 December 1975 (Washington, D.C., 1974 data), p. 2.

Fire hazards associated with certain plastics include the following:

- Rapid flame spread.
- Extreme heat when ignited.
- Large amounts of dense smoke. Generally, plastics that contain flame retardants will produce more smoke when forced to burn than untreated materials.
- Generation of toxic gases. As in the case of the other carbon-containing combustibles, carbon monoxide can be produced when plastics burn. Also, aldehydes, hydrogen cyanide, and hydrochloric acid may be generated, depending on the type of plastic (see Table II).

Detailed investigations of fire fatalities show that the combined effect of carbon monoxide, pulmonary injury, alcohol, and cardiovascular disease plays a major role in many fire deaths. Some 62 per cent of fire-related deaths occur in residential occupancies. According to some researchers about 80

Table II PLASTIC POLLUTANTS

Plastic	Use	Pollutants Resulting from Combustion
1. Polyethylene	packaging materials, pipe, cable insulation	carbon monoxide
2. Polystyrene	packaging materials, household goods, toys	carbon monoxide, carbon black
3. Polyvinyl chloride	pipes, films, flooring materials, furniture, electrical insulation	carbon monoxide, hydrochloric acid
4. Fluorine polymers	special hospital equipment corrosion-resistant or antifriction coatings	hydrogen fluoride, carbonyl fluoride
5. Nylon	fibers, gearwheels, household goods	carbon monoxide, nitrogen-containing gases,
6. Polyesters	plastic boats, lacquers, household goods	carbon monoxide
7. Phenolic molding compositions such as Bakelite	adhesives, handles, telephones	carbon monoxide
8. Polyacronitrile	fibers, rugs, household furnishings	hydrogen cyanide, carbon monoxide
9. Urethanes	foams, rubber, molded materials	hydrogen cyanide, carbon monoxide
10. Melamine resins	adhesives, lacquers, household goods	carbon monoxide, nitrogen-containing gases

per cent of the victims of fire are not touched by the flame but die from smoke inhalation.

Over 20 per cent of all plastics are used in the building industry. As this amount grows, the fire and smoke problem grows likewise. Large quantities of hydrochloric acids are released from buildings with burning polyvinyl chloride flooring and pipes, possibly causing severe corrosion of nearby equipment such as instruments, electronic apparatus, and machines made from certain metals. Hydrochloric acid will even attack concrete. In an analysis of the degradation products from flexible polyester plastics and polyurethane foams made from toluene diisocyanate (TDI), over thirty products were identified, including the highly toxic unreacted TDI.

Boettner and colleagues, in one study, ignited four types of different bedroom furnishings ranging from the conventional to highly flame-retardant.[1] In analyzing the effects they found these major substances: hydrogen, cyanide, carbon monoxide, and sulfur dioxide, all of which are considered to be very toxic. In the "improved room," high aldehyde concentrations were recognized as a significant hazard.

Other studies were carried out to determine the burning characteristics of a variety of upholstered furniture and floor coverings arranged in a typical sitting/dining room. The upholstered furniture included traditional (wooden framing with cotton padding), semimodern (latex foam on wood), and modern (polyester foam on wood and molded) items. It was found that peak concentration of carbon monoxide, carbon dioxide, nitrogen oxides, and hydrogen cyanide were directly related to the more modern furnishings. As the furniture was changed from traditional to modern types, the time required to reach the maximum concentrations of toxic gas decreased. The rate of oxygen depletion in the room was greater for modern furniture. Thus less time is available for escape in fires involving modern as opposed to traditional furniture.

Fumes from burning flame-resistant plastics are likewise highly toxic, especially polyurethane foam.[2] In addition such fire-retardant plastics as polyisocyanurate, polystyrene, ABS and ABS foam, and flexible polyurethane produce some lethal emissions other than carbon monoxide. Some emissions such as fine dust particles are known to enhance the toxicity of other products, whether they be gases or vapors. This appears to be true also for plastic combustion products.

Plasticizers

Dangers due to the presence of plasticizers in many plastic products should not be overlooked. A plasticizer is a chemical that increases a plastic's workability and capacity to stretch. Production of plasticizers in the United States exceeds one and a quarter billion pounds per year and world production is not quite twice that amount.[8] About 63 per cent of the plasticizers are phthalates, and 80 per cent of all plasticizers sold are used in polyvinyl chloride formulations. Some plasticizers are fungistats (they discourage fungus growth) and some are flame retardants. The main problem is that many plasticizers are capable of leaching from the plastics.

Phthalate plasticizers are shown to be of low toxicity when administered orally, but they either excite or depress the central nervous system. Plastics authorities admit that since these phthalates are not bound into the polymer chemically, they tend to "migrate" to the surface where they can be released by water, oil, and solvents or removed by abrasion. The National Aeronautics and Space Administration (NASA) banned the use of polyvinyl chloride in space capsules because the plasticizer leached out and condensed on lenses of fine optical instruments.

High concentrations of plasticizing and stabilizing compounds are found in auto interiors. A "new-car smell" is mainly plasticizers released from dashboard coverings, side panels, seat covers, and interior roof linings. Residues found on the outside of windshields of new cars exposed to strong sunlight have been identified as plasticizers and stabilizers.[4]

Widespread contamination of water-life systems by

phthalate ester plasticizers has been noted. Phthalate ester plasticizers have also been found in blood stored and filtered through plastic tubing and plastic bags. One plasticizer was found in both rat liver and human tissues.[5] The presence of plasticizers has been reported in milk[6] and in a deep fryer of a restaurant.[7] Whether the presence of these will lead to harmful effects is curently unknown.

The Vinyl Chloride Problem

Vinyl chloride is a synthetic organic compound which is important in the plastic industry. Its most popular use is a stepping stone (or a "monomer") in the production of polyvinyl chloride (PVC), a polymer. While PVC, which is used in a large number of plastic products (see Table III), is not known to be toxic as such, vinyl chloride (VC) is. VC is also known to leach out, especially during the early life of the PVC product. Various new methods for polyermizing VC can reduce this leakage, but unfortunately these are not yet widely utilized.

The first hint that VC is a cancer-causing substance came from the B. F. Goodrich Company in January 1974 when it was confirmed that since 1971 three workers at one PVC plastic manufacturing plant had died of angiosarcoma. This is a rare liver cancer disease accounting for about twenty-five deaths annually in the United States. The unusual incidence of three cases of a rare cancer in one locale alerted health officials to probe the association between PVC production and cancer occurrence. By May of 1974 the relationship between VC and cancer was established. By early 1976 the National Cancer Institute confirmed thirty-eight cases of angiosarcoma among workers with a history of occupational exposure, sixteen in the United States and twenty-two in Europe and Canada.

Table III   USES OF VINYL CHLORIDE PLASTIC

Building and construction	pipe, pipe fittings, and conduit flooring siding windows and other rigid profiles swimming pool lines lighting weather stripping rain water systems
Household furnishings	furniture upholstery wall coverings shower curtains, draperies garden hose appliances refrigerator gaskets
Consumer goods	photographic records footwear toys outerwear sporting goods such as beach balls baby pants
Electrical uses	coated wire and cable
Packaging	hardware and pharmaceutical packaging food packaging bottles coatings
Transportation	upholstery and seat covers vinyl tops auto floor mats
Miscellaneous	laminates medical tubing credit cards novelties

Besides being a proven carcinogenic agent, VC is known to induce gene mutations (a mutagenic agent) and is known to cause birth defects (a teratogenic agent). Other ailments as-

Table IV

FDA ANALYSIS OF VINYL CHLORIDE IN COMMERCIAL MOUTHWASHES

Brand	size (oz)	% alcohol	parts per billion of vinyl chloride
Cepacol	7	14	none
Cepacol	14	14	870
Cepacol	32	14	none
Colgate 100	12	17	6,300
Colgate 100	16	17	7,900
Giant Red	16	5	290
Blue	16	15	240
Amber	16	25	trace (est. 30)
Bioris (Dart Drug)	32	5	370
Scorol	32	18.5	770
Biorine	32	25	360

All samples purchased on October 23, 1974, except Colgate 100, which was purchased in 1971.

Source: Health Research Group Petition to the FDA, July 1, 1975.

sociated with VC exposures include mucous membrane dryness, epigastric pain, hepatitis, dyspeptic disturbances (indigestion), chronic bronchitis, ulcers, Raynaud's syndrome, scleroderma (type of skin disease), and allergic dermatitis. German experience with long-term VC exposure (one to three and a half years), not only showed circulatory, skin, and bone disorders, but also deafness, vision failure, giddiness and liver disfunction.

The awareness of toxic effects of VC has led to a series of governmental actions to protect workers, consumers, and inhabitants living near VC and PVC manufacturing plants. The first concern was the workers who made VC and PVC. Labor unions and occupational health officials called for more stringent exposure requirements. Presently the threshold limit for VC is one part per million (1 ppm). However, public-interest groups are pressing for a zero tolerance level saying that there are no levels below which cancer-causing effects do not occur with exposure to such a dangerous carcinogen.

Contrary to initial industry assertions that only small amounts of valuable VC were escaping into the outside environment, one random EPA sampling in mid-1974 showed detectable VC in air near a plant site. Responding to citizen prodding, the EPA carried on a comprehensive monitoring program for the next two years and found average daily VC exposures of less than one part per million (still worthy of concern). But in some twenty-four cases, concentrations ranged between 1 and 3 ppm, with one peak exposure at an astounding 33 ppm. EPA estimated in late 1976 that these levels have been reduced somewhat as a result of the Department of Labor's worker protection standard. However, there are about 4.6 million people living within five miles of existing plants (see Table V).

EPA realized that though no proof of immediate adverse effects to humans near VC plants has been established, the long latency period between exposure to carcinogens and the occurrence of observable effects made it prudent to reduce exposure levels as much as possible. The latency period may be twenty years or more, and VC production fifteen to twenty years ago was 10 per cent of what it is today. Thus the EPA designated VC as the fourth "hazardous air pollutant"* on October 21, 1976, and announced standards limiting air emissions of VC from all existing and new manufacturing plants. Commercial products containing VC already on the market shelf were recalled.

Restrictions on the use of PVC plastic has progressed far slower. As seen in Table III, a number of consumer items in widespread use have PVC packaging. Concern is also focused on food products where the FDA is reviewing leach rates of vinyl chloride from the contaminated PVC wrapping to different types of food and beverage products.

* Asbestos, beryllium, and mercury were so declared on April 6, 1973.

A number of factors affect the degree of exposure from the leaching of VC from PVC plastic:

a) the amount of VC residue in the plastic (this varies according to the polymerization method employed in making it);

b) the type of plastic article (a rigid form may release less than a more flexible variety);

c) the use of the plastic article;

d) the kinds of media in which the plastic material is in contact (water, air, or food);

e) the length of the contact of the plastic with the media (how long a consumer product stands in a confined space);

f) weather and heating factors which might aid in releasing the VC.

Polyvinyl chloride bottles account for 8 per cent of the total plastic bottle market. Of the other 92 per cent about 85 per cent is high-density polyurethane, 3 per cent low-density polyurethane, and 4 per cent other materials. Though there are some restrictions on the use of PVC bottles for alcoholic beverages, still some alcoholic products are on the market with these containers (see Table IV). In June 1975 the production of PVC bottles for food was 57.3 million pounds. PVC water pipe manufactures, another area of major concern, consumes about 400 million pounds of plastic product annually.

Another area of vital importance is the leaching of VC from plastics in storage rooms or automobiles. Automobiles, found to have VC levels of 1 ppm (the level argued as the limit for occupational safety), contain PVC seat coverings. EPA analysts say that considerable amounts of vinyl chloride may accumulate in homes with PVC floor tiles. Since the vinyl chloride is heavier than air, it tends to settle and remain near the floor especially in rooms which are infrequently used.

Table V PLANTS AFFECTED BY REGULATIONS

Producing Company	Plant Location
1. Air products, Inc.	Calvert City, Ky.
2. Air Products, Inc.	Pensacola, Fla.
3. Allied Chemical Co.	Baton Rouge, La.
4. B. F. Goodrich Co.	Calvert City, Ky.
5. B. F. Goodrich Co.	Avon Lake, Ohio
6. B. F. Goodrich Co.	Henry, Ill.
7. B. F. Goodrich Co.	Long Beach, Calif.
8. B. F. Goodrich Co.	Louisville, Ky.
9. B. F. Goodrich Co.	Pedricktown, N.J.
10. Borden, Inc.	Illiopolis, Ill.
11. Borden, Inc.	Leominster, Mass.
12. Borden, Inc.	Geismar, La.
13. Borden, Inc.	Springfield, Mass.
14. Continental Oil Co.	Aberdeen, Miss.
15. Continental Oil Co.	Oklahoma City, Okla.
16. Continental Oil Co.	Westlake, La.
17. Diamond Shamrock Corp.	Delaware City, Del.
18. Diamond Shamrock Corp.	Deer Park, Tex.
19. Dow Chemical Co.	Midland, Mich.
20. Dow Chemical Co.	Freeport, Tex.
21. Dow Chemical Co.	Oyster Creek, Tex.
22. Dow Chemical Co.	Plaquemine, La.
23. Ethyl Corp.	Baton Rouge, La.
24. Ethyl Corp.	Baton Rouge, La.
25. Ethyl Corp.	Houston, Tex.
26. Firestone Tire Co.	Perryville, Md.
27. Firestone Tire Co.	Pottstown, Pa.
28. General Tire Co.	Ashtabula, Ohio
29. Georgia-Pacific Corp.	Plaquemine, La.
30. Goodyear Tire Co.	Niagara Falls, N.Y.
31. Goodyear Tire Co.	Plaquemine, La.
32. Great American Chemical Corp.	Fitchburg, Mass.
33. Jennat Corp.	Torrance, Calif.
34. Jennat Corp.	Tucker, Ga.
35. Jennat Corp.	Somerset, N.J.
36. Keysor-Century Corp.	Saugus, Calif.
37. Monochem, Inc.	Geismar, La.
38. Occidental Petroleum Corp.	Burlington, N.J.
39. Occidental Petroleum Corp.	Hicksville, N.Y.
40. Pantasote Co.	Passaic, N.J.
41. Pantasote Co.	Point Pleasant, W. Va.

Producing Company	Plant Location
42. Pittsburgh Plate Glass Co.	Guayanilla, P.R.
43. Pittsburgh Plate Glass Co.	Lake Charles, La.
44. Robintech, Inc.	Painesville, Ohio
45. Shell Oil Co.	Deer Park, Tex.
46. Shell Oil Co.	Norco, La.
47. Shintech, Inc.	Freeport, Tex.
48. Stauffer Chemical Co.	Long Beach, Calif.
49. Stauffer Chemical Co.	Long Beach, Calif.
50. Stauffer Chemical Co.	Delaware City, Del.
51. Tenneco Chemicals, Inc.	Burlington, N.J.
52. Tenneco Chemicals, Inc.	Flemington, N.J.
53. Tenneco Chemicals, Inc.	Pasadena, Tex.
54. Tenneco Chemicals, Inc.	Pasadena, Tex.
55. Union Carbide Corp.	Texas City, Tex.
56. Union Carbide Corp.	Texas City, Tex.
57. Union Carbide Corp.	South Charleston, W. Va.
58. Vulcan	Geismar, La.

Besides being used in the making of plastics, VC has had another modern use which has been a cause for worry—that of a liquid propellant for aerosol sprays. Following discovery of its occupational dangers, VC was banned as a propellant in pesticide aerosol sprays by the EPA and from other uses by the FDA and the CPSC, notably in paints and hair products.

Citizens find it difficult to identify PVC plastics by inspection, and thus the need for PVC labeling is paramount. Vinylidene chloride, a plastic monomer, closely related to VC, and used in such food wraps as Saran Wrap, has been linked by Dr. Cesare Maltoni, of the University of Bologna, Italy, with the formation of kidney cancers in mice.[8] Dr. E. Cuyler Hammond, of the American Cancer Society, calls this an excellent candidate to be a carcinogen. However, there is no evidence at present of this leaching into food.

Nonhousehold Plastic Dangers

Because homemakers use plastic materials, a number of other pollution dangers occur. These are worth noting so as to understand the connection between indoor, occupational, and general environmental problems.

▪ *Depletion of nonrenewable resources:* The chemical industry is the heaviest drain on energy among the segments of American industry. About one half of the total chemical energy expenditure is used in making synthetic fibers, rubber, and other plastic materials. In fact, a major portion of the petrochemical industry is geared to furnishing raw materials for plastic manufacture. Irresponsibility on the part of producers as well as continuing consumer demand are the causes of this form of resource depletion.

▪ *Dangers in manufacture:* Many of the monomers, such as vinyl chloride, which are used in making plastics, are quite toxic. The large-volume production and consequent emissions threaten both the workers and the people living near production sites. Some major organic chemicals such as ethylene chloride, styrene, benzene, and vinyl chloride are highly toxic and must be controlled through strict environmental controls. These large-scale hazards often illustrate subtle dangers occurring within the home environment.

▪ *Dangers due to disposal:* Plastics will often remain for centuries in the environment. Many American flooded streams and rivers are dotted with plastic bottles and objects. Often these plastic items contain toxic substances which will leach out over a period of time. (Proper disposal of plastic materials is treated in Section J.)

▪ *Dangers in fabrication:* This is not only an occupational health problem but one for the home hobbyist as well (see Section H). Today's artists work with plastics using cements, heating elements for cutting, glues, solvents, and machines which generate dust; they are being exposed to toxic plastic chemicals.

Safety Precautions When Handling Plastics

▪ Plastics can be used for fuel but be cautious about when and where to burn them. Never burn plastics in an open fireplace or for cooking food. Do not breathe vapors from burning plastics.

■ As a general rule do not store food and beverages in plastic containers, especially PVC. Replace with glass and properly glazed pottery. Where possible, reduce the use of food packaging.

■ Never use plastic nonreturnable beverage containers. Alcoholic beverages may cause plasticizers to leach quite easily.

■ Weigh the hazards and benefits associated with mobile homes and campers which use large amounts of plastic materials. Read literature on flammability standards before making purchases.

■ If PVC flooring is being installed, ventilate the living quarters well for one month after installation. The same precaution should apply in a more modified manner for new PVC upholstered couches, chairs, and furnishings.

■ Determine whether one lives within five miles of a PVC or VC processing plant (Table V), and check with local environmental and state regulatory agencies to assure that the air is being monitored in the vicinity.

■ If the label does not indicate what kind of plastic is used in an item, ask the store manager; if he or she does not know, write to the manufacturer. Not all materials with the name "vinyl" on them are PVC products. If uncertain, ask what is meant by the label and whether vinyl chloride is used in making the product.

■ Petition regulatory agencies such as the Consumer Product Safety Commission and the Food and Drug Administration to ban PVC for certain uses or at least require proper labeling of PVC products.

■ When uncertain about the safety of plastic, find out from the following:

1) *National Highway Safety Administration*—sets flammability standards for interior of automobiles and buses.

2) *Federal Aviation Administration*—sets flammability standards for compartments of airplanes.

3) *Federal Trade Commission*—has ordered twenty-six

members of the plastics industry to discontinue marketing products that use the term "self-extinguishing" or "nonburning."

Phasing Down Plastic Use

A responsible environmentalist must remember the following sensitive areas when making judgments about plastic uses:

- Depletion of natural (fossil fuel) resources.
- Occupational health of industry workers.
- Disposal problems whether in combustion or in litter.
- Fumes and dusts arising in fabrication by home furnishers.
- Leaching of solvents and plasticizers upon installment or storage in home or motor vehicle.
- Fire hazards.

Weigh all these factors in making a choice. To state unequivocally that one should not use this or that item is hardly proper. In fact, the use of any item whether natural or synthetic most likely has certain disadvantages for the manufacturer or the laborer, for the consumer, for the general environment. Thus, we should simply reduce consumption for the betterment of our health and our environment. What we do consume we should consume wisely. Here are some points to consider in the use of plastics.

- Small disposable items such as packaging should be made of paper rather than plastic because of heavy energy use in plastic production and the resistance of these synthetics to natural decomposition.
- Where weight is a factor, as in automobiles and in camping and hiking equipment, plastic construction materials may actually be energy saving. Since plasticizers can leach out in the interior of autos, these auto interiors should occasionally be aired out, especially when new.
- In small nondisposable items (information cards, playing

cards, toys, and games) plastics may be more durable and could be legitimately substituted for paper items. Plastic garbage cans are less noisy than metal ones.

■ In choices of natural versus synthetic fibers, use a scale of qualities and select responsibly. Again durability and lack of energy expenditure in laundrying may make synthetics advantageous. (See Section C about flame-retardant safety problems.)

■ Plastic coverings may be justified on a garden in winter or in a compost pile.

■ Use wooden and natural fiber furniture and furnishings when possible for conservation and safety reasons. In some cases the durability or the lack of need for ironing may make synthetic fabrics comparable from an energy viewpoint. Where the home areas are properly ventilated, the safety factor is a less important consideration. But avoid PVC products in homes and auto interiors wherever possible.

REFERENCES

[1] E. A. Boettner, G. L. Weiss, and B. Weiss, "Combustion Products from the Incineration of Plastics," Final Report EPA Grant ♯EC-00386, PUB ♯PB-222-001/0 (Feb. 1973).

[2] Einhoem Petajan et al., "Extreme Toxicity from Combustion Products of a Fire Retarded Polyurethane Foam," *Science,* Vol. 187 (Feb. 28, 1975), pp. 742–44.

[3] Modern Plastics Encyclopedia (1972–73 ed.).

[4] K. P. Shea, "The New Car Smell," *Environment,* Vol. 13 (Oct. 1971), pp. 2–9.

[5] R. J. Jaeger and R. L. Ruben, "Plasticizers from Plastic Devices: Extraction, Metabolism and Accumulation by Biological Systems," *Science,* Vol. 170 (Oct. 23, 1970), pp. 460–61.

[6] J. Cerbulis and J. S. Ard, *Journal of the Association of Official Analytical Chemists,* Vol. 50, 646 (1967).

[7] E. G. Perkins, *Journal of the American Oil Chemists Society,* Vol. 44, 197 (1967).

[8] "Vinylidene Cloride Linked to Cancer," *Chemical and Engineering News,* Feb. 28, 1977, pp. 6–7.

Additional Sources

M. M. Birky, *Review of Smoke and Toxic Gas Hazards in Fire Environment,* Center for Fire Research, National Board of Standards, Washington, D.C.

"Standard Support and Environmental Impact Statement: Emmission Standard for Vinyl Chloride," U. S. EPA Research, Triangle Park, N.C. 27711 (Oct. 1975).

Q. QUICKSILVER (MERCURY) AND OTHER METALS

Homemakers may become exposed to various metals in either a pure or a combined form (see Sections D, H, L). Many of these are not harmful—and may even be beneficial in the amounts present—but others can cause health problems. Some of the more troublesome ones include:

Mercury

Like lead, mercury is both a heavy metal and an old pollutant. In fact mercury production—and perhaps pollution peaked about a century ago due to the widespread use of mercury in precious metal purification. Mercury was once used throughout the felt hat industry and was known to cause mental instability in some hatters, thus giving rise to the expression "mad as a hatter."[1]

For centuries inorganic mercury used in scientific work and in medicines has been known to damage human health. Inorganic mercury poisoning resulting from chronic exposure may manifest itself in adults in inflammation of the gums, metallic taste, diarrhea, mental instability, and tremors. Damage is done to the kidney and also to the liver and the brain.

Organic mercury compounds are newer. They are divided into two classes: the alkyl and aryl salts. The aryl salts seem to break down in the human body into inorganic mercury and behave accordingly. Alkyl mercury compounds, such as methyl mercury, which forms in silt deposits containing mercury compounds, may penetrate brain membranes, damaging them along with other parts of the body such as muscle and tissue. Symptoms are nonspecific at first, such as fatigue, headache, and irritability. Later, tremor, numbness of arms and legs, difficulty in swallowing, deafness, blurred vision, and loss of muscular co-ordination occur. A severe epidemic of "Minamata" disease, organic mercury poisoning, occurred in the late 1960s at Minamata Bay, Japan, where people caught and ate fish contaminated by mercury compounds.

The description of forms of mercurialism is not meant to frighten readers but to alert them to heavy metal health effects. Mercurialism may occur if "low level" exposure is of sufficient magnitude and duration. The best precaution is to reduce and eliminate any excessive intake of mercury, though it is impossible for us to be totally immune from small amounts of mercury in our environment.

Mercury has many industrial uses such as in chloralkali plants and the paper industry. Some mercury escapes and enters the environment, is converted to soluble organic mercury compounds, and enters the food chain by concentrating in such end products as fish, eggs, and meat. Coal-burning releases some mercury in the atmosphere. Each small contribution adds something to our total body burden of mercury.

Mercury may enter the home in many ways such as in mercurial medicines or spilled mercury from a broken thermometer. Phenylmercury acetate (PMA) is the most common form of mercury fungicide and has been used in commercial laundries particularly in diaper services to suppress molds. Also the paper industry uses mercury compounds to protect wood pulp, and traces of mercury may enter the home in the finished paper. However, the major indoor source of mercury pollution is in water-based paints, especially latex types where PMA is added as an in-can product stabilizer to inhibit growth of and attack by bacteria (at concentrations of 50 to 200 parts per million). In exterior paint products PMA is used as a mildewcide and fungicide in ranges of 250 to 2,000 ppm.

There is no necessity for interior latex paints to have mercury materials. Other biocides are known and used. A *Con-*

sumer Reports analysis of a number of latex paints found all but Sherwin-Williams to contain detectable amounts of mercury.[2] However, the mildew resistance of that brand was close to that of Dutch Boy which "had the highest mercury content in the paint film—35 per cent—of all the latexes tested." Sherwin-Williams has been producing mercury-free paints since 1970, and Sears no longer uses mercurials. Likewise, Tournene Paints have been using nonmercurial substitutes with satisfactory results.

As far back as 1957, researchers studied the volatility of mercury from paints used and found none. However, instruments used for minute detection have been greatly improved since that time. A 1972 re-examination of mercury emission's from latex paints showed exposure levels below the maximum acceptable concentration values[3] recommended for an adult for an eight-hour period, but the values were above those recommended by the Soviet Union for twenty-four-hour exposure for an adult.[4] Indoor mercury vapor concentration was many times greater than the ambient outdoors atmosphere. Also the 1972 study concluded that mercury-containing vapors will remain in the indoor atmosphere for a period of time.

The Environmental Protection Agency addressed larger mercury problem by dealing with sources of major pollution first, such as chloralkali plants and mercury pesticides. The agency issued notices of cancellations and tried to determine risks and benefits of numerous mercury compounds and uses. On March 22, 1972, EPA issued a notice of intent to cancel all registrations for mercurial pesticides. Proceedings continued for four years resulting in 4,466 pages of hearing transcript. On February 17, 1976, the agency concluded that the benefits of continued use of mercurial pesticides in paints and coating were not sufficient to outweigh the risks to human beings or environment. EPA added that alternatives *were* available.

On May 28, 1976, EPA Administrator Russell Train reversed the ban on mercury use in water-based paints, saying the original decision overestimated the over-all efficacy of nonmercurial substitutes. While this battle wages on, the best advice is to avoid indoor mercury paints.

Cadmium

Another biologically nonessential trace metal is cadmium. It is basically absent from the human body at birth but accumulates with time, its main effect being kidney malfunction. In Japan the ingestion of large amounts of cadmium in contaminated food and water supplies caused *itai-itai-byo* disease, which is marked by pain, softening of the bones, muscular weakness, and loss of weight.[5,6] Also there is postulated a link between death rates due to cardiovascular diseases and ambient levels of cadmium.[7]

As with many other chemical pollutants, the most acute damages are not to home dwellers but to those engaged in certain occupations. Eleven cases of cadmium intoxication were found in workers exposed to cadmium fumes at a Native American jewelry factory in Albuquerque, New Mexico. These people had symptoms of dyspnea, chest pain, nasal congestion, dry mouth, and dizziness.[8]

Foods are people's largest source of cadmium. Sea foods, grains and grain products, and meats, especially organs such as kidneys, are high natural sources of cadmium.[9] The processing of foodstuffs appears to increase the cadmium concentration. Cadmium-bearing wastes are also present in the water entering either directly or indirectly from land contaminated by airborne fallout, fertilizers, and agricultural chemicals. Thus drinking water may be contaminated with cadmium.

Cadmium concentration in tobacco is relatively high compared to other plants. An appreciable amount of cadmium present in the body may come from smoking or breathing in a smoke-filled room. Cadmium may also enter the home from the air via the particulates emitted by the various industrial processes using cadmium, the refining of zinc ore, the remelting of cadmium plated or galvanized scrap steel. Incineration of cadmium-containing sludges and combustion of coal and other fossil fuels are other sources of airborne cadmium.

Cadmium pigments in paints (usually the yellows and oranges) may also be a source of indoor cadmium pollution. Some paints warn that cadmium pigments are present and should not be used for painting children's toys or furniture reachable by the child. Furthermore, cadmium is sometimes used as a stabilizer in polyvinyl chloride (PVC) plastics. Though there is little reason to expect under normal conditions that household items will add appreciably to the cadmium body burden, homemakers should try to keep the metal out of the home as much as possible.

FROM LABEL ON PAINT CAN

Red, Yellow and Orange may contain cadmium and/or selenium. Do not apply on toys or other children's articles, furniture or interior surfaces of any dwelling or facility which may be occupied or used by children.

Beryllium

Beryllium is a toxic metal which has been responsible for an occupational disease called berylliosis. This severe pneumonia-like lung inflammation can occur after brief intensive exposure, or prolonged exposure to low concentrations of the fumes.[10] Certain mantle-type camp lanterns contain beryllium metal. Most of the beryllium becomes airborne during the first fifteen minutes of use of a mantle. Inhalation of these fumes can be hazardous.

Selenium

Both acute and chronic poisoning may result from inhalation of fumes or vapors of selenium compounds. Symptoms include nausea, vomiting, nervousness, tremor, dizziness, and fatigue. Liver damage also may occur.[10] Seldom are selenium compounds available in the home as such. However, some paint contains certain selenium compounds and should be avoided.

Decreasing Heavy Metal Pollution

▪ Avoid mercury-containing paints, especially for indoor use.

▪ If there is a mercury (liquid) spill in a closed room such as a laboratory or playroom, clean up as much as possible using a sheet of paper or thin scraper to gather together the droplets, and then draw up with a medicine dropper. After removing all visible mercury, scatter flowers of sulfur over the contaminated area.

▪ Be especially careful with mercury-containing medicinals.

▪ Never use cadmium or selenium-containing paints for baby toys or furniture.

▪ Allow new mantle-type camp lanterns to burn outdoors for some time (at least one-half hour) before bringing indoors.

REFERENCES

1 Neville Grant, "Legacy of the Mad Hatter," *Environment*, May 1969, p. 18.
2 "Exterior Trim Paints," *Consumer Reports*, Aug. 1973, p. 506.
3 Maximum allowable concentration is an exposure level recommended by the American Conference of Government and Industrial Hygienists (a time-weighted average of 50 mg/M^3).
4 Donald J. Sibbett et al., "Emission of Mercury from Latex Paints," American Chemical Society, Boston, Apr. 1972.
5 "The Cadmium Crisis," *Newsweek*, Vol. 68 (1971).
6 N. Yamagata and I. Shigematsu, "Cadmium Pollution in Perspective," *Bulletin of the Institute of Public Health*, Vol. 19, I-27 (1970).
7 Robert E. Carroll, "The Relationship of Cadmium in Air to Cardiovascular Disease and Death Rates," *Journal of the American Medical Association*, Vol. 198, No. 3, pp. 177–79.
8 Public Health Service, CDC, Atlanta, EPI-76-28-2 (April 2, 1976).
9 L. Bruckman et al., "Rationale Behind a Proposed Cadmium Air Quality Standard," Air Pollution Control Association, Boston, June 15–20, 1975. Paper 75-31.7.
10 J. M. Stellman and S. M. Daum, *Work Is Dangerous to Your Health* (New York: Vintage Books, 1972).

Additional Sources

J. R. Bertinuson, "Mercury and Its Compounds: Are They Dangerous?" OCAW Occupational Health and Safety Educational Series, Vol. 2, 1973.
M. Fleischer et al., "Environmental Impact of Cadmium," *Environmental Health Perspectives*, Vol. 7, May 1974, p. 253.

R. RADIATION POLLUTION

Radiation is an ominous concept to many. It has many shades of meaning to different people. It is best to begin by explaining the concept of radiation so as to understand what degree of concern is needed with potential sources of indoor radiation pollution.

Most radiation is energy moving through space as invisible electromagnetic waves. The frequency of these waves—the number of waves per second—helps determine the radiation characteristics and how it affects people. Frequency is a measure of classifying the various kinds of radiation (radio-TV, microwaves, infrared, visible light, ultraviolet, X rays, gamma) over a scale, from least energetic to most energetic, called the electromagnetic spectrum.[1]

The electromagnetic spectrum is divided into two principal categories of radiation, higher and lower energy forms—ionizing and nonionizing. Ionizing radiaton (X rays, gamma rays) has the ability to strip electrons from atoms, creating charged particles capable of disrupting life processes. Nonionizing radiation of longer wave length lacks sufficient energy to create charged particles but can disrupt life processes by other mechanisms. Other types of radiation are beta and alpha rays, which are energetic particles that can cause cancer (see later parts in this section).

Much of what is known about radiation's effect on people is the result of information obtained from large amounts of radiation exposure associated with occupational environments. Less is well known about the health effects of lower levels of radiation exposures, levels we are concerned with when

This chart indicates the electromagnetic spectrum, from the least energetic to most energetic.

Power	Radio-Television	Microwaves	Infrared	Visible Light	Ultraviolet	X Rays	Gamma Rays
		• ovens		• sun lamps			
		• radar		• lasers			

Least Energetic

Most Energetic

Non-ionizing Radiation

Ionizing Radiation

Longer Waves

Shorter Waves

speaking of indoor pollution sources. At present, there is no clear evidence that there are threshold levels of radiation below which no harmful health effects will occur. As measures are being taken to safeguard against high-level occupational exposure, the International Symposium of the Bioeffects of New Radiation is drawing attention to the health effects of low-level radiation. This area may prove to be more important to the average citizen.

A number of commonly used consumer appliances are potential sources of long-term, low-level radiation: television sets (both color and black-and-white), fluorescent lights, microwave ovens, heat and sun lamps, and black lights. If homemakers recognize these potential sources of radiation pollution, they can better assess their willingness to subject themselves to these risks and take precautions to minimize or eliminate the dangers.

Television

The television was the first electronic product which was recognized as a source of radiation danger in the home. The problem first surfaced around 1966 when a TV manufacturer discovered that certain large-screen receiver models were emitting X-ray radiation in excess of the National Council on Radiation Protection and Measurements recommended level for exposure. X-ray radiation can be created at high-voltage energies by electrons striking obstacles and then radiating energy, as in the vacuum receiver tubes of TV sets.

A survey was conducted by the Bureau of Radiological Health to determine the extent of public exposure to this potentially harmful radiation. The 1967–68 survey of the Washington, D.C., area revealed that 6 per cent of the black-and-white sets and up to 20 per cent of the color sets tested were found to emit radiation above the recommended maximum.

Reacting in large part to the nationwide concern about X-ray radiation from television sets, Congress enacted the Radiation Control for Health and Safety Act of 1968 to protect the public from *unnecessary* exposure from all electronic products. FDA's Bureau of Radiological Health (BRH) drew up standards which established the maximum allowable levels of radiation emission and regulated industry to comply with those emission levels.

Significant improvements in TV design have been made over the past decade reducing the likelihood of exposure. Old improperly operated television sets still may present potential harmful situations.

There is no absolute guarantee of safety provided by the emission standard. Health experts can make no assurances that even at low levels of radiation no harmful effects are produced. With this in mind it is prudent to view TV from a safe distance. When the problem first surfaced, the Surgeon General recommended at least a seven-foot viewing distance. This precaution still makes good sense.

Microwave Ovens

Thousands of people today use microwave ovens in their homes. By 1980, some estimates say there will be more than 5 million ovens in use in American homes, institutions, and commercial establishments. The wide marketability of these appliances implies that they must unquestionably offer some convenience. For home dwellers some convenience must be counterbalanced by doubts as to the reliability and safety of these products.

Microwaves are low-energy nonionizing radiation between radio waves and infrared heat waves on the energy spectrum. Absorption of microwave energy by many materials produces temperature rise. It is this absorbed energy which cooks the food. Metallic surfaces like oven walls, grids, and screens reflect microwave energy. Glass and nonmetallic wrapping material allow the waves to pass right through.

There are *no* dangers from food cooked in microwave

ovens. Microwaves do not make food or any other materials radioactive. Rather, the reasons for recent concern are:

a) Microwaves can interfere with normal operation of certain heart pacemakers, as well as other electric and electronic items.
b) The thermal effect of exposure to these waves may harm sensitive body cell tissue or organ function.
c) Microwave radiation can cause eye damage and cataracts and is suspected of causing other ailments including nervous exhaustion.
d) Low-energy, nonionizing radiation may also be capable of causing detrimental health effects not fully recognized or understood.

A fundamental concern about microwave ovens is excessive microwave leakage. Such leakage occurs because of defective design or construction, or when safety features required by law fail allowing the oven to operate when not properly closed. Other frequent causes of leakage include maladjustment of the oven door safety locks, abuse of door seals, dirt build-up around door seals, improper servicing, and failure to replace or repair worn-out door hinges or latches.

The Bureau of Radiological Health has issued a standard setting radiation maximum levels for microwave ovens manufactured after October 6, 1971. The standard also requires that ovens be equipped with at least two independently operating safety locks to shut off radiation as doors are opened. BRH has banned the use of ovens manufactured after August 6, 1974, if one or both of the locks fail to function. All ovens must carry labels certifying compliance with federal standards.

In 1974, under pressure from consumer groups, the BRH confirmed that a frequent cause for new radiation leakage was an improper seal around the door. They conducted tests on microwave ovens by placing a thin object between the door and oven so that the door would be closed without force and the oven would operate. The ovens were run at maximum critical conditions with no cooking load to simulate the greatest possible danger. It was found that 89 out of 203 ovens tested emitted levels that violated safety standards, with some registering very dangerously high levels of microwave emission. Consumer groups pushed BRH to require manufacturers to modify oven design to prevent the likelihood of operator exposure to harmful levels of leakage. In spite of this request the BRH determined that the industries' designs were acceptable, and caution labels on the product were sufficient to safeguard the public. Consumer groups objected. Adults were not very likely to receive proper protection and children who frequently use the ovens even less likely; infants can also be exposed to severe risk.

Since October 1975, the labeling caution has been required except when a manufacturer can convince the BRH that the warning is not applicable. In consumer testing of microwave ovens in June 1976, it was found that, as a group, new microwave ovens presented significantly less of a possibility of radiation leakage than did the best of the 1973 models.

In January 1977, the FDA discovered that 36,000 Hotpoint Versatronic and Cook Center ovens manufactured from November 1973 through October 1975 were possibly emitting excess radiation because of deterioration of door seals. As a result, General Electric had one year to locate and notify owners and make the repairs in the owners' homes without charge.[2]

A fundamental concern for exposure to microwave radiation from ovens remains. The BRH standards are being criticized in light of growing scientific concern about the health effects of low-level radiation.

Sun Lamps, Black Lights, and Other Lighting

The skin and eyes are sensitive to the radiations of near-visible frequencies including ultraviolet, near ultraviolet, and infrared. Ultraviolet (UV) radiations are emitted by black lights, broken or unshielded mercury vapor lamps, and fluorescent lights as well as by what is termed "UV lights." UV radiation wave lengths fall far below the level visible to the eye. These wave lengths are responsible for two of the most well known radiation effects—sunburn and snow blindness. In addition, exposure to UV radiation has been linked to incidence of skin cancer.

The cornea and the ocular media in the eye absorb UV radiation. The radiation causes photochemical changes, resulting in cell deaths at sufficient exposures. Because of the low metabolic level of the lens, damage is slow and cumulative. The lens contains no pain receptors to give warning. These minute reactions go unnoticed for years until their dark chemical products have accumulated as recognizable cataracts.

Black lights, and to some extent fluorescent lights, emit another invisible range of radiation, near ultraviolet (NUV). Black lights cause the eye lens to fluoresce, resulting in blurred vision, headaches, feelings of tiredness and discomfort. Long-term effects of NUV exposure probably include cataract formation and retarded cell growth, but study of this wavelength range has only just begun.[3] Occupational safety standards have been set for UV exposure, and the Bureau of Radiological Health (of the FDA) has expressed "deep concern" over black light radiation. However, no manufacturers' standards have yet been set for nonindustrial black lights.

Amber sunglasses best absorb the damaging UV frequencies and should be worn if exposure to black light cannot be avoided. Medicines commonly used for treatment of glaucoma sensitize the lens to darkening, so that glaucoma patients should be especially cautious.

Danger from the infrared (wave lengths beyond 700nm) radiations of sun lamps is great. Because sun lamps produce little visible radiations, it is easy to belittle the seriousness of manufacturers' warnings to limit exposure and keep eyes covered. Skin and retinal burns result from misuse of sun lamps.

Transmission Equipment

Microwaves coming from radar, television transmitters, and other electronic equipment may touch the lives of many home dwellers.[4,5] This came to light with reports that the Soviet microwave bombardment of the American Embassy in Moscow was making the people inside sick. The ambassador himself repeatedly suffered nausea and bleeding in the eyes.

National defense detection and guidance systems also emit microwaves. Dr. Milton Zaret, on hearing that Finns living in two southeastern districts were experiencing the world's highest rate of heart attacks, suggested that powerful Russian missile-detecting radars might be partly to blame. It has been found that the closer the Finns live to the border, the more heart attacks they suffer.[5]

Fire Detectors

Smoke and fire detectors are a new safety product whose installation may soon be required in all homes. While detectors that use a photoelectric device appear to offer no pollution problems, ionization-type detectors use radioactive materials that make them a potential hazard, especially when it comes to disposing of them. All battery-powered detectors contain radioactive materials while most alarms that are plugged or wired into house power are not radioactive types.

The radioactive materials in the ionization-type alarms are confined in metal containers designed to keep exposure to radioactivity to negligible levels. The container is supposed to withstand high temperatures and various accident conditions. While the designs have been tested to meet some safety criteria, only time and experience will tell whether the designs and quality of construction are fully adequate for radiation protection. Clearly, these devices should not be in the hands of casual tinkerers or curious children.

The radioactivity in these alarms lasts for thousands of years—centuries longer than the usual household device or even the houses they protect. The radioactive devices for that reason should not be casually thrown away into the environment. Similar materials produced in nuclear reactors must be carefully buried deep underground. The recommended disposal method is to return the device to the manufacturer, presuming it continues in business. The instruction books for some of these detectors do not mention proper disposal or even the presence of radioactive materials, leaving this vital information to a small label inside the detector. It remains a serious and presently unanswerable question whether homeowners or local fire officials will in fact properly dispose of these devices.

The radioactive fire alarms, in general, react slowly to smoky, smoldering fires which account for 75 per cent of home fire deaths. According to *Consumer Reports*, only one model of the radioactive devices reacts as sensitively to smoke as the photoelectric detectors.[6,7] If only one detector is used, the photoelectric type protects better than almost all radioactive alarms against the majority of fatal home fires, and presents none of the potential hazards of the radioactive devices. If radioactive alarms are added for a more complete fire warning system, careful handling and disposal are essential.

Glasses and Teeth

With the growing concern about the possibility of low-level radiation, two areas needing special caution are false teeth and eyeglasses. Traces of uranium have been mixed into the porcelain powder from which false teeth are made for over forty years. Concern was raised in the United States after the National Protection Board of Great Britain found such teeth made in England exposed the mouth to almost double the acceptable level of radiation. False teeth worn by an estimated 50 million Americans are radioactive. While they are regarded as not radioactive enough to cause harm, the FDA has found them radioactive enough to be considering an order to reduce uranium permitted in false teeth. The industry on its own has reduced uranium in porcelain by half.

One out of every ten American eyeglasses is radioactive. While levels are low some risk may accrue. Lenses are radioactive because zirconium oxides contaminated with radioactive elements are mixed into glass to improve optical resolution quality. The Army discovered this phenomenon when it found military equipment to be radioactive. They provided this information to the AEC Health Services Laboratory which found 91 of 440 test samples to be radioactive in varying degrees. A person wearing a contaminated pair of glasses sixteen hours a day could receive a radiation dose close to eight times higher than permitted by law.

Precautions

Natural radiation dangers cannot be eliminated, but we should guard against man-made radiation through a number of practical steps:

- If suspicious of having a faulty television set, have it checked for radiation leakage. It is worth the extra expense.
- Follow microwave oven manufacturer's instruction manual for recommended operating procedures and precautions.
- Examine the oven for evidence of shipping damage.
- Never insert objects around the door seal.
- Do not tamper with or inactivate the oven safety interlocks.
- Frequently clean oven cavity, door, and seals with mild detergent. Do not use scouring pads, steel wool, or other abrasives.
- Have oven regularly serviced by a qualified serviceperson for signs of wear, damage, or tampering.

- Stay at least an arm's length away from the front of the oven while it is on.
- For ovens manufactured prior to standards set October 6, 1971, the user should switch the oven off before opening the door.
- Follow instructions for use of sun or heat lamps.
- Don't install black lights in the home or workplace.
- Don't oversunbathe under either natural or artificial lighting.
- Shield ultraviolet lamps so that one cannot look directly into them.
- Don't overuse fluorescent lighting.
- Install opaque plastic over fluorescent lights. This sufficiently screens out the UV wave lengths which irritate the skin of UV-sensitive people.[8]
- Return faulty or discarded ionization-type fire detection equipment to manufacturer or to fire department.
- Home dwellers near powerful transmitters can do little more than move.
- Each citizen should learn about the potential hazards of microwave radiation. The EPA and other government agencies should be petitioned to monitor radiation levels in homes, especially near locations of sophisticated defense electronic equipment.

REFERENCES

[1] *FDA Consumer,* Sept. 1974, DHEW Publication No. (FDA) 75-8014, Washington, D.C.

[2] Staff Reporter, *Wall Street Journal,* Jan. 12, 1977.

[3] W. F. Van Pelt et al., "A Review of Selected Bioeffects Thresholds for Various Spectral Ranges of Sight," U. S. Department of Health, Education, and Welfare, Rockville, Md., June 1973.

[4] P. Brodeur, "A Reporter at Large (Microwaves)," *New Yorker,* Dec. 13, Dec. 20, 1976.

[5] S. S. Rosenfeld, "Radiation Sickness: Medical and Political," Washington *Post,* Jan. 7, 1977.

[6] "Smoke Detectors," *Consumer Reports,* Oct. 1976, p. 555.

[7] "Are Smoke Detectors Hazardous?," *Consumer Reports,* Jan. 1977, p. 52.

[8] A. Kobza et al., "Photosensitivity to White Fluorescent Lamps," *British Journal of Dermatology,* Vol. 89, 4 (Oct. 1973), pp. 351–59.

Additional Sources

"Radioactive Wastes," U. S. Environmental Protection Agency, Office of Public Affairs, Washington, D.C. 20460.

W. Moore, Jr., "Biological Aspects of Microwave Radiation: A Review of Hazards," Food and Drug Administration, Rockville, Md. 20852, July 1968.

"The Hazards of Ionizing Radiation," *Environmental Action Bulletin 7,* October 30, 1976.

P. W. Laws, "Medical and Dental X-rays, A Consumer's Guide to Avoiding Unnecessary Radiation Exposure," Public Citizen Health Research Group, Washington, D.C. 20036.

K. Z. Morgan, "Reducing Medical Exposure to Ionizing Radiation," *American Industrial Hygiene Association Journal,* May 1975.

"Is Microwave Leakage Hazardous?" *Consumer Reports,* Vol. 41, 319 (June 1976).

S. SOLVENTS

It is said that Thrasyas, the father of botany, was so skilled in the preparation of drugs, that he knew how to compound a poison which would . . . kill by a lingering illness. Theophrastus speaks of this poison, and says its force could be so modified as to occasion death in two, three, or six months, or even at the end of a year or two years; and the writings of Plutarch, Tacitus, Quintilian and Livy are full of instances of what seem to be the same kind of slow and occult poisoning.[1]

A solvent is a substance which dissolves another substance. The most familiar and universal of solvents is water. Water dissolves minerals and carries them in sap to the upper reaches of plants. In our cooking it dissolves sugar and salt.

While solvents may be gases or solids, our common experience is with liquids. In this section we shall deal with nonaqueous organic solvents prepared by the chemical industry for use in paint products (marine, epoxy, enamel or primer paints, stains, varnishes, shellacs, lacquers, thinners, and paint removers).

The particular pure or mixed solvent in a product is chosen because of a number of considerations:

economics—the expense of the material, where found in nature, amount of energy required, and number of manufacturing operations are important.

flammability—some solvents, like fluorinated and chlorinated hydrocarbons are relatively noncombustible, but some, like the ethers, are highly combustible.

volatility—related to the last property. The solvent must evaporate rapidly enough to allow paint and similar materials to dry in a reasonable time, and yet not so rapidly as to prevent even applications.

safe storage—some solvents decompose upon standing, and some need special transportation equipment or refrigeration.

solubility—some solvents will dissolve fats and oils easily while others will not.

From the above-listed properties it is evident why water is considered such a good solvent and why latex and other water-based paints have become so popular. Water is quite cheap; it has fairly good solvent properties for most nonoil-based materials; it does not burn; it is stored easily; and it evaporates in a reasonable time. Another property which has become important both in industry and in the home is the toxicity of the solvent, and here again the health and environmental consciousness of the consumer increases the popularity of water as a paint solvent.

The most commonly used hydrocarbon solvents employed in the formulation of paint products fall into the following general classifications:

Petroleum Ethers (Including Ligroins)

Petroleum distillate fractions are highly volatile, relatively cheap, and have fairly good solvent properties. These are generally highly flammable. They are not as toxic as aromatic compounds.

Aromatics

Simple aromatic compounds such as toluene, benzene, and xylenes are generally produced by reformulation processes at petroleum refineries. These are used in a host of synthetic chemical processes, especially in making plastics, high-octane gasoline, and synthetic fibers, and thus have a high demand. They are quite toxic and yet are very good solvents for paints.

Recent studies have implicated benzene as a possible cancer-causing compound.[2] On May 31, 1977, EPA listed benzene as the fifth hazardous air pollution agent requiring special regulation. Its severe toxicity has caused it to be used less frequently in paint formulation. However, some thinners still have benzene in them. Xylenes have a narcotic effect; intoxication can cause mental disorientation and depressed motor response. Xylenes like benzene have variable effects on the liver, kidney, and gastrointestinal tract.

Terpenes

Turpentine, depentine, pine oil, etc., have been known for many years for their solubility properties, which suits them well for use in paints. While not as toxic as many of the aromatic compounds, these do have resulting ill effects especially when ingested and must be handled with care. They are obtained commercially from natural resins and essential oils.

Alcohols

Alcohols such as methanol, ethanol, or propanol are usually volatile, pungent, colorless liquids. They are closer to water in solubility properties and are generally less toxic than aromatics. However, their ingestion may lead to serious complications.

Most alcohols are irritating to the eyes and upper respiratory tract. Allyl alcohol, in particular, can cause permanent eye damage. Alcohols may also damage the liver and kidneys, and sometimes the central nervous system. Methanol, which is often mistaken for ethanol (drinking alcohol), can lead to death if swallowed.

Esters

Esters such as ethyl acetate or butyl acetate are usually pungent colorless liquids with fruity smells. They are chemically comparable to inorganic salts and are formed from the chemical combination of organic acids and alcohols. They vary in volatility and are often quite expensive. Various acetates are frequently used in lacquer and paint solvents. They are generally more severe in toxicity than the alcohols. Exposure leads to irritation of the eyes, nose, and throat; these compounds have a narcotic effect. Prolonged inhalation may also cause pulmonary edema.

Ethers

"Cellosolves" and ethyl ether are excellent solvents for oils and resins. Requiring sophisticated chemical processes, these compounds are quite expensive. They vary considerably in volatility and flammability.

Ketones

Ketones such as acetone and methyl ethyl ketone are generally excellent solvents but vary considerably from low to moderate toxicity.

Halogenated Hydrocarbons

Methylene chloride, trichloroethane, carbon tetrachloride, chloroform, fluorinated hydrocarbons, etc., are highly used industrial solvents as well as dry-cleaning fluids. These materials do not burn, but they do have some severe toxic properties.

Effects

In 1973 an estimated 11,848 injuries resulting in acute emergency treatment were associated with paint products. A majority of these injuries resulted from acute poisoning and a number from chemical burns, most frequently damaging the eyes. Children are the most common victims of acute exposure to solvents. NIESS reports that 72 per cent of injuries requiring emergency medical care due to poisonous ingestion of paint and varnish thinners occurred among children four years of age or younger. Carelessness, especially with open containers where paint brushes are left soaking, is a major cause. Another is transferring solvents to unlabeled or mislabeled containers.

The eyes are a major target area for careless use of solvents. People often refuse to wear goggles. Solvents are splattered or reach the eyes by the hands and soaked objects. Skin contact with the solvents can cause dermal irritation or dermatitis. Some solvents enter the body through skin contact because they dissolve oily materials so easily. Inhalation of vapors from solvents can have an irritant effect on mucous membranes of the respiratory passage and can cause nausea, headaches, muscular weakness, and drowsiness. It can also impair motor response, lead to a loss of co-ordination contributing to increased accident proneness, and can cause mental disorientation and confusion. Severe intoxication may even lead to death.

One of the prime body organ targets of many solvents is the liver. This organ is the body's major chemical plant and is vital to life because it removes poisonous chemicals from the blood and aids in the digestion of food. When harmful chemicals enter the bloodstream, they go through the liver and are generally broken down into harmless chemicals and filtered out of the body by the kidneys. This process is called detoxification. If the toxic chemicals are not broken down by the liver, they may recirculate through the body. The liver can be severely damaged by many solvents which destroy liver cells. The destroyed cells are replaced by scarred tissue, which impairs the functioning of the liver. When enough liver cells are destroyed, the organ can no longer function properly. One symptom of liver disease is jaundice—a yellowing of the skin and eyes.

Besides toxic effects on human beings in the home, the presence of solvents in the atmosphere can enhance smog conditions in urban areas. Los Angeles County has measured the amounts of volatile solvent chemicals in the air and found that reduction of these solvents would significantly reduce the levels of smog in the area. Thus the county has enacted legislation regulating the degree of volatility of paints so as to reduce this source of pollution. Solvents such as benzene and carbon tetrachloride have been banned.[2]

Halogenated hydrocarbons are produced in large quantities in modern chemical plants and are often quite persistent in the environment, resisting ordinary breakdown to less harmful components. Extended exposure to these widely used solvents can cause liver and kidney damage. Many may stimulate the body's production of adrenaline, which may cause an irregular heartbeat, dizziness, fainting, or sudden death.

Methylene chloride, a common organic solvent, is used extensively in paint removers. It has been found to be metabolized *in vivo* to produce carboxyhemoglobin (COHb), which reduces the flow of blood oxygen in the human body. Exposure to methylene chloride vapors for two to three hours causes COHb levels of 5 to 15 per cent,[3,4] stressing victims with cardiac or pulmonary disease. One group reported levels of 26 to 40 per cent COHb after a six-hour furniture-stripping session in a large single-room basement with the outside doors and windows closed.[5]

The dangers of methylene chloride are more evident in the reported death of a retired man who had undertaken the hobby of refinishing furniture. The man suffered a heart attack and was hospitalized after stripping a piece of furniture. No connection was made between solvent level in the workplace and the attack. After recovery he returned to his hobby only to be once again admitted to the hospital with a more severe heart attack. Again no association was made between the use of paint remover and his illness. Six months later he again recovered enough to return to his hobby, and two hours after emerging from the workshop suffered a fatal attack. Methylene chloride was the culprit.

The case led to a study of the effects of the compound on healthy subjects. Researchers have found the carbon monoxide level in the blood to be related to exposure to methylene chloride paint remover vapors. Duration of low oxygen blood levels (higher carbon monoxide levels) and heart stress were extended by concurrent exposure to methanol, another common paint remover ingredient. Thus the potentially dangerous period can extend several hours beyond the exposure period.

As of yet the Consumer Product Safety Commission has not required a warning of the dangers of paint removers to be placed on the labels. Meanwhile, hobbyists and others, especially those with higher potential risk of heart trouble, will be threatened by these solvents.

Another area of concern when dealing with paint solvents is that of soft contact lenses. The same absorbency that allows contact lenses to retain medication can prove dangerous in the presence of strong vapors from solvents. Instead of being washed away quickly by tears, chemicals are absorbed and held against the eye until the lenses have been removed. Thus the time of exposure can cause considerable eye damage or irritation.

Solvent Precautions

Many solvents do not have adequate substitutes. It is best to treat them with respect when used.

▪ Read labels carefully before mixing and handling paint solvents.

▪ Use adequate equipment for body protection such as rubber gloves and goggles.

▪ Think ahead about how solvents will be used and know the first-aid remedies in case of accident.

▪ Don't smoke when using solvents, even when they are noncombustible.

▪ Respect body health and weaknesses. If lungs, skin, or heart might not be able to endure the insult of the paint remover or solvent, either ask a healthier friend to do the job or simply omit it. The painting operation may not be necessary, and there might be other ways of beautifying the home surroundings.

▪ When painting can be done outdoors (by moving furniture out), wait until weather is suitable. Work indoors only when ventilation is adequate, which means a very large airy room with a current of dry air. Don't work on hot or muggy days when the solvent build-up indoors could be appreciable. Turn off the air-conditioner and open windows. Use an exhaust fan.

▪ Don't overuse solvents, paint removers, and antirust agents—a tendency among many amateur painters. The same precaution also applies to paint thinners used to clean brushes. This cleaning operation is a prime occasion for solvent inhalation and contact.

▪ If the ingredients are not listed on the container, write to the company and ask what the product components are. Also contact the Consumer Product Safety Commission and the Federal Trade Commission about the lack of proper labeling.

▪ Don't work with solvents when wearing soft contact lenses.

▪ For persons with cardiac problems avoid using methylene chloride.

▪ Air out a newly painted room thoroughly. Don't sleep in such rooms for a few days until the smell has disappeared.

▪ Warn those using paint solvents about the dangers attached. People can seriously impair their health and suffer fatal consequences for lack of knowledge.

▪ Keep children out of the workplace where solvents are stored. Seal paint cans properly. Recognize that many children like the smell of certain paint solvents, and that aerosol varieties have been the source of sniffing abuses.

■ Get rid of aerosol spray paints. When the job involves painting in difficult places, do it some other way—for instance, by using an atomizer or small paint brush, by dipping the object in a pan of paint, or by partial painting.

■ Don't leave open containers of nonaqueous paint solvents for soaking paint brushes. It is better to clean immediately after use and then to place the brush in water to prevent unremoved paint from hardening the bristles. When difficult cleaning problems develop, use a cheap or old brush which can be discarded.

■ Never keep benzene-solvent mixtures around the house.

■ Label any used solvent properly and store safely. Don't use containers which may be mistaken for beverages.

Solvent Substitutes

■ Use water-based paint whenever possible. While some of these paints do have toxic substances present, they lack volatile solvents such as chlorinated hydrocarbons (methylene chloride, etc.) or petroleum distillates (xylene, benzene, toluene) which may be a severe threat to the human health of the painter or home dweller.

Scotch Brand Contact Cement (3M Corporation) "not to be sold in NY state"

DANGER: extremely flammable. Vapors may cause flash fire. Harmful if swallowed (or fatal). Vapor may ignite explosively. Prevent build-up of vapors. Open all windows and doors and cross-ventilation. Do not smoke or ignite any flame. Extinguish all flames and pilot lights. Turn off stoves, etc. . . . .

CONTAINS: petroleum distillates, acetone, toluene. Avoid prolonged breathing of vapors and prolonged repeated contact with skin. Avoid contact with eyes. Do not induce vomiting. Call physician immediately. Keep out of reach of children.

REFERENCES

[1] W. L. Chandler, "Physiological Action of Nitrobenzene Vapor on Animals," New York Agricultural Experiment Station, Cornell University Memoir, 20 (1919), pp. 405–72.

[2] T. J. Elias, Occupational Health, County of Los Angeles, Department of Health Services. Personal communication (1976).

[3] R. D. Steward, T. N. Fisher, M. T. Hosko, et al., "Carboxyhemoglobin Elevation After Exposure to Dichloromethane," Science, Vol. 176 (1972), pp. 295–96.

[4] R. D. Steward and C. L. Hake, "Paint Remover Hazard," Journal of the American Medical Society, Vol. 235 (1976), pp. 398–401.

[5] P. L. Langehennig, R. A. Seeler, and E. Berman, "Paint Removers and Carboxyhemaglobin," New England Journal of Medicine, Vol. 295 (Nov. 11, 1976), p. 1,137.

T. TOBACCO SMOKE

Over 50 million Americans, or one quarter of the total population, smoke cigarettes, pipes, or cigars. It seems that for those seeking the pristine tobacco smoke-free indoor environment, there are few places to go. This has given rise to a new breed of environmentalists—perhaps the first organized group seeking to curb indoor pollution—who are demanding their nonsmoker rights. It is quite common now to find plane and bus passengers and store and restaurant customers insisting on a smoke-free environment. At the beginning of various meetings people will ask that smokers either move to certain sections or refrain from smoking altogether. Social pressures which entice people to smoke now compete with nonsmokers' counterpressures.

Smoke in the Home

Smoke is more than a nuisance. Some 30 to 40 million Americans are thought to be sensitive to tobacco smoke and to react adversely to varying amounts of it in the air. Beyond the discomfort that many people experience—the burning of eyes from cigar smoke and the choked feeling in a cigarette smoke-filled room—there are the more serious health risks which afflict the smoker. These include higher risks of lung cancer, emphysema, and heart disease.

The health of the nonsmoker is also compromised by exposure to tobacco smoke. The nonsmoker—often without choice—becomes a passive smoker and pays a penalty due to pollution by the smoker. Effects of smoke to the smoker have been well known and documented, though perhaps not enough to motivate many smokers to abandon their cigarettes. The health impact on the nonsmoker is generally less well recognized, and so there has been a neglect of nonsmoker rights until recent years.

A burning cigarette produces both mainstream and sidestream smoke. The physiological effects of tobacco smoke on the smoker and the nonsmoker are distinguished by the exposure to each of these types of smoke. Mainstream smoke comes from the butt of the cigarette and is directly inhaled into the lungs. It primarily affects smokers. Sidestream smoke coming from the tip of the cigarette affects both smoker and nonsmoker. To some extent mainstream smoke, when exhaled by the smoker, enters the atmosphere and can also be breathed by the nonsmoker.

Mainstream smoke contains an intense dose concentration of particulate matter, tobacco tars, and nicotine, which enter into the lung area of the inhaling smoker. Tobacco tar is well known to tobacco workers in the field, who find their hands turn black with a sticky goo after handling tobacco for only a few minutes. When these tars enter the lungs through inhalation of the smoke, some of the identifiable cancer-causing chemicals are left on the lung tissue. Mainstream smoke may be accurately designated as "carcinogenic."

Sidestream smoke fills the surrounding air as the cigarette burns. An average cigarette produces about twenty-four seconds of mainstream smoke, yet burns for twelve minutes, all the while generating sidestream smoke which goes into the surrounding air. As a smoker inhales, two thirds of the smoke goes into the surrounding environment and becomes a significant source of pollution to the nonsmoker. The amount of smoke from cigars and pipes is even higher.

While sidestream smoke is less intense in particulate matter than is mainstream smoke, sidestream smoke contains 2 times more tar and nicotine, 3 times as much 3,4-benzopyrene (a carcinogenic aromatic compound found in smoke), 5 times as much carbon monoxide, 50 to 100 times as much ammonia, and up to 2 times as much cadmium from the smoldering tip of the cigarette as does mainstream smoke.

The criteria for establishing smoke as carcinogenic are based on dose-response levels of cancer-causing substances in the air. While the secondary effects of smoke on the non-smoker probably do not cause greater risk of lung cancer, emphysema, or cardiovascular heart disease, carcinogenic and cocarcinogenic chemical compounds do exist in all tobacco smoke, and the threshold level required to increase risk of ill health is not clearly defined. While high risks are associated with high concentrations of particulate matter, it is not known whether low risks are associated with lower concentrations, as from sidestream smoke. Exposure of even lesser concentrations of this particulate matter may have some debilitating effect on a number of people. Thus the detrimental effect of sidestream smoke on the health of smoker and nonsmoker alike is of keen interest to conscientious indoor environmentalists.

Factors which can influence the dose exposure of the to-bacco smoke to the nonsmoker include: the amount of smoke produced, the depth of inhalation, the number of cigarettes smoked, and, time spent in smoking. Perhaps another significant factor is the type of tobacco used in the cigarette.

Dr. Gio B. Gori, of the National Cancer Institute, says that if smokers were willing to use low-hazard cigarettes, the intake of dangerous cigarette components might be lowered to limits that "could make the resulting risk of disease virtually undetectable."[1] From dose-response analyses of several scientific studies, Gori has estimated daily intake limits for certain components of smoke. These daily limits are about 150 milligrams of tar, 10 milligrams of nicotine, 950 micrograms of nitrogen oxides, 1,500 micrograms of hydrogen cyanide, and 450 micrograms of acrolein. Carbonylhemoglobin values—which relate to the intake of carbon monoxide—should not exceed normal base-line values of 4.8 per cent.

Through new growing, harvesting, and curing practices,

smoke dilution devices, and tobacco extraction and transformation methods, "low-hazard" cigarettes can be produced. The appropriate technology has been developed.[2] Gori says that if low-hazard cigarettes are developed by 1990, they may save 200,000 to 600,000 lives per year. He reasons that antismoking education has met with only partial success and it is important to protect individuals who continue to smoke despite all warning.

The most preponderant response by nonsmokers to tobacco smoke is one of general irritation. Of 271 people surveyed in one study on the effects of tobacco in passive smokers—persons involuntarily inhaling smoke in the ambient air—68 per cent complained of headaches, 47 per cent of sneezing, 50 per cent of running noses, 44 per cent of nasal obstruction, 47 per cent of a flare-up of sinusitis, 48 per cent of coughing, 44 per cent of wheezing, and 73 per cent of one or other eye symptom such as watery, burning, red, smarting, and itching eyes.[3]

General effects on passive smokers can also be more serious. Parents who smoke can aggravate symptoms and even trigger attacks of asthma in their children who may be asthmatic. Nonasthmatic children whose parents smoke suffer respiratory illnesses such as bronchitis and pneumonia twice as frequently as young children whose parents do not smoke.[4] For the expectant mother who smokes in her later stages of pregnancy, the likelihood of her child being born small and weak is markedly increased. The fetus may suffer from oxygen debilitation. Carbon monoxide forces oxygen out of the mother's red blood cells and cuts down the supply of oxygen to the baby. Other maladies such as bronchitis and angina pectoris are found to plague nonsmokers because of exposure to tobacco smoke.

Nearly three thousand compounds have been identified in cigarette smoke, but only a few have been related to health hazards. Nicotine is a toxic substance found only in tobacco smoke. It is a poisonous alkaloid which is used for insecticides. Nicotine is a cardiovascular constrictor which is potentially very hazardous after an exerting activity. It has been related to atherosclerosis cardiovascular disease, and is especially harmful to persons with existing respiratory problems. Nicotine increases the likelihood of ventricular arrhythmia, blood clotting of arterial walls, higher blood pressure, and faster pulse. Nonsmoker blood level content of nicotine has often doubled in rooms with smokers.

Another material found in tobacco smoke is nitrogen dioxide, a sharply irritating gas that can damage the lungs. Considered by some as dangerous in amounts exceeding 5 parts per million (ppm), it has been recorded in amounts of 250 ppm in average cigarette smoke. It is known to cause emphysemalike diseases in rats and to destroy cellular and subcellular structures. Other nitrogen oxides also play a role in the development of pulmonary diseases.

Eye irritation from tobacco smoke is caused by the chemical acrolein. This yellowish or colorless pungent liquid has been used as a tear gas in chemical warfare. Highly toxic, its threshold level is 0.1 ppm.

In addition, tobacco smoke contains ammonia, hydrogen sulfide, benzene, formaldehyde, acetylene, ethylene, methane, ethane, propane, and other compounds which are asphyxiants. A number of insecticides are present in small amounts which have been carried over from the tobacco-growing process. Vinyl chloride and 3,4-benzopyrene, which are carcinogenic agents, are present in tobacco smoke in small amounts. Highly toxic hydrogen cyanide is also present.

Smoking generates very hazardous levels of poisonous carbon monoxide gas. Carbon monoxide is dangerous because it combines with the hemoglobin in the blood to produce a complex called carbonylhemoglobin which interferes with the normal oxygen-carrying ability of the blood. The lack of sufficient oxygen can increase stress on the heart, impair reflexes, and threaten the health of sufferers of chronic bronchitis, pulmonary and coronary heart diseases. Carbon monoxide remains in the blood for three or four hours.

Thirty minutes in a smoke-filled room will cause an increase in the carbon monoxide level of a nonsmoker's blood pressure and pulse rate. Researchers have found that smoking seven cigarettes in one hour in a ventilated room created a carbon monoxide level of 20 ppm. Federal Air Quality Standards sets the outdoor limit concentrations of carbon monoxide at 9 ppm. Smoking ten cigarettes in an enclosed space such as a car can produce an air carbon monoxide level of 90 ppm. The carbon monoxide concentration level of a nonsmoker doubled in the first hour and redoubled in the second hour. Unlike oxygen the carbon monoxide persists in the body hours after a nonsmoker leaves a smoke-filled environment.

These carbon monoxide levels impair the ability of some persons to distinguish relative brightness, and to judge intervals of time. Carbon monoxide can cause distress to a person already suffering from a respiratory disorder, and can increase the level of physiologic stress of the heart of both healthy persons and victims of high-risk heart ailments.

What to Do About Tobacco Smoke (and Smokers)

For those whose "tobacco smoke problems" are caused by the habits of others the following hints may be helpful:

■ If there are smokers in the house, declare smoke-free zones where fresh air is sacred. Perhaps the smokers should be relegated to the bedroom or a special smoking room set apart for them.

■ If no one smokes in the house, make some "no smoking" signs and install them at strategic locations around the house. Discard ash trays and learn to say no when someone asks whether they may smoke. This should also apply to marijuana-smoking visitors.

■ If persons do smoke in your home, systematically air out the house so that the outdoors might dilute the foul atmosphere.

■ Make a fuss about smokers who violate passenger vehicles and no smoking areas of restaurants. Make a scene, if necessary, to assert nonsmoker rights. Ask public establishments to create no-smoking zones.

▪ Support:

Action on Smoking and Health (ASH)
P.O. Box 19556
2000 H St. N.W.
Washington, D.C. 20006

Group Against Smoking Pollution (GASP)
Greenbelt, Md. 20770

▪ For smokers, try tips to stop found in "Danger—
Cigarettes," produced by the American Cancer Society; if
you cannot find the will power to stop, at least smoke
fewer cigarettes, choose a brand with low tar and nicotine,
don't smoke an entire cigarette, and take fewer draws and
shallower puffs.[5]

Nonsmokers' Rights: Recommendations of the Third World Conference on Smoking and Health (Excerpted)

Exposure to tobacco smoke is aggravating and sometimes
harmful to nonsmokers and adds to the problems of those
who have recently stopped smoking. Restricting areas where
smoking is permitted in public places will provide important
incentives to those who are trying to stop smoking and to
others who have stopped and require support to remain free
of tobacco. Therefore, it is recommended that, as a part of
national health policy, the use of tobacco should be viewed as
behavior that is destructive to self and to others, and to im-
plement this aspect of policy by appropriate legislation, regulation, and voluntary action, there should be a deliberate and
systematic enlargement and guarantee of nonsmoking areas in
all public places including places of employment. Nonsmokers
should always have the right to work in smoke-free
areas. . . .

That it be recognized that unrestricted tobacco smoking in
enclosed areas creates a health hazard for millions of persons
with a wide variety of medical susceptibilities and conditions,
and causes physical irritation and discomfort to the majority

of nonsmokers and therefore, that legislation be introduced, and that existing legislation be enforced, to protect the right of the nonsmokers and to shield them from the hazards and irritations of passive smoking; and that such legislation include the banning of smoking in public places such as cinemas, libraries, shops, trains, buses, and conference rooms.

That all federal and state governments world-wide immediately take steps to restrict smoking in all enclosed public places where people work or play.

That business, industry, and employee organizations should accept responsibility for their employees' health by providing health education programs regarding mortality and disability related to cigarette smoking, and that smoking cessation and nonsmokers' rights activities should be included in these programs.

That programs aimed at creating a social environment in which smoking is unacceptable be developed and implemented.

That all organizations and associations concerned with matters of smoking and health should utilize their resources for, and provide their wholehearted, vigorous, and unequivocal support to, legislative, administrative, and other measures or initiatives for the protection of the health of nonsmokers.

That all organizations and associations concerned with matters of smoking and health should set an example for the societies they serve by taking and enforcing all necessary and appropriate measures for the protection of nonsmokers, including the prohibition of smoking in their offices, at their conferences and workshops, and on the part of any persons representing them professionally or officially at any function or activities.

That local, regional, and national voluntary health organizations and national professional medical associations be made aware of the need for, and encouraged by the sponsors of this Conference to adopt and enforce, reasonable regulations within their jurisdictions to adequately protect individuals' lungs and health.

That all facilities in health care systems be made aware of the need, and encouraged by the sponsors of this Conference, to adequately protect individuals' lungs and health within their jurisdictions.

That smoking by members of the medical and nursing staff of hospitals be prohibited, and that other members of the staff who smoke do so in segregated areas, and that smoking by visitors to nonsmoking patients be prohibited.

That there should be a general prohibition against smoking throughout most of the medical environment, and that this should apply to all staff and patients. . . . That hospitals ban smoking in all semiprivate rooms, wards, clinics, waiting rooms, cafeterias, and other public places within the hospital and prohibit the sale of cigarettes on hospital property. Smoking in hospitals should be restricted to limited designated areas out of view of patients and the general public.

That professional medical practitioners concerned with the health of children (i.e., pediatricians, family practitioners, and pediatric nurses) be made aware by the sponsors of this Conference that the rights of nonsmoking patients are being ignored daily. . . .

Tobacco Substitutes

The best substitute for tobacco smoke is clean fresh air. Some good commercial substitutes for tobacco exist on the market. The smoker who wishes to try these can ask the physician or druggist about them. Also try having a supply of celery sticks, carrots, or chewing gum on hand.

REFERENCES

1 "Low-tar Cigarettes May Indeed Eliminate Risk," *Chemical and Engineering News,* Nov. 1, 1976, p. 5; also by personal communication.

2 *"Low-risk Cigarettes: A Prescription,"* Gio Gori, *Science,* Dec. 17, 1976, p. 1,243.

3 Norman Epstein, "The Effects of Tobacco Smoke Pollution on the Eyes of the Non-smoker," Third World Conference on Smoking and Health, New York, June 4, 1975.

4 J. R. T. Colley, "Influence of Passive Smoking and Potential Phlegm on Pneumonia and Bronchitis in Early Childhood," *The Lancer,* Nov. 2, 1974.

5 Center for Science in the Public Interest, *99 Ways to a Simple Lifestyle* (Garden City, N.Y.: Anchor/Doubleday, 1977), #69, "Stop Smoking Cigarettes."

Additional Sources

The following pamphlets are produced by the American Lung Association:

"Your Lungs"
"Smoking and Two of You"
"Second Hand Smoke"
"Emphysema"

U. UTENSIL COATINGS

All Americans experience the need for preparing a jiffy meal at home in order to get away to the next appointment. Food processors, quick to capitalize on the age of rush-rush, have come to the rescue with packaged dinners, speedy appliances, and a plethora of other "aids." A number of these "helps" really endanger human health or contaminate the environment. A leading candidate for the first place on this list is the aerosolized utensil coating, which is simply a combination of corn oil or lecithin and a propellant, generally Freon-11 and Freon-12 (see Section A).

A Kitchen Problem

These aerosol sprays must be singled out because they kill about seventy-nine people a year, 63 per cent of the reported deaths from aerosol sprays.[1] The victims are generally youth in the teens who experiment with getting cheap "highs." The grapevine suggests that heaven is waiting in a paper bag filled with Pam or some other aerosol spray lubricant. They are playing Russian roulette, that if a parent uses this food product it must not be too dangerous. Mild odors belie the seriousness of their risk.

As mentioned in other sections of this book, a heavy dose of an aerosol product will cause cardial arrhythmia, ventricular fibrillation, and alveolar capillary blocks. One theory of the cause of frequent deaths from the practice is that the alveoli (the air sacks in the lungs) get coated and this impedes the transfer of vital oxygen to the brain and thus leads to quick death.

Besides such fatal abuses of aerosol utensil coatings, there is the ongoing danger of container explosions at temperatures over 120° F., a very real danger since utensil coatings are generally kept near a hot stove. In 1975 a two-year-old child was killed by an exploding Pam can.

Besides the obvious dangers and abuses associated with utensil coatings, there is economic incentive for getting rid of them. About 70 per cent of the contained product is actually the propellant part of the delivery system. So the heavy weight of the can may be misleading to the average consumer who thinks he or she is really getting a bargain—or at least an even deal—by buying the product. A CSPI survey of various cooking minerals taken at a Washington, D.C., Safeway Supermarket in mid-1976 will show why:

"Numade" vegetable oil	$0.71/pound
Olive oil	1.71/pound
Shortening	0.71/pound
Pam aerosol spray	2.12/pound
Cooking Ease	2.05/pound

Remembering that aerosol sprays are predominately propellants, the actual cost of the oil is about $6.36/pound, which is somewhat more expensive than the best cuts of meat.

The environmental incentive for getting rid of these sprays is the heavy resource and energy requirements for making the product. It has been found that the energy required for preparing, processing, and delivering a comparable unit of regular cooking oil is about one fifth of that required for aerosol spray utensil coating.[2]

Stop Use of Aerosol Utensil Coatings

Few items found in the home have been known to be as misused as aerosol utensil coatings. Take up the cause; take some individual and some citizen action steps:

▪ Get rid of any such aerosol sprays and resolve never to buy another.

▪ Get relatives and friends, especially those with teen-age or even pre-teen-age youth, to do the same.

▪ Alert teachers in the neighborhood of the dangers of aerosol spray sniffing by youth. (It might not be wise to approach the subject with young people unless there is some assurance that the discussion and explanation will not encourage experimentation.)

▪ Notify the local supermarket manager that aerosol utensil coatings should not be marketed.

▪ Petition the Food and Drug Administration to remove aerosol spray lubricants from the list of approved foods, because of the number of cases of deliberate misuse.

▪ Organize a boycott of aerosol product sales.

▪ Lobby for municipal, state, and federal legislation to ban aerosol utensil coating products.

Using Simple Utensil Coatings

▪ Use shortening, vegetable oil, or lard for ordinary home cooking purposes.

▪ For cube trays use a 50-50 mixture of corn oil and peanut oil for coating both the tray and the dividers.[3]

Pam—Stops Food from Sticking
(Boyle-Midway, Inc., New York)

Made of lecithin, a pure vegetable product, with propellant.
WARNING: Use only as directed. Intentional misuse by deliberately concentrating and inhaling the contents can be harmful or fatal. Keep out of reach of children.
Contents under pressure. Do not puncture or incinerate. Avoid spraying in eyes. Keep away from excessive heat. Do not store in direct sunlight or where temperature is above 120° F. Do not spray on heated surfaces, near open flames or into the oven.

REFERENCES

[1] Empire State Consumer Association, Inc., Letter to the Consumer Product Safety Commission, May 21, 1975.

[2] A. Pierotti et al., "Energy and Food," CSPI Energy Series X, Washington, D.C., 1977.

[3] N. Stark, *The Formula Book* 2 (Kansas City, Kans.: Sheed Andrews & McMeel, Inc., 1975), p. 41.

Additional Sources

See Section A for references, especially "Aerosol Sprays" by Barbara Hogan et al., CSPI Publications, 1976.

V. VEGETATION IN THE HOME

Nothing enhances the quality of the household environment more than the judicious use of plants. Outside the home, they not only beautify the yard but afford privacy and protection against unwanted heat and light, air pollution, and winter winds. Indoors, vegetation freshens and humidifies the air, imparting a grace and warmth to the starkest of surroundings. In addition, it absorbs noise and, in some cases (e.g., herbs), provides food for the table.

Unfortunately, plants can also be toxic to members of the household. In 1974, for example, some 6,500 such poisonings of small children were recorded by American health officials.[1] This figure does not account for thousands of unreported children's cases, adult poisonings, or the 13 million victims of plant allergies.[2] The scope of the medical hazard is further reflected in the number of potentially toxic species—possibly as many as 8,000.[3] A few of these may find their way into the household as bouquets, special wild-flower arrangements, house plants, Yuletide decorations, supplemental food sources, and yard and garden plantings. Humans and pets may be exposed to their toxins and allergens through ingestion, skin contact, and inhalation of pollen or combustion vapors (e.g., the smoke from burning poison ivy). Physiological reaction can range from mild discomfort (stomach upset, skin rash, nasal congestion) to serious, sometimes fatal disorders (depression of circulatory and central nervous systems, violent purgation, kidney inflammation, convulsions, and heart failure).

The commercial florist industry maintains that severe poisonings—at least from cultivated plants—are rare, and that only a few species pose a genuine threat to the household. This position is highly questionable in light of the statistics noted above. Of course, there are instances when a poisoning is mistakenly attributed to a specific plant instead of a pesticide residue it contains. It is also true that the dangers of certain species have been the subject of prolonged controversy, as in the case of the popular poinsettia. The Society of American Florists has commissioned studies which reportedly exonerate this Yuletide favorite from its lethal reputation in certain quarters.[4] Nevertheless, the plant remains on the toxic list of some medical authorities.[5] While consumers may have difficulty in evaluating the charges and countercharges, they would do well to observe the warning of the New York State Consumer Product Safety Commission: ". . . poinsettia leaves, like those of many other plants, may cause varying degrees of discomfort if eaten, and *should be placed out of the reach of small children*" (emphasis added).[6]

Children are indeed especially susceptible to botanical poisoning. Colorful berries and flowers may be irresistible to the curious eye and eager hand of the young. It is quite easy for children to confuse toxic plant leaves and fruits with common household foods. Bulbs and seeds stored around the house may also whet a toddler's appetite. Outdoors there are many opportunities for youngsters to use the stems of harmful plants for skewering meat and marshmallows, or to suck nectar from poisonous blossoms.[7]

Even though adults are usually more discriminating about what they eat, they too can be quite vulnerable. Anyone, for example, who touches dumb cane (*Dieffenbachia,* an indoor plant common to many homes and offices) may pick up toxic sap from a bruised leaf or stem. If this substance is transmitted to the mouth, severe burning and choking can result.

Check the Safety of Plants

People of all ages should become familiar with any poisonous plants in their area which might be brought into the home or yard (see Table I). It will be helpful to keep the following points in mind:

▪ Certain parts of a plant may be innocuous (or even edible) while other parts may be highly toxic. The leaves of the tomato and rhubarb plants, for example, are poisonous and should never be used for brewing herb teas. The elderberry of wine and jelly fame grows toxic shoots that children occasionally use—with dire consequences—for blowguns and whistles.

Table I
TYPICAL POISONOUS PLANTS IN THE HOME AND GARDEN*

Plant	Poisonous Part	Toxic Hazard
Amaryllis (house, flower garden)	bulb	internal poison
Angel's trumpet (ornamental shrub)	all parts, especially seeds, leaves	internal poison, eye contact
Azalea (see Mountain laurel)		
Belladonna (garden ornamental)	berries, leaves, roots, flowers	internal poison
Caper spurge (yard and garden ornamental)	sap	dermatitis, internal poison
Chinaberry (ornamental tree)	fruit, leaves	internal poison
Christmas rose (flower garden)	roots, leaves	dermatitis
Crown-of-thorns (house, patio)	sap	dermatitis, internal poison
Dieffenbachia (dumb cane) (house, yard, and garden ornamental)	leaves, stems	internal poison

* As the heading indicates, this list does not contain all poisonous cultivated plants, nor does it cover wild varieties that may be brought into the house. Derived from: U. S. Department of Health, Education, and Welfare, Public Health Service, Food and Drug Administration, *Typical Poisonous Plants* (Washington, D.C.: U.S.G.P.O., 1976); and James Hardin and Jay Arena, M.D., *Human Poisoning from Native and Cultivated Plants* (Durham, N.C.: Duke University Press, 1974).

Plant	Poisonous Part	Toxic Hazard
Duranta (ornamental shrub)	berries	internal poison
Foxglove (flower garden)	roots, leaves, seeds	internal poison
Gas plant (ornamental shrub)	all parts in the presence of sun and water	dermatitis
Giant hogweed (house)	sap	dermatitis
Glory lily (yard and house)	all parts, especially tubers	internal poison
Golden chain (shrub or small tree)	flowers, seeds	internal poison
Hyacinth (house, flower garden, lawn)	bulb	internal poison
Jequirity bean (the beans of this semi-tropical plant are often used as rosary beads, toys)	seeds	internal poison, wound contamination
Lantana (patio and lawn ornamental)	fruit, especially if unripe	internal poison
Lily of the valley (flower garden)	roots, leaves, flowers, fruits	internal poison
Mistletoe (woodland Christmas decoration)	berries	internal poison
Monkshood (flower garden)	roots, seeds, leaves	internal poison
Mountain laurel (yard ornamental)	leaves, twigs, flowers, pollen grains	internal poison
Narcissus (house, yard)	bulb	internal poison
Oleander (ornamental evergreen)	twigs, flowers, green or dry leaves	internal poison
Pencil tree (house, patio)	sap	internal poison
Philodendron (house)	leaves, stems	internal poison
Rhododendron (see Mountain laurel)		

Plant	Poisonous Part	Toxic Hazard
Rhubarb (flower and vegetable garden)	leaves	internal poison
Rubber vine (ornamental vine)	all parts	internal poison
Sandbox tree (ornamental tree)	sap, seeds	internal poison
Tansy (herb garden)	leaves, flower heads	internal poison
Tung oil tree (ornamental tree)	all parts, especially seeds	internal poison
Yew (evergreen shrub)	all parts	internal poison

▪ The toxicity of some species is somewhat seasonal. The berries of pokeweed become less poisonous as they ripen (and are quite harmless when properly cooked). Even the common Irish potato can be toxic when eaten green.

▪ Plants that are toxic to one animal species may not be to another. People should therefore never rely upon the feeding habits of animals as a guide to edible plant selection.[8]

▪ Safe selection of woodland flora for indoor arrangements and herb pots requires thorough plant identification. After considerable itching and burning, hikers have belatedly discovered that the pretty red and yellow leaves they have been collecting were poison oak in autumnal disguise. More seriously, poison hemlock has occasionally been mistaken for parsley, anise, and parsnip plants.[9]

Plant allergies are also a form of poisoning in the broadest sense.[10] Individual sensitivity to eating certain foods (e.g., nuts) or touching specific plants (e.g., geraniums) may produce such symptoms as swelling, nausea, and skin irritation. Perhaps the most well known allergen, however, is pollen, which inflames the mucous membranes of the respiratory tract. Although this type of hay fever is generally considered more a nuisance than a disease, it does occasionally develop into asthma. Flowering plants should not be brought into a house or sickroom unless it is known that the occupants are free from such allergies.

Air conditioning can filter out almost all pollen from outdoor sources.[11] Because this is an expensive and sometimes impractical solution, homeowners should keep their properties and neighborhoods clear of ragweed and other nuisance plants.

It is also necessary to look at the "mechanical" hazards plants create. Thorns, spikes, and spines (e.g., roses and cacti) can inflict painful wounds and secondary infections on both admirer and passer-by. The placement of potted plants should receive considerable forethought.

A Note on Plant Foods

Occasionally it is desirable to replenish the nutrients which cultivated plants absorb from the soil during their growth cycle. To do this, many gardeners and house plant enthusiasts have followed the lead of large commercial farms by relying heavily on chemical fertilizers. Repeated applications of these strong substances, however, can burn plant roots and eventually deplete soil fertility. Besides, fertilizers are quite caustic to humans as well, particularly if ingested. They leach out of gardens and lawns to contaminate water supplies with their suspected carcinogenic properties (see Section W).

A significant number of plants, including most indoor varieties, do not require much soil enrichment at all. Many people mistakenly assume that an extra dose of fertilizer will cure whatever ails their plants. In some cases, ironically, toxic build-up of chemical salts may be the cause of the problem.[12] Since gentler, organic substitutes for these energy-intensive compounds are readily available, plant lovers would do well to use commercial fertilizers sparingly or not at all.

Vegetation Alternatives

Because of the great diversity of plants on the market, it is not difficult to find nontoxic species for the home and garden. Consult a local florist, university biology department, poison control center, garden club, public library, or county extension agent to become familiar with the problem varieties (see Table I). If at all uncertain about the toxicity of a plant in the home, be sure to keep it (or seeds and bulbs) out of the reach of children and pets.

Edible herbs are an excellent choice for the indoor gardener. They not only make an aesthetic contribution to the decor but liven up mealtimes in salads and teas. Among those herbs commonly grown inside are basil, chives, savory, parsley, thyme, marjoram, and mint.[13]

Plant lovers should also be careful to identify uncultivated varieties that are brought into the home. Children in particular should be instructed to eat only easily recognized fruits and berries, such as blueberries, gooseberries, cranberries, blackberries, dewberries, strawberries, huckleberries, citrus, plums, apples, and grapes.

Before buying the next load of commercial fertilizer for indoor or outdoor application, the plant enthusiast should consider the following safer alternatives:

animal manure
green manure (plowed-under clover and alfalfa)
seaweed and kelp
activated sludge (not always recommended for food plants, especially root crops, because of possible heavy metal contamination)
sawdust and wood chips
hay, straw, and peat moss
blood meal and dried blood
grass clippings
fish meal and fish scraps
phosphate rock and colloidal phosphate

REFERENCES

1 "Categories of Substances Ingested by Children Under 5 Years of Age. Reported by Poison Control Center for 1974." U. S. Department of Health, Education, and Welfare.

2 James Hardin and Jay Arena, M.D., *Human Poisoning from Native and Cultivated Plants* (Durham, N.C.: Duke University Press, 1974), p. 9.

3 William G. Carmichael, Director, Florist Information Committee, Society of American Florists and Ornamental Horticulturists, telephone interview, Jan. 7, 1977.

4 Robert P. Stone and W. J. Collins, "Euphorbia Pulcherrima: Toxicity to Rats," *Toxicon*, Vol. 9 (1971), pp. 301–2.

5 Hardin and Arena, *Human Poisoning*, pp. 8, 14, 115.

6 As summarized in "A Clean Bill of Health for the Poinsettia Plant," prepared by the Florist Information Committee, Society of American Florists.

7 Hardin and Arena, *Human Poisoning*, p. 5.

8 Ibid.

9 *Typical Poisonous Plants*, Public Health Service, Food and Drug Administration, U. S. Department of Health, Education, and Welfare, 1976, p. 15.

10 Harden and Arena, *Human Poisoning*, p. 9.

11 J. Spiegelman and H. Friedman, "The Effect of Central Air Filtration and Air Conditioning on Pollen and Microbial Contamination," *Journal of Allergy*, Vol. 42 (1968), pp. 193–202.

12 Joan Faust, *The New York Times Book of House Plants* (New York: Quadrangle Books, 1973), pp. 29–30.

13 Ibid., p. 186.

W. WATER CONTAMINANTS

Water, water everywhere, and (sometimes) not a safe drop to drink. While we have come to accept good drinking water as a fact of life, about 36 per cent of Americans have some health problems with water, and an even higher percentage of the world's population has chronic trouble with it. Only a small part of the water of the world is drinkable, and steps must be taken to protect it from contamination.

A Human Necessity

Water bears the commerce of our biological life. All chemical reactions necessary for life occur in water; our nutrients are carried through our bodies in an essentially water medium. In fact our bodies average 65 per cent water by weight, and over 80 per cent of the brain's weight is water.[1]

Our bodies require clean unpoisoned water, but so do our industries and power plants. These processes result in toxic wastes, pathogenic effluents, and wasted heat—all to be borne by water. Many remember the threatened streams and rivers of the 1960s—clogged with detergent suds residues above while below algae fed off phosphates from detergents.

The human body requires about three liters of water a day. This comes to 200 billion liters over-all in the United States in a year. But compared to the thirst of industry and agriculture, the amount we need to survive is paltry. The consumption of water to produce food and materials is about 1,000 liters per year per American. In 1974 United States steel production[2] used 11 trillion liters of water. World-wide use of water for steel production is about 85 trillion liters. American industry and agriculture annually gulp over 300 trillion liters of water, injecting into it some of the 12,000 known toxic industrial chemicals, waste heat, excess fertilizer, and biological contaminants.

Industry chemical emissions are joined by consumer discharges from cleaning, laundering, toilet use, and spraying. In fact the average American pollutes over 12 million liters of water in a lifetime.[3] Coupled with this is the fact that, of all the water around us, only 1 per cent is fresh and much of that is not easily available for human use. Thus fresh, available water is recycled and purified. People living on such rivers as the Mississippi—particularly those around New Orleans—drink water which has been cycled through power plants, steel mills, chemical factories, washing machines, bath tubs, and toilets.

Recognition of the need for available potable water has been a perennial problem especially in urban areas. The Romans built aqueducts to bring distant fresh mountain water to Rome. Large cities like London have had countless major water-borne epidemics. Community water supplies were protected and treated in the period after the Civil War to avoid such diseases as typhoid, cholera, and dysentery. By 1914 federal water standards were established by the Public Health Service.

Our water systems are currently designed to handle bacterial infection. Statistics reflect this. About 25,000 people die world-wide daily from water-borne disease while only 200 Americans died between 1961 and 1973.[4,5] These death statistics, however, do not tell much about our 50,000 community water systems. Because we have widespread and readily available medical facilities, deaths from sickness are expected to be low. Thus sicknesses, rather than deaths, give a more significant insight into the conditions of our nation's water supplies.

In the same twelve-year period (1961–73) an estimated 54,000 Americans became ill from drinking water.[6] In 1972 about 3,500 people were stricken with illness in Pico Rivera,

California, and in 1964 about 16,000 became ill in Gaines-
ville, Florida. More recently, 5,000 residents in Sewickley,
Pennsylvania, got acute gastrointestinal illness from contaminated drinking water.[7] In 1969 the Holy Cross College foot-
ball team contracted infectious hepatitis through drinking
water. Some 97 cases of typhoid, a scourge of the past, were
reported in a Florida migrant labor camp in 1973.

These illnesses are not surprising when other statistics are
considered. HEW surveyed 969 water systems around the
country in 1970 and found that:

1) 36 per cent of the 2,688 individual samples taken exceeded the minimum standard for bacteriological or
   chemical pollutants.
2) 56 per cent of the systems evidenced physical supply
   problems such as inadequate disinfection capacity,
   poorly protected ground-water sources, etc.
3) 9 per cent of the samples contained bacterial contamination of potentially dangerous quality at the consumer's tap.[8]

Thus even though our systems are designed to eliminate
bacterial contamination, many do not, while others go unchecked. The chance for a big disaster is real. Alameda, California, almost had one, except for a combination of luck and
alert citizens. Alameda's water officials tested water for bacteria only every two weeks. Once water samples were taken, another two weeks passed before samples were analyzed and results reported. In this instance, dangerous levels of bacteria
were found and a "boil your water" order issued. But the people had been exposed to bacteria for up to four weeks.
Officials initially claimed no cases of infection, but further citizen investigation uncovered a number of unreported illnesses.
Citizens worked to ensure that everyone was aware of the
need to boil the water. They since have organized and now
have safer water.[9]

But are the citizens of Alameda or other American cities
really safe? Perhaps not. In addition to bacteria, at least five

additional categories of dangerous substances are in some of the waters: viruses, runoff materials, organic materials, heavy metals, and other contaminants.

Even if bacteria are killed by the chlorine added to the water, viruses may not be. Polio, infectious hepatitis, and influenza are all viral infections. The extent of the problem is not known since viral standards do not exist and monitoring is not done. Dirty, muddy water from unchecked drainage from construction can protect bacteria in water from the chlorine. Runoff from feed lots and animal wastes can carry bacterial and chemical contaminants.

The remaining categories are specific to complex industrial-consumer societies, and may well be the end of them. Many hundreds of new chemicals annually reach our market shelves. Once used, these chemicals must go somewhere—usually into the air and water systems. Further, the dumping of billions of tons of liquid waste from manufacturing chemicals and consumer products places massive amounts of new untested substances into our waters. Some of the dangers are now identified; many will be identified decades later as the long-range (chronic) effects turn up.

Alone, a citizen can't do much about these substances. Boiling water removes some of the organic substances and kills the bacteria but most of the chemicals that remain need special treatment.

Organic compounds, many of which did not exist at the turn of the century, are now known to cause serious health problems. The EPA concluded from a 1975 study that at least 496 organic chemicals can be found, or are suspected of being present, in water in various locations in the United States. About 88 organic chemicals were found in water from the Mississippi River alone.

New Orleans is known to have the third highest rate of kidney cancer and the sixth highest rate of bladder and urinary cancer of the 163 metropolitan areas studied. Over-all, New Orleans has the second highest incidence of all cancers in the United States and the third highest rate for cancer mortality.[10] Water has long been held suspect.

An EPA study squarely hit one of the factors—carcinogens were found in New Orleans drinking water. The Environmental Defense Fund concluded that there was a statistically significant relation between cancer mortality in Louisiana and drinking water obtained from the Mississippi River. This was true for cancer of the urinary organs and cancer of the gastrointestinal tract.[11] As of 1975 carcinogens have been found in 32 per cent of the 80 cities surveyed by the EPA throughout the United States.[6]

Even worse, the treatment systems, designed to eliminate pollutants, may actually be adding some of the carcinogens.[12] Certain organic compounds containing chlorine (e.g., chloroform and carbon tetrachloride) cause cancer. Most American purification plants use chlorine to kill bacteria. Chlorine may combine with organic compounds contaminating the water and generate highly carcinogenic, chlorine-containing organic compounds. In most cases, industrial wastes are the major causes of these compounds. However, certain organic home products such as detergents and cleaning chemicals enter the water system, creating potential purification problems.

Heavy metals are an area of intense concern in water pollution. These include mercury, selenium, cadmium, arsenic, iron, chromium, and barium. About 90 per cent of the water supply systems monitored in 1969 were not tested for heavy metals. The EPA's study of the Mississippi River water found and traced many toxic metals to industrial discharges into the river. But heavy metals can also come from the pipes delivering the water to the home. Lead from water pipes have been found in tap water in Boston and Seattle. Cadmium, found along with zinc in galvanized pipes, can also leach into the water.

Though many heavy metals are needed in very low concentrations for health, they have deadly effects if ingested in higher concentrations. Lead poisoning is often characterized by "headache, hyperactivity or unusual lethargy, aggressiveness, loss of appetite, anemia, vomiting, stereotype repetitive behaviour as manifested by excessive grooming, high motor activity, short attention span, low frustration tolerance, hyperexcitability and impulsiveness. Depending on the degree of poisoning, any or all the symptoms may become chronic. Undiagnosed lead poisoning can lead to mental retardation or severe brain damage, cerebral palsy, blindness, kidney disease, convulsive disorders and death."[13] (See Section L.)

Mercury caused the painful and deadly Minamata disease in Japan that killed and crippled people who had eaten contaminated fish and shellfish. Initial mercury poisoning symptoms such as numbness, slurred speech, unusual aggression, and tunnel vision evolve to deformed limbs, memory loss, and ultimately death (see Section Q). Ingestion of small amounts of cadmium can have severe health effects, which are also discussed in Section Q. Chromium and arsenic are also dangerous in larger concentrations and may do severe body damage.

Other pollutants may also contaminate water. Asbestos, now recognized as one of the most ubiquitous of carcinogens, can be found in our air, homes, clothing, wine, and drinking water. Over 200 billion tons of asbestos-bearing mine tailings were dumped into Lake Superior by the Reserve Mining Company. Drinking water in nearby Duluth was subsequently found to contain asbestos. The drinking water of San Francisco has asbestos present, and the drinking water of Boston, New York, Philadelphia, Atlanta, Chicago, Dallas, Kansas City, and Denver are under suspicion. The price paid in human health for drinking asbestos-contaminated water is not yet fully known (see section B).

Road deicing salts (usually sodium and/or calcium chloride) drain into local water supplies, and increase the sodium content of the water, presenting particular problems to people with high blood pressure, obesity, and cirrhosis of the liver.

Nitrate fertilizers have increased fourteen-fold since World War II. These and other nitrate pollutants may contaminate water supplies, especially from runoff from farm fields, gardens, lawns, and golf courses. Nitrate and other nitrogen-con-

taining compounds may enter the bloodstream and tie up hemoglobin oxygen-carrying sites, causing asphyxiation—the
blue baby syndrome.

Algicides used in swimming pools can be dangerous chemicals. These are usually salts of heavy metal compounds which
kill algae. Careful filtration and regular pool-cleaning reduce
the need for these compounds and their contamination of
sewage systems.

Water Watch

Strategies and actions similar to those used to reduce air
pollution work to solve water pollution problems as well.
Both individual and local group actions have been successful
to some degree. In addition, the goals of the 1972 Water Pollution Control Act are most ambitious: The nation's water
will be clean enough for swimming, other recreational uses,
and the propagation of fish, shellfish, and wild life by July 1,
1983; there will be no more discharges of pollutants whatso-
ever by 1985. An offshoot of the act is the National Pollution
Discharge Elimination System (NPDES), which identifies
and registers pollutants and sets limits on the amount and
content of effluents.

When it comes to good drinking water, the average citizen
can do several things:

▪ Organize a citizen group in the locality. It is easier to
work for the improvement of drinking water quality as a
group. Organizations add clout, have visibility, disperse the
work load among members, and generally are more effective
than isolated individuals.

▪ Find out about the local water system:

1) The water supply: Is it downstream from extensive
farming operations which use pesticides? Is it downstream
from manufacturing plants which discharge pollutants into
the water system? Do these plants have permits required by
the NPDES? Does drinking water come from wells? Are

there nearby sources that are discharging pollutants into the underground water table?

2) The treatment plant: Is the plant approved or only provisionally approved by the EPA, and if the latter, why? Are measures being taken to make the system fully acceptable? How frequently are water samples taken and analyzed? Are the results of such analyses made public? Are warning procedures established in case of danger? Is the water tested both at the tap and at the plant?

Have local high school or college students run tests on water? If the school has advanced placement courses in chemistry and biology, both students and equipment should be available to do the analyses.

3) The treatment plant staff: Who has the ultimate responsibility for supplying the local drinking water? Are there conflicts of interest? What are the experience and credentials of the treatment plant staff? Are they doing a proper job in purifying the water? Is the staff adequate enough for the task?

■ Do's and Don'ts for the home:

1) Use water from the cold water tap for drinking and cooking. Hot water may contain more metals and pipe impurities.

2) Conserve water by fixing leaking pipes and faucets. Reduce toilet flushing by placing a filled plastic jug in the water tank.

3) When installing drinking water pipes, make sure they are not lead or asbestos cement.

4) If there is some suspicion that there is contamination of the local water supplies, have the water tested.

5) The general rule is "Don't use bottled water!" Both the EPA and the USGAO in evaluating bottled water plants found some samples contaminated with bacteria and some with heavy metals. New laws covering bottled water are on the books but do not cover certain organic chemicals and pesticides in water; they do not regulate intrastate bottled water

at all. In some cases bottled spring or mineral water may be high quality.

6) Don't buy water filters and purifiers. These ultimately turn into breeding grounds for bacteria. If the water needs purification, boil it before drinking.

Water Source Alternative

Build a cistern and collect rain water only after roof has washed off during heavy rain. In heavily polluted areas longer lengths of time are required to wash out pollutants.

REFERENCES

1 William Davis and Eldra Pearl Solomon, *The World of Biology* (New York: McGraw-Hill, 1974).

2 *The U. S. Factbook—The American Almanac* (New York: Grosset and Dunlap, 1976).

3 Philip Nobile and John Deedy, eds., *The Complete Ecology Factbook* (Garden City, N.Y.: Anchor/Doubleday, 1972).

4 Remarks by the Honorable Russell E. Train, Administrator, USEPA, before Los Angeles World Affairs Forum, Dec. 16, 1976.

5 Robert H. Harris and Edward Von Brecher, "Is the Water Safe to Drink?," *Consumer Reports*, June 1974.

6 "A Drop to Drink—A Report on the Quality of Our Drinking Water," USEPA, June 1976.

7 "Drinking Water in Pennsylvania," Citizens' Advisory Council, Nov. 15, 1976.

8 House Committee Report on the Safe Drinking Water Act (Report No. 93-1185), 1970.

9 Robert H. Harris and Edward Von Brecher, "Is the Water Safe to Drink?," *Consumer Reports*, July and Aug. 1974.

10 Samuel S. Epstein, M.D., "Potential Carcinogenic Hazards Due to Contaminated Drinking Water," *Biological Control of Water Pollution* (Philadelphia: University of Pennsylvania Press, 1976).

11 "The Implication of Cancer-causing Substances in Mississippi River Water," Environmental Defense Fund, Nov. 8, 1974.

12 T. A. Belair, J. J. Lichtenberg, and R. C. Kroner, "The Occurrence of Organohalides in Chlorinated Drinking Water," USEPA.

13 "Get the Lead Out," Citizens' Advisory Council to the Pennsylvania Department of Environmental Resources, Oct. 1974.

Additional Sources

"Toward Cleaner Water," USEPA, reprinted May 1974.

"First Things First—a Strategy Against Water Pollution," USEPA, Sept. 1974.

Gladwyn Hill, "Cleansing Our Water," Public Affairs Pamphlet No. 497, Public Affairs Committee, Inc., 1974.

"Lead and Metal Retardation," *Science News*, Apr. 5, 1975.

T. Page, R. H. Harris, and S. S. Epstein, "Drinking Water and

Cancer Mortality in Louisiana," *Science*, Vol. 193(4247), July 1976, pp. 55–57.

House Committee Report on Safe Drinking Water Act, No. 93-1185.

H. A. Schroeder and Luke A. Kramer, "Cardiovascular Mortality, Municipal Water and Corrosion," *Archives of Environmental Health*, Vol. 28 (June 1974).

Henry A. Schroeder, M.D., "Cadmium, Chromium and Cardiovascular Disease," *Circulation*, Vol. 35 (Mar. 1967).

F. W. Stitt, M. D. Crawford, D. G. Clayton, and J. N. Morris, "Clinical and Biochemical Indicators of Cardiovascular Diseases Among Men Living in Hard and Soft Water Areas," *The Lancet*, Jan. 20, 1973.

Robert and Leona Train Rienow, *Moment in the Sun* (New York: Ballantine Books, 1967).

"Manual for Evaluating Public Drinking Water Supplies," USEPA.

"Public Health Service Drinking Water Standards and Appendix," Pub. No. 956, 1973 (rev.), USEPA.

"Community Water Supply Study," 1970, USEPA.

"Safe Drinking Water for All: What You Can Do," Publication 247, 1973, the League of Women Voters, 1730 M St. N.W., Washington, D.C. 20036.

"The Water you Drink: How Safe Is It?" Publication 246, 1973, the League of Women Voters.

D. Ton That, "Water," *Development Forum*, Vol. 4, No. 9 (Dec. 1976), p. 4. United Nations Centre for Economic and Social Information, Geneva.

"A Summary and Evaluation of Selected State Drinking Water Systems," Environmental Defense Fund, Dec. 2, 1974.

"Controlling Hazardous Pollutants: In Inland Waters," 1975, the League of Women Voters.

Water Pollution Control Handbook: A Citizen's Guide to the Federal Water Pollution Control Act Amendments of 1972, Vols. 1 and 2.

B. Reid and G. Speth, "Project on Clean Water," 1973, Natural Resources Defense Council, Washington, D.C. 20036.

X. EXTRA CHEMICALS AROUND THE HOME

Since the average home today has more chemicals present than the average chemical laboratory one hundred years ago, one might expect that there are many danger spots which have not been covered by the preceding sections. The information in his book will hopefully serve to gain control over a certain fraction of the 20 million injuries that result from consumer product use each year. Some 40 per cent arise from use of recreational equipment; 12.5 per cent from home fixtures; 16 per cent from appliances, heating and cooking devices, home and yard tools and equipment.

Dangers Through Ingestion

Ingestion of chemicals has been cited throughout as a leading hazard in the polluted home. Of all the ways toxic materials may enter the human body (mouth, nose, eyes, wound, skin, tactile) ingestion is the most common route for small children, who invariably want to taste any foreign solid or liquid around the house. Table I lists the twenty-five major categories of substances most frequently ingested by children. Of the fifteen not yet covered by this book, eight are medicines, three are cosmetic substances, and two are health supplements. Coverage of these nonaerosolized cosmetics and medicines is beyond the scope of this book. "Chemicals" and "miscellaneous products" are the categories which remain.

The "miscellaneous products" category accounts for less than 4 per cent reported cases of ingestion poisonings in children. It includes the following: alcoholic beverages, ink,

Table I

CATEGORIES OF SUBSTANCES MOST FREQUENTLY INGESTED BY CHILDREN UNDER 5 YEARS OF AGE
Reported by Poison Control Centers for 1974

	No.	Per cent	Section
1. Plants (excluding mushrooms and toadstools)	6483	6.9	V
2. Soaps, detergents, cleaners	5474	5.8	K
3. Aspirin	4837	5.1	X
adult	750		
baby	3195		
unspecified	892		
4. Vitamins, minerals	4577	4.8	X
5. Antihistamines, cold medicines	3783	4.0	X
6. Perfume, cologne, toilet water	3385	3.6	
7. Household disinfectants, deodorizers	2944	3.1	J
8. Insecticides (excluding moth balls)	2879	3.0	I
9. Miscellaneous internal medicines	2761	2.9	X
10. Psychopharmacologic agents	2237	2.4	X
11. Household bleach	2361	2.5	O
12. Liniments	2045	2.2	X
13. Miscellaneous analgesics	2095	2.2	X
14. Cosmetic lotions, creams	1844	1.9	—
15. Hormones	1811	1.9	X
16. Glues, adhesives	1680	1.8	H
17. Liquid polish or wax	1620	1.7	F
18. Fingernail preparations	1632	1.7	—
19. Miscellaneous external medicines	1602	1.7	X
20. Miscellaneous products	1574	1.7	X
21. Corrosive acids, alkalies	1543	1.6	X,O
22. Rodenticides	1378	1.5	I
23. Paint	1350	1.4	S,Q,L
24. Chemicals	1335	1.4	X
25. Antiseptic medication	1216	1.4	X

Source: U. S. Department of Health, Education, and Welfare, National Clearinghouse for Poison Control Centers, "Tabulations of 1974 Case Reports" (Bethesda, September 1976), p. 2.

matches, snake and insect poisons, moth balls, animal and insect repellents. Of these, moth balls present a special problem for children because of their candylike appearance. Their powerful toxicity makes use of the new crystal form preferable.

The "unassorted chemicals" category accounts for 1.4 per cent of the cases. It includes chemical encounters such as that of a New York family whose silicone dishwasher sealant exuded an arsenic compound onto their dishes. The family members suffered stomach pains, low-grade fever, and weakness before the cause was finally traced to their newly applied General Electric silicone sealant. The hot water had leached the compound, originally intended as a fungicide.[1]

Other Dangers

Other substances may be dangerous for reasons other than ingestion, namely: ice-melting compounds, fire extinguishers, and fireworks.

Ice-melting Compounds, especially sodium and calcium chloride, are often found in cooler climates, in garages and storage rooms. Calcium chloride, which works faster than common salt, is hygroscopic, removing moisture from the hands. Stored calcium chloride picks up moisture, and the solution formed can ooze over cabinets and tables and cake easily. Ice-melting compounds are quite toxic to vegetation around the house.

Fire Extinguishers are lifesaving devices which belong near entrances and other accessible places in every house. They should never be tinkered with, but should be checked regularly. After the death of an Oregon woman in July 1972 from a broken fire extinguisher, the FDA banned the use of carbon tetrachloride extinguishers in the home. The local fire department can be called to check any suspect extinguishers.

[1] "Poison Control Center Receiving Calls on Taking Tests for Arsenic," New York *Times,* Dec. 29, 1976.

Fireworks are good for social celebrations when activated by experienced persons, but are unfortunately a source of serious injury to many. While injuries are only one-tenth those from firearms, a firecracker around the home can unsettle the nerves and cause serious burns.

Precautions:

A chemical is always dangerous to the inexperienced person. For this reason the best substitute for a household chemical is to remove and properly dispose of it when not needed. Proper storage and handling precautions mentioned in other sections should be observed. For the special classes which were singled out, one might do the following:

Alcoholic beverages: Keep out of reach of children, and use milder drinks.

Ink: Use ball-point pens. They require more plastic and natural resources but are safer than ink bottles and fountain pens, especially in a home with children.

Matches: Be cautious. Use lighters where children are present.

Moth balls: Keep sealed properly for both economic and health reasons. They disappear when left in the open.

Animal and insect repellents: Use sparingly. If needed for protection, keep stored properly. Liquid and salve forms of insect repellents are better for health and environment than aerosolized types.

Fireworks: Let the town and municipal pyrotechnic experts put on the fireworks, which have no place in the home. Pack supper and take the children to watch the public displays. They will probably enjoy it as much, and the neighbors will be spared the wear and tear of Fourth of July fireworks at home.

Ice-melting compounds: Do not use deicers which do not have contents labeled on the package. Use sand instead, which is cheaper and easier on the environment. Remember that salt will kill shrubs and plants when the snow has melted and the rains come.

Fire extinguishers: Use those approved by the local fire department. Replace outdated ones and check regularly those which are approved. It's good insurance.

Medicines: Keep in high places away from the reach of children. Throw away old and unlabeled medicines. Try to use only what is needed.

PEOPLES ISOPROPYL RUBBING ALCOHOL

Isopropyl Alcohol 70%

Rubbing ▪ Bathing ▪ Massaging

This preparation is made from Isopropyl Alcohol and does not contain nor is it sold as a substitute for Ethyl or Grain Alcohol.

FOR EXTERNAL USE ONLY

Flammable

If taken internally severe pain and serious bodily injury may result.

For customary use of external Rubbing Compounds

Unbreakable plastic bottle

KEEP OUT OF REACH OF CHILDREN

Y. YULETIDE AND OTHER DECORATIONS

Most people decorate their homes on special festive occasions such as birthdays, Halloween, and religious occasions like Christmas or Hanukkah. While these decorations can also add a dash of atmosphere and cheer, there is again the risk of overdoing a good thing. Witness the homes where every corner is lined with Christmas lights, heralds of the advent of the season of commercialism.

Decoration Dangers and Wastes

But there is an added danger from special decorations that is associated with their temporary nature. Many of the streamers and tinsel are combustible and can easily attract the small hands of infant visitors. Paper streamers hanging around a party room can become fuel for the carelessly discarded cigarette and tinder for a major house fire. Greenery used for decoration such as Christmas trees, evergreen branches, wreathes, garlands, and mistletoe tend to dry out and in many cases are made of resinous materials which literally burst into flame when a lighted match or cigarette is near. The fresh-cut evergreen tree gives off a pleasant aromatic odor and conjures up memories of childhood delights and expectations, but it is a fire hazard when allowed to dry out during the holiday season.

A good decoration for either a season or an occasion is the bouquet of flowers or the potted plant (see Section V). Flowers can be dried and fireproofed and are a delight to the eyes during the long winter months.

Another decorative item which can be potentially dangerous is the candle. Few people dispute that candles, especially hand-carved and molded ones and those of multicolors and various scents, are excellent gifts for friends. But often candles either are arranged in combustible settings (an evergreen wreath or a cardboard stand) or are placed in a spot where they may ignite furnishings when lit. Candles frequently trigger the hidden pyromaniac streak found in both young and old. The German practice of lighting candles on a Christmas tree should be seriously questioned from a fire-prevention viewpoint.

Outdoor decorative gaslights are major energy wasters. The gaslight when left burning during the day—as many are—can consume more gas during the year than needed to cook meals for five families. This betrays a lack of individual and civic conservation consciousness. While the gaslight is not emitting many contaminants when solely decorative, it draws from a limited pool of energy needed for cooking and warmth. Quite frequently the decorative gaslight is overshadowed by a strong electric street light.

Decorative packaging is another luxury item which adds to the total garbage burden of the community and requires energy to make and process. This is especially true where packaging is not easily reused. The beautiful bows and ribbons are decorative delights but last such a short time at present-opening moments.

CHRISTMAS AND TRU SCENT FROSTY SPRAY
(Essex Chemical Corporation Consumer Products Division, Orange, Conn.)

Caution: Contents under pressure. Store can upright in cool place not over 120° F. Do not puncture or throw into fire or incinerator. Keep out of reach of children. Do not spray near food.

A final note must be given to dangerous convenience items, especially those in aerosol spray containers. These help speed decorating but also help spread hazardous gases throughout the household. This includes the artificial snow for Christmas trees and cocktail glass chillers. These health and ecological disasters should be avoided.

Yuletide Safety Hints

Decorating and party preparation take planning. Be sure to exclude in those plans all possible decoration dangers. The following hints may aid in making the home safer:

■ If a rooted Yuletide tree cannot be used, attempt to fireproof the tree. *The Formula Book* recommends one cup of ammonium sulfate, one-half cup boric acid, two tablespoons borax, and eight tablespoons of 3 per cent hydrogen peroxide[1] (all generally obtainable from drugstores or garden supply places). This can both be sprayed over the tree and put in the cup at the base of the tree. It reduces fire hazard and preserves the needles. Remember, the fireproofing chemicals are harmful when ingested, so keep out of reach of children.

■ Never use aerosol decorative and party materials such as spray snow and cocktail glass chillers.

■ Sparkle batting made from asbestos should never be used.

■ Certain forms of Yuletide greenery can be toxic (e.g., mistletoe, yew, jequirity bean). Keep these out of the reach of small children. (See Section V.)

■ Even though Europeans still use candles for the soft glowing effect on their Yuletide trees, remember that these are major fire hazards. Candlemaking is a favorite holiday activity. Use textile wicks. Don't place candles where combustible materials are present. Use a noncombustible stand or base.

■ Be sure that tinsel, silver and gold icicles, cotton or sparkle batting, glass ornaments, and satin balls are fireproof. Where children might be expected near the tree, place delicate glass balls or other breakable items out of their reach. Tinsel cord made from popcorn is quite safe. Fireproof all homemade decorations.

Yuletide Alternatives

■ Think of using an artificial Christmas tree. These will last almost indefinitely with proper care and storage, and save money over the long haul. Check when purchasing for the following qualities: flame-retardance, ease in assembly, sturdy stand, storage carton, coded branches and poles, and a minimum five-year warranty.

Artificial trees lack the pleasant smells of live ones but save on energy and resources in the following operations: seeding, growing trees, fertilizing, care during growth, protection, cutting, transporting to market, carrying home on purchase, and sending to the disposal site. The tree is a renewable resource, but it takes varying amounts of nonrenewable fossil fuel to perform these operations, which greatly exceed those of artificial trees.

■ If the pull of tradition is too strong and the family demands a live tree, buy one with roots from the local nursery. Put the tree in a pot of moist soil. After the holiday season, plant the tree outdoors where it becomes a nice addition to the shrubbery. Since it does not dry, there is not as much danger of a fire hazard. Select the type with care, depending on what is wanted in the yard and what will grow in the particular region—Japanese black pine, Norway spruce, fir, cedar, hemlock, etc. If it can't be used after the season, donate it to a park or nonprofit institution.

■ Gifts signify a remembrance of others. They also reveal lifestyle aspirations. Give fewer "things." See that the gifts are durable, or are experiences such as a recording, a magazine subscription, or membership to a museum. Give something natural, such as a house plant or potted herb, rather than synthetic (see Section V). Make the gift suggest conservation habits: cloth napkins and napkin rings, a picnic basket set, cloth dish towels, and used books. Give donations to needy public-interest groups.[2]

▪ Use leftover fabric, wallpaper, comics, or magazine cut-outs for wrapping paper. Recycle used ribbons, bows, and decorative wrappings.

▪ Reduce the number of indoor and outdoor ornamental lights. Ornamental gas lamps which burn continuously throughout the year are major natural-gas wasters. Tell friends or neighbors to shut them off voluntarily. If this fails, take the matter to the municipal council for imposition of a conservation ordinance.

▪ Birthday accessories are part of the atmosphere of any party. When not stored as keepsakes, reuse at the next birthday.

REFERENCES

[1] Norman Stark, *The Formula Book 2* (Kansas City, Kans.: Sheed Andrews & McMeel, Inc., 1976), p. 33.

[2] "The Compendium Newsletter," Dec. 1976–Jan. 1977, 2315 Westwood Blvd., Suite 1, Los Angeles, Calif. 90064.

Additional Source

Alternative Christmas Catalog, 1924 E. 3rd St., Bloomington, Ind. 47401.

Z. ZOOLOGICAL WASTE AND DISEASE

It is difficult for many of us to acknowledge the health hazards created by pets in our homes and communities. Despite occasional reports of rabies and turtle salmonella, we remain largely oblivious to the pervasive public health problems that domesticated animals engender. Such complacency undoubtedly grows out of affection for the animals which share our homes and submit to our affection and caresses. Our intimate bond with pets, however, makes us particularly vulnerable to zoonoses, the diseases that animals transmit to human beings.

Animal Waste

The biggest problem is animal waste. The favorite urban pastime, "walking the dog," is what the British more aptly describe as "fouling the footpath"—a forty-dollar offense in London. It has been estimated that in New York City alone, animals deposit some 150 tons of dung and 114,000 gallons of liquid waste daily.[1] Some of these pathogenic deposits eventually wash into waterways that may already carry a heavy load of feed-lot waste, street runoff, industrial effluent, fertilizer, pesticide, and municipal sewage. The remainder stays under foot to offend the nose and eye and, more alarmingly, to breed parasites and illness.

The *Toxocara* parasite, for example, is a roundworm commonly found in dogs and cats. The excrement of these pets can contain vast numbers of microscopic *Toxocara* eggs that stick to the soles of shoes and the hair of animals rolling in contaminated dirt. Puppies are particularly prone to smear parts of their coats with dung, which can be transferred in imperceptible amounts to an affectionate owner's hand.[2]

Feces that are not immediately disturbed by people, pets, or heavy rain eventually decompose and enter into the soil layer. The *Toxocara* eggs, however, can survive there for years, even against the onslaught of rain and cold weather.[3] As excrement accumulates in an area regularly littered by animals, the chances for human contact (e.g., playing children) with the parasite increase. British researchers were recently startled to find that a random survey of the country's public lands revealed that one out of four dirt samples were contaminated with *Toxocara* eggs.[4]

Once a person ingests the eggs, they hatch and invade body tissues, such as the lungs, liver, kidneys, brain and spinal cord, and eyes. The victim may experience fever, lethargy, body aches, anemia, and possible blindness and convulsions. Unfortunately these symptoms are hard to diagnose because the roundworms do not produce new eggs that can be detected in the stool of their unnatural human host.[5]

Toxocara is controlled to some extent by worm pills, which can be given to puppies six weeks after birth and every three months thereafter. Negligent pet owners and stray animals perpetuate the public health problem, however. It has been estimated that as many as 20 per cent of the children in some rural areas of Louisiana are hosts to these parasites.[6] The most obvious cases are among small children who eat dirt from pet pens and shelters. We have already seen, however, that *Toxocara* is not confined to the countryside. The residents of urban areas are also threatened by the accumulated wastes of unwormed pets and abandoned animals living in restricted open space. One study revealed that half of the *Toxocara* patients surveyed owned neither dog nor cat—a finding that suggests how far the hazard has spread beyond pet owners themselves.[7]

Histoplasmosis is another disease that is frequently transmitted via zoological waste to people having no direct contact

with animals. Once thought of as a rural midwestern phenomenon, this malady has been recently detected in more ur-
banized areas throughout the country. Some medical authorities estimate that some 30 million Americans have contracted
histoplasmosis, although many never exhibit any symptoms.[8]

The problem originates with tiny fungus seeds (spores) that
thrive in dark and damp places. Ideal environments for their
growth include caves, belfries, barns, old chicken houses, and
other roosting areas where the droppings of birds (e.g., pi-
geons, starlings, chickens) and bats accumulate. When the
contaminated soil in such places is disturbed, these spores
may become air-borne and inhaled. In one case, members of
a boy scout troop contracted histoplasmosis while cleaning up
a dusty park area where starlings frequently roosted.[9]

Once the spores are inhaled, they can damage lung cells
and lymph nodes and precipitate calcium deposits. Prolonged
exposure to contaminated dust can lead to fever, fatigue,
weight loss, chest pain, coughing, and—rarely—hemorrhaging
and death. While most infected individuals experience mild or
negligible reactions, the potential for serious illness exists for
significant numbers of people, particularly children and older
men.

Toxocara and histoplasmosis are only two of more than one
hundred diseases that can be contracted from animals or animal waste. Others include psittacosis (parrots, parakeets, and
barnyard fowl), brucellosis (dogs, cattle, swine), leptospirosis
(dogs, mice, swine), actinomycosis (cats, dogs), toxoplas-
mosis (cats, birds), acariasis (many pets), tunga infections
(dogs, swine), cat scratch fever (cat, dogs), and African
green monkey disease.[10] Animals can also expose humans to
such infectious diseases as tuberculosis and diphtheria.

Zoological Guidelines

Because of the pathogenic potential of domesticated animals, we should consider the total impact of pets on our
home before we acquire them. We should ask ourselves:

1) Will there be a waste-disposal problem? Taking the animal outside to use the curb merely shifts the burden to the community.

2) Does the pet under consideration appear healthy? Has it been protected from diseases and parasites common to its species?

3) Will there be a noise problem for neighbors? Strident dogs, birds, etc., are a sure prescription for poor community relations.

4) Will the animal be likely to bite, scratch, or threaten visitors and passers-by? Lawsuits and medical bills can boost the cost of a pet dramatically.

5) Are there superior alternatives?

Some consideration should also be given to the impact of living conditions on the pet itself. It may be inhumane, for example, to confine large working or sporting dogs to a small apartment or pen for extended periods of time.

Once a decision is made to acquire a pet, the owner should resolve to maintain a sanitary environment for the animal and to keep it free from parasites such as worms, fleas, ticks, and lice. Always wet down the floors of bird roosting areas before sweeping, so that dusty droppings will not be stirred aloft.[11] Hand washing after contact with pets and their pens, cages, or shelters obviously reduces the chances that any infection will be transmitted.

Be cautious with the use of pet supplies. Cat litter boxes, pet medication, flea powder, aerosol sprays (which should be avoided in any case), and pet food dishes should be kept out of the reach of small children. Apply powders in well-ventilated areas—preferably out of doors.

Those of us who are animal lovers should seriously consider neutering our pets where any opportunity for breeding exists.[12] Millions of abandoned dogs and cats are exterminated each year at local animal shelters. It is difficult for a pet owner to foresee all the chances for mating that occur over the lifetime of an animal, and even harder (sometimes) to find homes for the litters spawned by such accidents. Re-

member that the proliferation of pets places a growing
strain upon global food resources in a time of acute hunger
problems for many of the world's peoples.

Zoological Alternatives

Because many animals have relatively short life spans, there
are usually a number of occasions to reconsider our commit-
ment to pet ownership. Despite the pollution potential of animals, some people can certainly justify pets for companionship, safety, or assistance (e.g., Seeing-Eye dogs). In these
cases, it is still possible to minimize the adverse impact of animals on the home environment. In addition to observing the
hygienic precautions noted earlier, prospective owners can
take other measures, such as acquiring smaller, more docile
pets. (Goldfish are probably more appropriate for apartment
living than great Danes). Adoption of unwanted animals is
preferable to the purchase of those intentionally bred. People
living in congested areas may want to farm out their pets pe-
riodically to friends in the countryside.

Those who are in any way undecided about pet ownership
should examine their motivation for assuming such a major
responsibility. Security, for example, is a prime incentive for
buying large dogs in high crime areas. Rather than confine
such animals to a house or small yard, however, it may be
equally effective—and certainly more humane—to use alternative protective measures (additional locks, peepholes, alarm
systems, better exterior lighting, and self-defense courses).
For companionship as well as safety, individuals living
alone may find that taking on boarders and housemates may
afford better protection against crime than a watchdog.

REFERENCES

1 Morley Safer, "Where Has My Little Dog Gone?," *60 Minutes,* Vol. 8, No. 21 (New York: Columbia Broadcasting System, May 16, 1976), transcript, p. 7.
2 Dr. Iris Krup, ibid., p. 10.
3 Safer, ibid., p. 9.
4 *British Veterinary Journal,* Vol. 131, No. 6 (Nov.–Dec. 1975), pp. 627–38.
5 John Dent, M.D., and G. M. Carrera, M.D., "Eosinophilia in Childhood Caused by Visceral Larva Migrams," *Journal of the Louisiana State Medical Society,* Vol. 105, No. 7 (July 1953), p. 13.
6 Safer, "Where Has My Little Dog Gone?," p. 10.
7 *British Veterinary Journal,* Vol. 131, No. 6 (Nov.–Dec. 1975), pp. 627–38.
8 "Histo (Histoplasmosis): The Facts," National Tuberculosis and Respiratory Disease Association, Nov. 1971.
9 Ibid.
10 See "Epidemiological Aspects of Some of the Zoonoses," U. S. Department of Health, Education, and Welfare, n.d.
11 "Histo."
12 See Center for Science in the Public Interest, *99 Ways to a Simple Lifestyle* (Garden City, N.Y.: Anchor/Doubleday, 1977), ⅜38, "Question Pets and Pet Food."

HAZARDOUS SUBSTANCES DETERMINATION

Several ways in which a substance can come under the requirements of the Federal Hazardous Substances Act are:

(1) A substance that may cause substantial injury or illness through any customary or reasonably foreseeable handling or use and that falls into any of the following categories is classified as hazardous and is required to bear appropriate labeling if it is packaged for or intended for use in or around the home:

(a) TOXIC/HIGHLY TOXIC. A substance is toxic if it can cause injury or illness when ingested, inhaled, or absorbed through the skin. Highly toxic substances are those proven through laboratory testing to be particularly lethal. (Example: Certain liquid furniture polishes are toxic.)

(b) EXTREMELY FLAMMABLE/FLAMMABLE/COMBUSTIBLE. These three degrees of flammability are based on the conditions under which a substance will ignite or the rate at which it burns. Gasoline, for example, will ignite even at sub-zero temperatures and thus is extremely flammable. Substances igniting only when held at a temperature above 150° F. are not defined as flammable or combustible under the law.

(c) CORROSIVE. Corrosive substances cause destruction of living tissue on contact through chemical action. (Example: Certain drain cleaners are corrosive.)

(d) IRRITANT. An irritant is a noncorrosive substance that produces inflammation of living tissue after immediate, prolonged, or repeated contact. (Example: Some laundry detergents are irritants.)

(e) STRONG SENSITIZER. Strong sensitizers may be divided into two groups. A strong *allergic* sensitizer will make some people extremely sensitive to its presence after they are once exposed to it. Thus a person who comes into contact with such a substance for the first time will show no ill effects, but on a subsequent contact (even with an insignificant amount of the substance) may show a strong allergic reaction. A strong *photodynamic* sensitizer will make some people, after exposure to it, extremely sensitive to sunlight or its equivalent. The area of sensitivity may be general or limited to the point of contact with the sensitizer. (Example: Formaldehyde is a strong allergic sensitizer.)

(f) A substance that GENERATES PRESSURE through heat, decomposition, or any other means. (Example: aerosol cans.)

(g) Any RADIOACTIVE substances not regulated under the Atomic Energy Act of 1954 that are judged by the Consumer Product Safety Commission to be hazardous enough to need LABELING.

(2) Toys and other articles intended for use by children that are found to have electrical, mechanical, or thermal hazards may be designated as hazardous substances. These hazards are defined separately in Federal Hazardous Substances Act Regulations published by the commission. (Examples: electrical toys with shock hazards, dolls with accessible straight pins, toy ovens with excessively high temperatures.)

Source: "The Federal Hazardous Substances Act," No. 55, *Fact Sheet,* U. S. Consumer Product Safety Commission, Washington, D.C., May 1975.

APPENDIX 2

PLACES FOR INFORMATION

FEDERAL

Consumer Product Safety
   Commission
1750 K St. N.W.
Washington, D.C. 20207

Protects consumers against
unreasonable risks and injury
associated with consumer
products

Director
Office of Consumer Affairs
Department of Health,
   Education, and Welfare
Washington, D.C. 20201

Investigates problems of
general concern for
consumers

U. S. Environmental Protection
   Agency
Washington, D.C. 20460

For indoor pollution problems

FEDERAL INFORMATION CENTERS*
STATE LOCATIONS

ARIZONA

Phoenix
(602) 261-3313
Federal Building
230 N. 1st Ave.
85025

CALIFORNIA

Los Angeles
(213) 688-3800
Federal Building
300 N. Los Angeles St.
90012

* Federal Information Centers, Spring 1977, General Services
Administration, Washington, D.C. 20405.

Sacramento
(916) 449-3344
Federal Building and
   U. S. Courthouse
650 Capitol Mall
95814

San Diego
(714) 293-6030
880 Front St.
92188

San Francisco
(415) 556-6600
Federal Building and
   U. S. Courthouse
450 Golden Gate Ave.
94102

COLORADO

Denver
(303) 837-3602
Federal Building
1961 Stout St.
80294

DISTRICT OF COLUMBIA

Washington
(202) 755-8660
7th & D Sts. S.W.
Room 5716
20407

FLORIDA

Miami
(305) 350-4155
Federal Building
51 S.W. 1st Ave.
33130

St. Petersburg
(813) 893-3495
William C. Cramer
Federal Building
144 1st Ave. South
33701

GEORGIA

Atlanta
(404) 221-6891
Federal Building
275 Peachtree St. N.E.
30303

HAWAII

Honolulu
(808) 546-8620
U. S. Post Office and
   Courthouse and Customhouse
335 Merchant St.
96813

ILLINOIS

Chicago
(312) 353-4242
Everett McKinley Dirksen
   Building
219 S. Dearborn St.
60604

INDIANA

Indianapolis
(317) 269-7373
Federal Building
575 N. Pennsylvania St.
46204

KENTUCKY

Louisville
(502) 582-6261
Federal Building
600 Federal Place
40202

LOUISIANA

New Orleans
(504) 589-6696
Federal Building
701 Loyola Ave.
70113

MARYLAND

Baltimore
(301) 962-4980
Federal Building
31 Hopkins Plaza
21201

MASSACHUSETTS

Boston
(617) 223-7121
J.F.K. Federal Building
Cambridge St.
02203

MICHIGAN

Detroit
(313) 226-7016
Federal Building and
    U. S. Courthouse
231 W. Lafayette St.
48226

MINNESOTA

Minneapolis
(612) 725-2073
Federal Building and
    U. S. Courthouse
110 S. 4th St.
55401

MISSOURI

Kansas City
(816) 374-2466
Federal Building
601 E. 12th St.
64106

St. Louis
(314) 425-4106
Federal Building
1520 Market St.
63103

NEBRASKA

Omaha
(402) 221-3353
Federal Building and
    U. S. Post Office and
    Courthouse
215 N. 17th St.
68102

NEW JERSEY

Newark
(201) 645-3600
Federal Building
970 Broad St.
07102

NEW MEXICO

Albuquerque
(505) 766-3091
Federal Building and
    U. S. Courthouse
500 Gold Ave. S.W.
87101

NEW YORK

Buffalo
(716) 842-5570
Federal Building
111 W. Huron St.
14202

New York
(212) 264-4464
Federal Office Building
26 Federal Plaza
10007

OHIO

Cincinnati
(513) 684-2801
Federal Building
550 Main St.
45202

Cleveland
(216) 522-4040
Federal Building
1240 E. 9th St.
44199

OKLAHOMA

Oklahoma City
(405) 231-4868
U. S. Post Office Building
201 N.W. 3rd St.
73102

OREGON

Portland
(503) 221-2222
Federal Building
1220 S.W. 3rd Ave.
97204

PENNSYLVANIA

Philadelphia
(215) 597-7042
Federal Building
600 Arch St.
19106

Pittsburgh
(412) 644-3456
Federal Building
100 Liberty Ave.
15222

TENNESSEE

Memphis
(901) 534-3285
Clifford Davis Federal Building
167 N. Main St.
38103

TEXAS

Fort Worth
(817) 334-3624
Fritz Garland Lanham
Federal Building
819 Taylor St.
76102

Houston
(713) 226-5711
Federal Building and
   U. S. Courthouse
515 Rusk Ave.
77002

UTAH

Salt Lake City
(801) 524-5353
Federal Building
125 S. State St.
84138

WASHINGTON

Seattle
(206) 442-0570
Federal Building
915 2nd Ave.
98174

If none of the foregoing is nearby, residents of the following thirty-nine cities can call the local number given and be connected by toll-free tie line to a center:

ALABAMA

Birmingham: 322-8591
Mobile: 438-1421

ARIZONA

Tucson: 622-1511

ARKANSAS
Little Rock: 378-6177

CALIFORNIA
San Jose: 275-7422

COLORADO
Colorado Springs: 471-9491
Pueblo: 544-9523

CONNECTICUT
Hartford: 527-2617
New Haven: 624-4720

FLORIDA
Fort Lauderdale: 522-8531
Jacksonville: 354-4756
Tampa: 229-7911
West Palm Beach: 833-7566

IOWA
Des Moines: 282-9091

KANSAS
Topeka: 295-2866
Wichita: 263-6931

MISSOURI
St. Joseph: 233-8206

NEW JERSEY
Trenton: 396-4400

NEW MEXICO
Santa Fe: 983-7743

NEW YORK
Albany: 463-4421
Rochester: 546-5075
Syracuse: 476-8545

NORTH CAROLINA
Charlotte: 376-3600

OHIO
Akron: 375-5638
Columbus: 221-1014
Dayton: 223-7377
Toledo: 241-3223

OKLAHOMA
Tulsa: 548-4193

PENNSYLVANIA
Allentown/Bethlehem:
  821-7785
Scranton: 346-7081

RHODE ISLAND
Providence: 331-5565

TENNESSEE
Chattanooga: 265-8231
Nashville: 242-5056

TEXAS
Austin: 472-5494
Dallas: 749-2131
San Antonio: 224-4471

UTAH
Ogden: 399-1347

WASHINGTON
Tacoma: 383-5230

WISCONSIN
Milwaukee: 271-2273

For ordering government
  documents:

Superintendent of Documents
  Government Printing Office
  Washington, D.C. 20402

National Technical Information
  Service
  5282 Port Royal Rd.
  Springfield, Va. 22151

TYPICAL POTENTIAL HOUSEHOLD HAZARDS IN A RETAIL MERCHANDISE CATALOGUE

1. Tree fertilizer spikes
2. Insecticides for tree fogging devices
3. Carbon dioxide cartridges for bikes
4. Chain lube spray for motorcycles
5. Lithium grease
6. Gear grease
7. Brake fluid
8. Motor oils
9. Engine flush liquid
10. Auto-body repair
    a. aerosol spray can primer
    b. cream hardener
    c. epoxy repair kit
11. Batteries
12. Fire extinguishers
13. Polyurethane wood finish spray
14. Epoxy spray enamel
15. Wood stain
16. Masonry coating
17. Crack stop
18. Concrete etching acid crystals
19. Antiskid sand additives
20. Heavy-duty cleaners
21. Paint remover
22. Acrylic latex caulk
23. Brush cleaner
24. Mildew wash
25. Swimming pool chemicals
26. Water conditioners
27. Toilet bowl cleaner
28. Portable toilet antifreeze (propylene glycol)
29. Propane torch kits
30. Silicone
31. Rug shampoo
32. Laundry detergents
33. Boat supplies
    a. polyester materials
    b. epoxy materials
    c. epoxy marine enamel
    d. semisoft point (cuprous oxide)
    e. water repellents

APPENDIX 4

ACRONYMS

BOM	Bureau of Mines
BRH	Bureau of Radiological Health (FDA)
CPSC	Consumer Product Safety Commission
CSPI	Center for Science in the Public Interest
CU	Consumers Union
DOC	Department of Commerce
DOI	Department of Interior
DOT	Department of Transportation
EPA	Environment Protection Agency
ERS	Economic Research Service (USDA)
FDA	Food and Drug Administration
FEA	Federal Energy Administration
FIFRA	Federal Insecticide, Fungicide and Rodenticide Act
GNP	Gross National Product
NAS	National Academy of Sciences
NASA	National Aeronautics and Space Administration
NBS	National Bureau of Standards
NTIS	National Technical Information Service
OTA	Office of Technology Assessment
SIC	Standard Industrial Code
USDA	U. S. Department of Agriculture

INDEX